IMMIGRATION AND ETHNIC CONFLICT

By the same author

COLOUR PREJUDICE IN BRITAIN
THE COLOUR PROBLEM
POSTWAR IMMIGRANTS IN CANADA
MIGRATION AND RACE RELATIONS IN AN ENGLISH CITY
READINGS IN RACE AND ETHNIC RELATIONS (*editor*)
ADJUSTMENT OF IMMIGRANTS AND THEIR
  DESCENDANTS (*with W. E. Kalbach*)

Immigration and Ethnic Conflict

Anthony H. Richmond
Professor of Sociology
York University, Toronto

St. Martin's Press   New York

© Anthony H. Richmond 1988

All rights reserved. For information, write:
Scholarly & Reference Division,
St. Martin's Press, Inc., 175 Fifth Avenue, New York, NY 10010

First published in the United States of America in 1988

Printed in Hong Kong

ISBN 0–312–01159–8

Library of Congress Cataloging-in-Publication Data
Richmond, Anthony H., 1925–
Immigration and ethnic conflict/Anthony H. Richmond
p.   cm.
Bibliography: p.
Includes index.
ISBN 0–312–01159–8: $30.00 (est.)
1. Canada—Immigration and emigration.   2. Racism—Canada.
3. Canada—Race relations.   4. Australia—Immigration and
emigration.   5. Racism—Australia.   6. Australia—Race relations.
I. Title.
JV7225.R533   1988   87–16119
304.8'71—dc19   CIP

THE LIBRARY
ST. MARY'S COLLEGE OF MARYLAND
ST. MARY'S CITY, MARYLAND 20686

THE LIBRARY
ST. MARY'S COLLEGE OF MARYLAND
ST. MARY'S CITY, MARYLAND 2068e

Contents

List of Figures and Tables	vi
Preface and Acknowlegements	vii

1	Introduction: Ethnic Conflict and Post-Industrialism	1

PART I   IMMIGRATION

2	Structural Change and the Sociology of Migration	29
3	Socio-Cultural Adaptation and Conflict in Immigrant-Receiving Societies	49
4	Immigration and Unemployment in Canada and Australia	67
5	Third World Immigrants in Canada	81

PART II   RACISM AND MULTICULTURALISM

6	Environmental Conservation and Immigration: A New Racist Ideology?	95
7	Canadian Unemployment and the Threat to Multi-culturalism	107
8	A Canadian Dilemma: Bilangualism, Multiculturalism or Racism?	125

PART III   ETHNIC NATIONALISM

9	Ethnic Nationalism: Social Science Paradigms	141
10	Ethnic Nationalism and Post-Industrialism	167

End-notes	183
Glossary of Terms	187
Select Bibliography and References	191
Name Index	209
Subject Index	223

List of Figures and Tables

Figures

1.1	Conflict in post-industrial societies	6
2.1	Model of conflict, order and change	43
4.1	Canada: numbers unemployed, percentage unemployment and number of immigrants destined to the labour force, 1951–65	69
4.2	Canada: numbers unemployed, percentage unemployment and number of immigrants destined for the labour force, 1966–82	70
4.3	Australia: numbers unemployed, percentage unemployment and number of immigrants destined for the labour force, 1966–82	71
5.1	Immigration to Canada by region, 1971–82	82
5.2	Immigration to Canada by world area, 1983	83
5.3	Third world immigrants in Canada, 1981	84
10.1	Power, legitimation and social integration	169
10.2	Power and legitimacy in a *Gemeinschaft* society	170
10.3	Power and legitimacy in a *Gesellschaft* society	171
10.4	Power and legitimacy in a *Verbindungsnetzschaft* society	174

Tables

4.1	Percentage of labour force unemployed, 1971, and index of unemployment by sex and birthplace for 'rest of Canada' and Australia	72
4.2	Percentage and index of unemployment by sex and birthplace for Metropolitan Toronto and Melbourne, 1971	74
4.3	Indexes of unemployment for foreign-born, by sex and period of immigration for 'rest of Canada' and Australia	76
4.4	Longitudinal survey data re-analysis: percentage unemployed by length of residence in Canada	78

Preface and Acknowledgements

I wish to thank colleages, staff, and students at York University, Toronto, who, for more than twenty years, have provided intellectual and practical support in my various research endeavours and the Social Science Research Council of Canada which funded many of the projects. I also appreciated the invitation to spend a sabbatical, 1984–85, at St Antony's College, Oxford where Professor Kenneth Kirkwood's weekly seminar on Race Relations provided a stimulating forum for discussion. I am indebted to my wife for valuable editorial assistance in the preparation of this volume.

The following acknowledgements are due:

Chapter 2 is a revised version of a paper originally presented at the meetings of the International Sociological Association, Research Committee on Migration, held in Dubrovnik, June 1985.

Chapter 3 was first commissioned by UNESCO and is reprinted by permission from *International Social Science Journal*, 1984, (36), 519–86.

Chapter 4 is reprinted by permission from *International Journal of Comparative Sociology*, 1984, (24), 243–45.

Chapter 5 is a revised version of a paper first presented at a the CICRED/ICM Joint Meeting on International Migration, held in Geneva, June 1984.

Chapter 6 is reprinted, with permission from the Smithsonian Institution, from R. S. Bryce-Laporte (ed.), *Sourcebook on the New Immigration: Implications for the United States and the International Community* (New Brunswick, New Jersey: Transaction Books, 1980).

Chapter 7 is reprinted with permission from *Journal of Canadian Studies,* 1982, (17), 81–90.

Chapter 8 is a revised version of a paper presented at the meetings of the British Association of Canadian Studies, held in Edinburgh, April 1985.

viii   *Preface and Acknowledgements*

Chapter 9 was originally commissioned by UNESCO, Division of Human Rights and Peace in 1984, and is printed with permission.

Chapter 10 is reprinted with permission from *Ethnic and Racial Studies*, 1984, (7), 4–18.

ANTHONY H. RICHMOND

1 Introduction: Ethnic Conflict and Post-Industrialism

The central theme of this volume of essays is the nature of immigration and ethnic conflict in post-industrial societies that have experienced large-scale movements of population since the Second World War, creating ethnically diverse 'multicultural' societies. The concept of a post-industrial society has been widely used, for more than twenty years, to describe the rapidly changing characteristics of contemporary economic and social systems influenced by modern computerised technologies including automation, robotics, rapid transportation and satellite communications. Key features include the importance of scientific knowledge, an emerging technocratic elite, a system of management based on information systems, and the growth of the tertiary sectors of industry, at the expense of agriculture and manufacturing. Early forecasts, based on far too optimistic scenarios, also anticipated a period of material affluence, a decline in the importance of work as a major activity and its replacement by the constructive use of leisure and entertainment (Touraine, 1971; Bell, 1973; Toffler, 1971; 1981). The technocratic society was seen as transcending political boundaries and was likely to lead to a convergence of the economic and political systems of capitalist and communist countries as well as spreading to the Third World (Kerr; 1960; 1983).

Following my earliest studies of post-war migration to Canada, I advanced the view that international migration was profoundly influenced by post-industrial developments. Migration, together with other forms of occupational and social mobility, was a necessary feature of post-industrial societies. It was 'anachronistic to assume that migrants will settle permanently in a particular country or locality' (Richmond, 1967:278). Easy and cheap transportation, together with an awakening consciousness of economic opportunities elsewhere, and the possibility of escape from oppressive political regimes, resulted in large scale movements of population. Personal and mass communication networks promoted aspirations to migrate.

2 Introduction: Ethnic Conflict and Post-Industrialism

At the same time telephones and jet aircraft provided the means by which people maintained close ties with family and friends, as well as awareness of changing economic, political and social conditions in their former country and in other places. Consequently, high rates of re-migration and return were typical of post-industrial societies (Richmond, 1969).

The term *transilient* was adopted to describe the more highly qualified and professional migrants who did not necessarily acculturate or integrate into the receiving society. On the contrary, they moved frequently and were often the catalytic influence that induced significant economic and social change wherever they went. Teachers, scientific workers, as well as the professional and managerial employees of large corporations, were prominent in this category. It has since become evident that highly qualified personnel are not the only ones to exhibit high rates of re-migration and return. Receiving countries have made increasing use of skilled and unskilled manual workers who work under short-term contracts, or have only temporary residence status. Nevertheless, many 'temporary' workers seek to bring families and remain for longer periods. The distinction between 'permanent' and 'temporary' migration is no longer clear (Kubat, 1984).

It was suggested (Richmond 1969:271–281) that the term *verbindungsnetzschaft* might be appropriate to describe the key principle of social organisation in post-industrial societies. (The neologism may not be good German but it was meant to convey a whole spectrum of social phenomena associated with social and communicaton networks in advanced societies that no word in English adequately conveys.) Territorially based comunities, or *Gemeinschaft* were typical of pre-industrial societies and formally organized bureaucracies, or *gesellschaft*, were characteristic of industrialised societies. However, while post-industrialism did not completely replace older forms of social organization, the instantaneous transmission of information fundamentally changed social structures and the locus of power in modern societies. It also created a potential for more widespread conflict. Glazer and Moynihan (1975:25) noted that 'the international mass media network rapidly spreads the story and symbols of ethnic discontent'. Marshall McLuhan (1964), who invented the term 'global village', would have been more accurate if he had described such a communications network as a 'global babel' or 'global bedlam', such is the potential for conflict and confusion which it creates. Selective access to the networks and control over their

Introduction: Ethnic Conflict and Post-Industrialism 3

informational content also produces a concentration of power and the ability to manipulate the consciousness of those involved. Terrorists and other dissident groups have made extensive use of the media as a means of drawing world attention to their demands.

POST-INDUSTRIALISM AND SOCIAL CONFLICT

The early prognosis of social change, based upon the concept of a post-industrial 'revolution', have been criticised on a variety of grounds. Kumar (1976;1978) argued that recent economic and technological changes do not constitute a radical departure from trends that have been evident since the industrial revolution. The application of science and technology, improved communications and transportation, the increasing substitution of capital for labour, and the growth of the service sector are not new. However, it is true that these trends have been accelerated in the second half of the twentieth century.

Sociological studies of post-industrial change have also been criticised for their exaggeration of the role of a technocratic 'knowledge elite' in forecasting social trends and advising politicians and planners concerned with economic and social policy. Economists and other social scientists have been actively involved in the governmental decision-making process, either by serving in office themselves, or by contributing to various governmental commissions and advisory bodies. Their advice is not always heeded but, when applied, has singularly failed to anticipate major crises or to offer practical solutions to economic and social problems. Eva Etzioni-Halevy (1985) argues that those who thought that post-industrialism, and related advances in the natural and social sciences, would inevitably lead to 'progress', were wrong. On the contrary, there is widespread poverty, conflict, alienation, rioting and terrorism. The much vaunted 'leisure oriented' society predicted by Bell (1973), and expressed in more utopian form by Toffler (1970;1981), has taken the form of chronic unemployment on an unprecedented scale, throughout the world. Furthermore, superpower confrontation has led to a spiralling arms race, the horror of nuclear 'deterrence' and numerous conventional wars and civil turmoil in various regions of the globe.

The unemployment experienced in post-industrial societies in the 1970s and 1980s is the outcome of several sets of factors whose impact coincided. They included technological redundancy due to the deve-

4 Introduction: Ethnic Conflict and Post-Industrialism

lopment of less labour-intensive methods of production and distribution of goods and services; 'deindustrialisation', and structural changes in the distribution of the labour force, particularly shifts from primary and secondary to the tertiary and quaternary sectors of industry; an increase in the number of people seeking employment consequent upon the end of the 'baby boom', together with the liberation of the next generation of women who continue to work outside the home, while limiting their families or having no children. Finally, among major factors contributing to unemployment were the fiscal policies adopted by most governments concerned with fighting inflation and endeavouring to reduce budget deficits. Social programmes and 'welfare state' expenditures were cut while spending on the military, 'defence' projects and 'space research' was maintained at unprecedentedly high levels. The number of people in poverty grew while the material and social conditions in 'inner cities' deteriorated.

In a society where advanced technology theoretically makes it possible for almost all manufactured goods to be produced by robots, and services to be provided by automated and computerised systems, technological redundancy is endemic. A fundamental structural contradiciton arises from the enormous productive potential of such a system and the deficiency in demand resulting from massive unemployment and under-employment. The situation is exacerbated by the gross inequality in the distribution of power and resources, resulting in a differential impact of such technological change on various continents, countries, regions and classes.

Conflict, in some shape or form, is the normal condition of any society. A social system without conflict exists only in the imaginations of fiction writers and utopian ideologues. Without conflict there is no freedom, no dissent and no power to bring about change. Conflicts arise from several different sources among which competing interests, the differential distribution of power or resources, and the opposition of fundamental beliefs and values are the most common. Normally, integrative mechanisms handle such conflicts. Institutional sub-systems exist to reconcile differences, mediate disputes, legitimate authority, allocate resources and to achieve a workable degree of distributive justice. When contradictory forces exist within a social system such integrative processes may not be sufficient to prevent conflict from manifesting itself in violent form.

Conflict and contradiction are two related terms but they are not synonymous. Contradictions exist within a society when its funda-

Introduction: Ethnic Conflict and Post-Industrialism   5

mental organizing principles, its central institutions or core value systems, are disjunctive. The rational pursuit of one set of goals, or the use of the most efficient means to a desired end, has perverse and generally unforeseen effects on other positively valued objectives. This can lead to system degeneration and sometimes total collapse. When this happens certain conflicts are impossible to resolve without radically changing the whole system. Conflicts arise between individuals and collectivities pursuing their respective goals. Contradictions exist when institutions and value systems are incapable of responding to the challenge which such conflicts generate. Rex (1981:120) prefers to use the term 'system conflict', rather than 'contradiction' for such phenomena. He identifies conflicts between actors in particular institutions, conflicts in one institution that are reflected in another, and inter-institutional dominance, as examples of 'system conflict'.

Giddens (1979:143) identified the disjunction between private appropriation and socialised production as one of the primary contradictions of modern capitalism. He also located contradictions between the private and public spheres of civil society and the state, and between the emerging global polity and economy on the one hand, and the internal consolidation of 'nation-states', on the other (Giddens, 1984). In post-industrial societies there is a further contradiction between automated production and private consumption. In the industrial phase of capitalism the 'work ethnic' provided the legitimation for receiving income, other than that from accumulated wealth. The 'welfare state' represented a transitionary stage, in which a variety of transfer payments were made to those not in the paid labour force, in order to rectify particular inequities, according to principles of distributive justice. The bureaucratic mechanisms established in the last fifty years to achieve these goals are proving inadequate in societies where a large proportion of the able-bodied can no longer be guaranteed employment, because post-industrial technologies have made them redundant.

In developing a 'critical theory' of advanced capitalist societies, Habermas (1976) identified the economic, political and socio-cultural sub-systems of society as the points of origin of crises which could, in some circumstances, lead to delegitimation of the state and political eruption. A somewhat modified and adapted interpretation of this view is represented in Figure 1.1. The development of multinational companies and oligopolistic markets, often with the active support of governments aiming to protect their own resource industries, farming

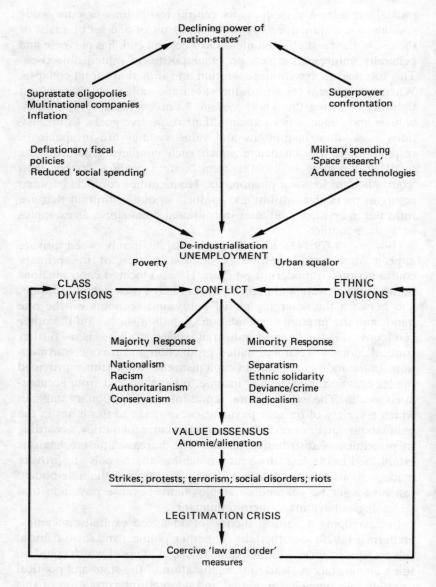

Figure 1.1 Conflict in post-industrial societies

Introduction: Ethnic Conflict and Post-Industrialism

and manufacturing sectors, limits competition and raises prices, thus contributing to inflation. Measures intended to combat inflation create unemployment and exacerbate class conflicts. The state is no longer seen as a benign or neutral arbiter and its administrative system becomes de-personalised, as bureaucratic 'rationality' and 'cost-effectiveness' become ends in themselves. Traditional, bureaucratic and charismatic authorities cease to be effective and are challenged by leaders claiming to represent oppressed classes and ethnic minority groups.

There is always a danger of reifying 'systems' and attributing to them a causal status that properly belongs to the individuals who participate in them, particularly those, who through the dominant roles they play, exercise significant power over others. However, social systems and organisations persist over time, existing prior to the individuals who participate in them. The latter must be socialised into the performance of appropriate roles, including both dominant and subordinate ones. The bridge between individuals and systems is the experience of *internalisation* (or as psychoanalysts prefer *introjection*). People learn system norms and goals, incorporate them into their personalities and then act as if they were autonomous. Organizational means and ends become individual sources of motivation and conformity becomes its own reward. External sanctions reinforce obedience but are only needed when 'duty' and 'conscience' fail. Systems which exhibit contradictory tendencies create a source of strain for the individuals concerned. They endeavour to resolve cognitive dissonance, frustration and conative stress by various reaction formations and psychological tension release mechanisms. The form these reactions take depend on whether the individual or group concerned is part of the dominant class or majority group in society, or a member of a subordinated class or minority group.

Majority group responses to stress, typical of those who have wealth, exercise power, enjoy privileges and seek to maintain their status within a society, include heightened 'nationalism' and jingoistic attitudes, support for imperialistic ventures and reluctance to accept the loss of former colonial territories. Such reactions are often accompanied by racist attitudes, support for anti-immigration policies and generally 'authoritarian' responses to social conflict. They are frequently part of a political programme that is seen as 'neo-conservative', appealing to those who feel threatened by rapid social change.

8   *Introduction: Ethnic Conflict and Post-Industrialism*

Minority responses to social crises and conflict are complementary to those of majority groups. Class lines are hardened and ethnic solidarity increases. Subordinated groups demand a larger share of resources and greater control over distribution. Regional and ethnic separatist movements may arise seeking greater autonomy and self-government. When legitimated constitutional channels and democratic processes fail to deliver the desired results, some minority group members may engage in peaceful protest and endeavour to bring about change through constitutional and democratic means. Others may be alienated from the system altogether and resort to various forms of deviant behaviour ranging from violent protest, riots and disturbances, to crimes against persons and property, symbolic of the 'oppressive' social order, and/or organised terrorism and subversion. Under these conditions the state is faced with a major 'legitimation crisis'.

The most usual reaction of a government to any perceived threat to its stability and survival is a coercive one. 'Law and order' must be maintained. In support of this the police force may be strengthened and issued with more powerful weapons. Special strategic forces may be trained to deal with civil disturbances and terrorist activities. Civil liberties may be curtailed and the mass media censored. The judiciary may be called upon to mete out tougher sentences and political prisoners may be subject to special restrictions. Such a typical response of governments to perceived threats to the existing social order assumes the form of a 'positive feedback', which actually exacerbates the conflict. As Figure 1.1 indicates, coercive 'law and order' measures reinforce existing class and ethnic divisions contributing to the further alienation of disadvantaged groups. If allowed to continue indefinitely, such a vicious spiral of conflict could lead to civil war and a collapse of the existing social order. It is important to emphasise that there is nothing deterministic or inevitable about such a tendency. Human behaviour is reflexive and self-regulating. The possibility exists for a reversal of the conflict and a resolution of the contradiction, but the longer it continues and the more entrenched the opposing forces, the greater the probability of perpetuating the crisis.

International Migration and Social Conflict

Contemporary developed societies have failed to respond to the challenge of post-industrialism and the structural changes necessi-

Introduction: Ethnic Conflict and Post-Industrialism 9

tated by a political, economic and social revolution which resulted in the creation of a *global* polity, economy and society. No country, whether surrounded by water or not, can function as an island in the modern world. Enormous pressures to migrate have been generated. There are movements from the less developed and poorer countries to those whose economies are expanding, or which historically appeared to provide better economic opportunities. Within and between industrialised countries there are large gross movements of population that take the form of an exchange, with little net gain or loss. There are short term movements from 'peripheral' to 'core' areas, within the context of an international labour market that increasingly exploits the human and material resources of developing countries for the benefit of the wealthier ones (Richmond and Verma, 1978; Petras, 1981). To these forces must be added the consequences of political dissent, revolution and oppression which give rise to a growing number of refugees and expellees, seeking asylum and permanent settlement elsewhere. There is an inherent contradiction between the maintenace of sovereignty by separate states and their integration into a global society, in which such migratory pressures exist. The contradiction is epitomised in the U.N. *Charter of Human Rights*, Article 13 of which recognises a universal right to emigrate, but no corresponding right to be admitted elsewhere!

One of the consequences of an interdependent world economy, and the incorporation of formerly autonomous states into a world system, is that people follow the lines of communication which already link them across international boundaries, including former colonial ties and trading relations. Distance is no longer a barrier to communication or to population movement, in an age of transistor radios, satellite television transmissions and jet aircraft. The motive to migrate, the knowledge of possible destinations and the means to achieve the goal of emigration are now almost universal.

During periods of rapid economic growth industrialised countries sought workers abroad, either for permanent settlement or on a temporary basis. When recession occurred many aimed to repel or discourage those who sought entry, whether for economic or political reasons. Legislative barriers, border controls and draconian measures designed to restrict immigration and permit deportation and 're-patriation', were widely adopted. Such measures generally proved useless against the massive movements of population that occurred throughout the world. Authoritarian measures, designed to insulate

10 *Introduction: Ethnic Conflict and Post-Industrialism*

advanced industrial societies from the consequence of gross economic inequalities and the political upheavals which they generate, led to the problem of illegal and undocumented migrants, whose numbers increased everywhere. Although most marked in the case of Mexicans endeavouring to enter the United States, the problem of unwelcome visitors, surplus 'guestworkers', homeless expellees, stateless refugees and unwanted settlers, is widespread. The experiences of countries such as Canada, Australia and the United Kingdom, are indicative of the conflicts and contradictions inherent in the immigration process.

IMMIGRANTS IN CANADA

Measured in terms of its geographic area, Canada is the second largest country in the world. However, its population of some twenty-five million people is concentrated in approximately ten per cent of the land area, much of which is wilderness. Canada's wealth has depended upon the exploitation of its natural resources. Even the Arctic tundra is a potential source of oil and minerals. In 1981, 76 per cent of the population was urbanised, that is to say living in concentrations of 1000 people or more. However, only the metropolitan areas of Toronto and Montreal exceeded three million people. Immigrants constituted 16 per cent of the population. Three out of four of the foreign-born lived in cities of over 100 000 compared with less than half of the non-immigrant population. From the beginning of colonial settlement Canada has depended heavily upon immigration as a source of population growth. Between 1951 and 1971 the population grew at an average rate of 2.2 per cent per annum, of which approximately a third was due to net migration. In more recent years the rate of growth has declined to one per cent per annum, of which about 20 per cent can be attributed to net migration.

A key factor influencing the development of Canada's polyethnic, multicultural society has been the presence of the French who have constituted between a quarter and a third of the population since Confederation. Although French-speaking minorities are found throughout the country the largest concentration is in Quebec, where 82 per cent of the population of six and a half million is francophone. Although Britain has remained the largest single source of immigrants to Canada, those of British origin have declined relative to the growing numbers from other countries. Twenty-eight per cent of the

Introduction: Ethnic Conflict and Post-Industrialism 11

population is now of neither British nor French descent. Native Peoples (Status and non-Status Indians, Inuit and Metis) number about 500 000 or 2 per cent of the population. In the post-Second World War period, up to 1961, Europe provided the major source of immigration and Italy was the second largest country of origin. Between 1961 and 1971, immigration from Britain and Italy continued but other, non-European, countries, such as India and Jamaica, began to contribute. The trend toward Third World immigration increased proportionally in the following decade, although the absolute number of immigrants declined in response to less favourable economic conditions. Nevertheless, gross immigration averaged 144 000 per annum during the 1970s and net migration accounted for 1.15 million people who had arrived in the ten years preceding 1981.

While pursuing a positive immigration policy, Canada exercised strict control over those who were admitted for permanent settlement. In addition to health and security checks, immigrants were selected with a view to their potential economic contribution. Although agriculture and other primary industries continued to be highly productive they depended less on labour-intensive techniques. Consequently, immigrants gravitated toward the expanding secondary and tertiary industries, particularly in the larger metropolitan centres. For more than twenty years immigrants to Canada have been selected on the basis of 'points' earned on the basis of education, occupational qualifications, knowledge of English or French and assessment of the 'occupational demand' factor in Canada. Although family re-union and humanitarian considerations have also been taken into account, the dominant criterion has been economic.

Given the selective nature of the immigration policy it is not surprising that immigrants to Canada were, on average, better educated, had higher occupational status and larger incomes than the Canadian-born. In 1981, the most recent immigrants tended to be the best educated, including those from Asia and other Third World countries. Of those who came between 1971 and 1981, 15 per cent had University degrees compared with 8 per cent of the non-immigrants. The foreign-born were relatively over-represented proportionally in professional, technical, clerical, manufacturing, sales and service occupations. Compared with the Canadian-born, they were under-represented in farming and other primary occupations, together with transportation. The 1980 income of immigrants was ten per cent higher than that of other Canadians (Statistics Canada, 1984).

12   Introduction: Ethnic Conflict and Post-Industrialism

Previous studies showed that the advantage of the foreign-born, after controlling for age and education, was largely a consequence of their relative concentration in metropolitan areas. Similar benefits were enjoyed by the second generation (Canadian born of foreign parentage) who generally achieved substantial educational and occupational mobility (Richmond and Kalbach, 1980).

However, there were important exceptions to the generally high socio-economic status of immigrants in Canada. Immigrants from southern Europe, including Italy, Greece and Portugal, were generally sponsored by close relatives and were not required to meet the same criteria as independent immigrants, in terms of education. They tended to fill the less prestigious jobs in manufacturing and construction. Furthermore, recently arrived immigrants often had difficulty translating their educational qualifications into credentials acceptable to Canadian employers and licensing authorities. For example, many refugee doctors were unable to obtain the hospital internship which is necessary before being licensed to practise medicine in Ontario. Immigrants and refugees arriving from the mid-1970s onward faced a slow-growth economy with rising unemployment and inflation. As a result, the incidence of poverty among the foreign-born was closely related to length of residence. In 1980, 9 per cent of pre-1961 immigrants, living in families, fell below an official 'low-income line', compared with 16.5 per cent of the recent arrivals and 13 per cent of the Canadian-born. Persons living alone had a higher incidence of low income which was particularly acute among elderly immigrants (Richmond and Kalbach, 1980; Statistics Canada, 1984).

At first sight, it seems that immigration into Canada has not generated major sources of conflict, despite evidence that ethnic prejudice and racist attitudes are present, and that there is minority support for extremist organizations such as the Western Guard and Klu Klux Klan (Henry, 1978). Successive public opinion surveys have shown Canadians believe that, at times of economic recession, immigration should be curtailed but not completely stopped. There has been widespread sympathy for the plight of refugees and general support for policies of 'family reunion'. The policy of 'multiculturalism within a bi-lingual framework', first announced by the Federal Liberal government in 1971, continued to be supported by the Progressive Conservative and New Democratic parties, although the emphasis shifted from promoting non-official language maintenance and cultural activities to combating racism and, more recently, encouraging ethnic minority business enterprise.

Introduction: Ethnic Conflict and Post-Industrialism 13

Nevertheless, there are certain inherent contradictions in the policies currently pursued and some potential conflicts which could become more serious. Firstly, Canada has become increasingly dependent upon the use of temporary employment visas to meet shortages of labour, particularly in the poorly paid agricultural and service sectors. Since 1973 the number of visas issued annually has risen from 84 000 to 144 000 (in 1984), representing an annual addition of more than 50 000 'person-years' annually to the Canadian labour force, when the duration of the permit is taken into account. Workers admitted for a limited duration are not supposed to bring their families. Although temporary workers contribute to unemployment insurance, pension plans and other 'welfare' services, through taxation and other deductions from pay, they are rarely able to benefit from them. Temporary workers are generally tied to a particular employer, or industry, and liable to deportation if they lose their job. Working and housing conditions are often poor. Although Britain and the USA supply some temporary workers, these countries are of declining importance relative to Asia, the Pacific, Latin America and the Caribbean. At the end of their officially approved stay in Canada, some fail to return and become part of an 'underground' illegal movement, open to threats and exploitation.

Secondly, the very success of longer term immigrants in achieving high socio-economic status could generate a 'backlash' in those regions of the country that have suffered most from the global economic crisis, or have never enjoyed the prosperity that Ontario experienced in the post-war period. Regional disparity is a major problem in Canada, as in other industrial societies. Successive governments have endeavoured to encourage investment in the Maritime Provinces and in other 'hinterlands', where unemployment has been traditionally high. At one time, oil exploration held out hope for some areas but the declining world price of energy has shattered those expectations and created problems for formerly prosperous provinces, such as Alberta, which remains a major oil producer. British Columbia, which attracted a high proportion of British immigrants in the post-war period and, more recently a substantial influx of Chinese and Sikhs, has also experienced above average unemployment.

Thirdly, there is growing concern at the scale of 'youth unemployment' and the under-employment of young people, with and without academic qualifications and specialised training. This is a universal problem in contemporary advanced industrial societies (OECD,

14   *Introduction: Ethnic Conflict and Post-Industrialism*

1981). Ethnic minorities are likely to be more seriously disadvantaged in the competition for jobs, particularly where there is prejudice and discrimination against 'visible minorities'. Precisely because Canada has relied heavily upon the importation of skilled and professional workers from abroad it has been slow to develop training in those trades and industries that offer the best prospects in a post-industrial age. There was a rapid expansion of post-secondary education in the 1960s and 1970s but the emphasis was on the more academic programmes.

Fourthly, the growing politicisation of ethnic minority group interests, and their links to extra-territorial opposition movements, is a potential source of conflict. Global crises are increasingly reflected in the internal politics of contemporary societies and Canada is not insulated from these events. Superpower confrontation, Middle Eastern wars, revolutions in Central and South America, political upheaval in Asian and Pacific regions, religious and sectarian conflict in other countries, are all reflected, in microcosm, in Canada. Refugees from before and after the Second World War, together with more recent arrivals, look to the Canadian government and people for support in dealing with war criminals, in redressing grievances and dealing with oppressive regimes abroad. Past injustices are added to concern for human rights and other issues in the present day. Opposition is not limited to peaceful demonstrations but is sometimes reinforced by bigotry, hate literature and telephone tapes, harrassment, graffiti, terrorist threats and bombings. So far, the scale of these activities has remained small, compared with some countries, but the potential for more serious conflict remains.

Finally, the representation of immigrant and other ethnic minorities in the power structure of Canadian society raises questions of equality and distributive justice. Although the proportion of French and Jewish minorities in the economic elites has increased over the last twenty years, other ethnic groups are still under-represented in the highest positions in corporations, government bureaucracies, labour unions, political parties and the mass media (Porter, 1965; Clement, 1975; 1977). There has been a growing concentration of economic power in certain multinational companies. American and other foreign ownership of Canada's resource and manufacturing industries, and the issue of a possible 'free trade' agreement with the United States, is a source of concern to those who wish to ensure independence for Canada's cultural industries and freedom to pursue national interests, economic and political, rather than accept American domination.

Introduction: Ethnic Conflict and Post-Industrialism 15

IMMIGRANTS IN AUSTRALIA

Australia is a thinly populated continent which has relied heavily on immigration as a source of population growth. Like Canada, it has vast areas that are regarded as uninhabitable for climatic or ecological reasons. The majority of people live in the coastal cities and other urban areas. Since the Second World War, the population has doubled from 7.6 million to over 15 million. Net migration contributed one third of the growth (Borrie, 1975; Price, 1984). Unlike Canada, the population was ethnically homogeneous until after the Second World War, the large majority of immigrants having come from the British Isles. Post-war refugee movements, and a later shift to southern Europe as a source of immigration, led to a greater ethnic diversification. In 1947 it was estimated that 90 per cent of the Australian population was of British ethnic origin, but by 1978 it was 77 per cent. The majority of the remainder were of European descent but there was a growing Asian population which constituted a little over 2 per cent. About 1.5 per cent are Aborigines or Pacific Islanders. Religious diversity also occurred with the growth of Greek Orthodox, Jewish and Muslim minorities (mainly from Turkey and the Middle East), adding to the traditional Protestant and Catholic population (Price, 1979; ACPEA, 1982).

Political, including strategic, considerations played a part in determining Australia's immigration policies in the post-war period but economic needs were the primary concern. At first, Australia was less selective than Canada, in terms of education and qualifications. However, as the effects of post-industrial changes were felt, Australia adopted a system of assessment similar to the 'points' system used in Canada. By 1971, immigrants in Australia were on average better educated than the Australian-born population, although there was considerable variation by birthplace. The highest level of qualification was exhibited by immigrants from Britain, the United States, New Zealand, western Europe and various Third World countries. Compared with Canada, Australia recruited more skilled manual workers and technicians, whereas Canada admitted more professionally qualified men and women (Rao, Richmond and Zubrzycki, 1984).

Despite the educational qualifications of immigrants in Australia, overall occupational status was lower for the foreign-born. There was considerable variation by birthplace and period of immigration. Whereas all cohorts of immigration equalled or exceeded the occupational status of the native-born in Canada, only the pre-1946 immi-

16   *Introduction: Ethnic Conflict and Post-Industrialism*

grants did so in Australia. British, American, New Zealand and Asian immigrant males in Australia achieved levels equal to or exceeding that of the Australian-born, but all other nationalities fell below the average in 1971. Immigrant women were even less successful, those from Greece, Italy and Yugoslavia having the lowest status (Richmond and Zubrzycki, 1984). Earnings were generally lower than those of the Australian-born, except for British and American immigrants, although household incomes were maintained at or above the Australian average, largely because of higher labour force participation rates by immigrant women. Recent immigrants from Southern Europe had below average incomes, as length of residence increased the number of dependent children rose, compelling some women to give up work. Consequently, the incidence of family poverty was higher among the earlier cohorts (Richmond and Zubryzycki, 1984:125; Cox and Martin, 1975).

Initially, Australia adopted attitudes and policies that emphasised rapid cultural and linguistic assimilation, or Anglo-Australianisation, of immigrants. However, as ethnic diversity increased, the necessity for a pluralistic approach was recognised. Educational institutions, welfare services, the mass media, industry, commerce and political parties were all obliged to respond to the special needs of non-English speaking migrants (Martin, 1978). Eventually, the Australian government followed the Canadian example and officially adopted a policy of 'multiculturalism'. In 1977, the Australian Ethnic Affairs Council drew up a 'charter' which suggested key principles for a successful multicultural society. They were 'social cohesion', 'cultural identity' and 'equality of opportunity and access'. To these were added, later, the principle of 'equal responsibility for, commitment to and participation in society' (ACPEA, 1982).

Multiculturalism, as a set of policy prescriptions proved to be more controversial in Australia than in Canada (Hawkins, 1974; 1982). Although not without critics in both countries, it was harder to persuade the Australian public, previously committed to a 'white Australia policy', that fundamental changes were needed if immigrants and their children were to be fully integrated into Australian society on a basis of equality. Immigration policies came under fire on various grounds, from threatening the delicate ecological basis of a society which lacked water resources, to more conventional objections such as aggravating unemployment and providing a source of cheap labour. Others considered that any substantial increase in the

Introduction: Ethnic Conflict and Post-Industrialism

Asian population would fundamentally alter the essentially British traditions of Australian society, and produce a hostile backlash from the British and European settlers and their descendants, particularly when unemployment was rising (Blainey, 1984).

The education of ethnic minority children in schools proved particularly controversial. In the immediate post-war years little attention was paid to the question and non-English speaking children were expected to fend for themselves. Later special programmes for English as a second language were introduced. From the 1970s onward there were growing demands for the teaching of ethnic minority languages in the public school curriculum. Recommendations to this effect were made by various government committees although implementation proved difficult (Bullivant, 1973; 1985; Smolicz, 1978). The issue of educational achievement and access to opportunity appeared to be subordinated to that of imparting information about diverse cultural life-styles and promoting inter-cultural understanding.

An examination of the political dimension of ethnicity in Australia reveals a number of areas of actual or potential conflict. As in Canada, ethnic minorities are under-represented (or altogether absent) from the power elites of Australian society. A well-established landed aristocracy that traces its ancestry to the earliest colonial settlers has succeeded in maintaining a dominant position, in terms of wealth and prestige (Encel, 1970; Higley, Deacon and Smart, 1979). It is largely a Protestant group of British ancestry, privately educated and self-perpetuating through marriage, inter-locking directorships and selective recruitment.

Ethnic stratification extends downward from the elites through the professional and managerial strata to the manual working classes, where non-English speaking immigrants are relatively concentrated. Ethnic politics are also class politics. 'No general theory of working-class politics can have any validity in Australia which does not encompass the behaviour and attitudes of ethnics' (Jupp, 1984: 11). The major political parties vied with each other for the 'ethnic vote' but immigrants are under-represented among those elected to political office. Multi-lingual broadcasting became a controversial issue in the late 1970s. Seen at first as a way of courting immigrants and influencing the ethnic vote, a government-funded body was established to regulate and promote radio and television programming in languages other than English. The development was opposed by

18   *Introduction: Ethnic Conflict and Post-Industrialism*

those who saw ethnic media as divisive and likely to create 'cultural ghettoes' (Bostock, 1984: 111).

Australia's geo-political situation is a vulnerable one. This became particularly evident at the time of the Vietnamese and Campuchia refugee crises. Australia was close enough to the scene to experience the arrival of 'boat people' on its shores and to serve as a country of first asylum for a number of those escaping from the aftermath of the war in Vietnam and political upheavals in Portuguese Timor. Australia quickly moved to regularise the flow of Indochinese refugees under the Orderly Departure Programme. By 1985 it had accepted approximately 100 000 Indo-Chinese refugees. Other nearby areas of political instability could create pressure on Australia to accept more people escaping from places such as Sri Lanka (Price, 1985).

Unemployment levels in Australia have risen in recent years but remain low compared with Britain, Canada and many Europen countries. Nevertheless, youth unemployment is serious among some groups, such as Turks and Lebanese, and could lead to disaffection and alienation if it persisted. The degree and extent of ethnic conflict in Australia will depend upon its success in making the necessary adjustments to post-industrial technology and the structural changes that this will involve. The relative concentration of some immigrant groups in traditional manufacturing and construction industries will make them more vulnerable to unemployment in the future.

IMMIGRANTS IN BRITAIN

Britain faced a significant demographic crisis after the Second World War. Its population was ageing and dependency ratios remained high, even after the end of the 'baby-boom'. To this was added the consequences of net outward migration over several decades. Apart from one or two exceptional years (such as 1960–61 and 1972), the country experienced a net loss of population by migration to other countries, including traditional 'Old Commonwealth' destinations, such as Canada and Australia. As these countries were generally selective in their admission policies, taking only those who were young, healthy and with some educational or occupational qualifications, this represented a slow drain of skills and energies, only partly compensated, numerically, by the entry to Britain of immigrants from various parts of the world. By 1981, 6.2 per cent of the

Introduction: Ethnic Conflict and Post-Industrialism 19

population of almost 53 million was born outside the United Kingdom and approximately 40 per cent of these came from so-called 'New Commonwealth' countries, mainly India, Pakistan, East Africa and the Caribbean. The term 'immigrant' in Britain has been used almost synonymously with 'Black' or 'Asian', although numerically immigrants from Ireland, Europe and other foreign countries, together with 'Old Commonwealth' countries, such as Canada and Australia, outnumber them. There is a growing second and third generation of Black and Asian descent who tend to be identified also as 'immigrants'. In 1983, it was estimated that almost one million people born in the UK were of West Indian or Asian descent, in addition to the 1.3 million born abroad (OPCS, 1984: CRE, 1985).

Despite the scale of its immigration, Britain has remained insular in its outlook and isolationist in its policies. Immigrants from the 'New Commonwealth' were not welcomed, or effectively woven into the fabric of a polyethnic, multicultural society. Britain was reluctant to admit those who by race or culture, did not fit the image of a traditional 'white anglo-saxon' population. Those who were allowed to settle faced widespread prejudice and discrimination. Personal and institutional racism persisted, even toward the second and subsequent generations born in Britain of immigrant parents or grandparents. In part, this was a consequence of other conflicts which arose out of structural changes and the contradictions generated by post-industrial developments, particularly in the political and economic systems.

In the political sphere, Britain experienced a relative decline in its power and influence after the Second World War. This was only partly a consequence of the 'loss of Empire', following the achievement of independence by India and, later, by almost all the former British colonial dependencies. It was also related to the rise of the United States and the Soviet Union as 'superpowers', and the military subordination of most European countries to the NATO alliance. Notwithstanding the British government's insistence upon an 'independent deterrent', the country became one of a number of client-states whose sovereignty was severely limited by the emergence of a world military order.

Economically, there was a similar decline in status and with it feelings of insecurity. Britian no longer ranked as a leader in economic growth or technological innovation and its traditional markets, closely linked to its position in the Commonwealth, gave way to those of Europe. Whatever benefits membership in the

20   *Introduction: Ethnic Conflict and Post-Industrialism*

European Common Market may have provided, Britain is now subject to external bureaucratic regulation of its economy and to direction by the European Court on certain issues, such as those relating to human rights. Its negotiating strength within the Community has declined and the result has been a significant loss of sovereignty in economic as well as political matters. Its access to North Sea oil postponed the time when material standards would be seriously jeopardised, but the price of oil on the world market (as well as that of other commodities) has been artificially maintained through state supported oligopolies. Faced with a declining world demand oil has proved to be a precarious prop for an ailing economy.

Technological advances in transport, communications, computers and robotics made redundant large sectors of British industry, and those who worked in them. The post-industrial economy, with its emphasis on the tertiary sector and highly qualified personnel, was slow to develop in Britain, where coal mining, shipping and secondary manufacturing industries were the traditional sources of employment and wealth. Following a short-lived expansion in these industries, after World War II, with consequent shortages of labour, there was a steady decline in output and manpower in these traditional sectors. In the decade 1973–83 steel production fell by 44 per cent, and coal by 10 per cent, with much greater reductions in output planned for the next decade. The manufacture of automobiles fell by 42 per cent and of merchant ships by 50 per cent in the same period, with predictable consequences for employment levels in the cities and regions of the country dependent on these industries. Altogether unemployment levels reached unprecedented levels, rising from 2.2 per cent of the labour force in 1973 to 11.2 per cent in 1983, resulting in three million people being without work. (This is probably an under-estimate due to changes in the method of counting the unemployed).

The size of the male labour force in employment fell by almost two million in ten years, while the number of employed women actually increased slightly, reflecting the growth in service industries and part-time employment, typical of post-industrial societies. Immigrant workers in Britain were relatively hard hit by the structural changes which took place in the economy, from the early 1970s onward. This was particularly true of men. Some immigrant women and their daughters were able to take advantage of the employment opportunities created in the tertiary sector, particularly the health service and

Introduction: Ethnic Conflict and Post-Industrialism 21

in catering and domestic work. Although these were low paying occupations they were less affected by unemployment.

The experience of Black and Asian immigrants and their descendants in Britain, since the end of World War II, illustrates the problems faced by many western societies, adapting to the crises and conflicts associated with post-industrial changes, on the one hand, and with racial diversification consequent upon immigration, on the other. The transition from a society exporting population to other parts of the Commonwealth, to one in which there was a multi-way flow of people to and from many parts of world, resulted in violent disturbances, beginning in Nottingham and London in 1958 and subsequently repeated at intervals in many other cities, the most serious outbreaks occurring in 1981 and 1985 (Richmond, 1960; Scarman, 1981; Benyon, 1984; 1986). These manifestations of deep-seated conflict in British cities reflected a combination of class and ethnic factors, exacerbated by the economic crisis and government fiscal policies. The prejudice and discrimination experienced by racial minorities in Britain reflected the resistance of that society to fundamental change. Britain's wealth and power was founded on the industrial revolution and imperialist exploits of a previous age. It has yet to come to terms with the demographic, technological, economic and cultural realities of today's post-industrial world.

The Black and Asian population in Britain has been seen by some sociologists, using a Marxian analysis, as a 'reserve army of labour', and an element in a continuing class conflict between 'workers' and 'capitalists' (Phizacklea and Miles, 1980). Other researchers anticipate the emergence of an 'underclass', potentially fomenting revolution by its identification with Third World liberation movements (Rex and Tomlinson, 1979). Both these theoretical perspectives find some empirical support, but they do so by focusing on the extreme examples of industrial conflict and through studying neighbourhoods, such as Harmondsworth in the Midlands, which have the highest concentrations of unskilled Black workers. In so doing, the influence of a growing middle class is ignored. Black and Asian immigrants and their descendants growing up in Britain are *relatively* segregated by region and concentrated in inner city neighbourhoods. They are also over-represented in manual occupations, as well as among the unemployed. Nevertheless, the Caribbean and Asian populations in Britain are distributed across a broad spectrum of society. They include men and women at all levels of socio-economic status, from doctors, nurses, lawyers, teachers and managers, to those self-

Introduction: Ethnic Conflict and Post-Industrialism

employed in small businesses, together with clerical workers and skilled tradespeople. Unskilled service personnel and labourers are proportionally over-represented, but they are not a majority among the immigrant population, or the second generation (Brown, 1984).

The one thing that all Black and Asian minorities have in common is the persistent exposure to the racial prejudice and discrimination that pervades British society. In any explanatory model of ethnic relations, racism is an autonomous factor not merely an epiphenomenal by-product of economic forces alone. The outward manifestations of racism in Britain cannot be reduced simply to competition for housing, jobs or other 'scarce resources', however severe such competition may be. Nor can it be explained away as merely a form of status differentiation, much less the 'false consciousness' of those who do not recognise their true economic interests. Racism is deeply embedded in the institutional structure of western societies and has been internalised in the personalities of those who live and work within and through those instituions. So endemic is the phenomenon that even those who espouse 'liberal' attitudes and advocate 'rational' solutions, generally fail to recognise the bias in their own perceptions and prescriptions. The latter often take the form of a greater emphasis upon 'law and order' measures, the need for discipline and social controls, or community relations programmes designed for 'tension management' and the containment of conflict, rather than its resolution. Such policies fail to attack the roots of the problem. Measures intended to combat ethnic prejudice and racial discrimination, or to remove the disadvantages faced by those living in inner cities, are often 'too late and too little'.

When immigrants from the 'New Commonwealth' reversed the former migratory pattern and came to settle in Britain, attitudes toward them, cultivated in an earlier 'colonial' period, persisted. These ranged from outspoken racism to a somewhat paternalistic concern for the welfare of newcomers. 'Common sense' dictated that the traditional 'British way of life' would be threatened by large scale Black and Asian immigration, which needed to be limited in the interests of the community as a whole. (Lawrence, 1982). Nationalism asserted itself in terms of the prior 'rights' of the indigenous 'English' over 'alien' invaders. Exclusionary policies were seen as necessary but the 'integration' of those who had been admitted already was also imperative. The extreme proponents of 'Keep Britain White' advocated more restrictive immigration laws and the repatriation of ethnic minorities. Even those who rejected such

Introduction: Ethnic Conflict and Post-Industrialism 23

policies, and condemned the violent demonstrations of the National Front, maintained a substantial measure of social distance from the immigrants. These attitudes persisted even toward the second and subsequent generations whose education and acculturation has taken place in a British environment. Children growing up in multi-ethnic Britain 'learned to be prejudiced', at home, in school and in the community (Davey, 1983). They followed the example of the adult world where the mass media reinforced, and sometimes inflamed, racial hatred through selective reporting (Hartman and Husband, 1974).

Education and the Second Generation

In a post-industrial society education and training are the key to employment and occupational achievement. Equality of opportunity for secondary and post-secondary education is essential if ethnic minority groups are to achieve upward social mobility and eventual access to positions of status and power within the society. Educational achievement is often closely related to that of parents. When the latter have higher education, a combination of material and social considerations tend to given children a 'head start' in life. Parental support and encouragement make it more likely that children of the better educated middle-class families will do well in school and continue their education.

Evidence from early studies of Black and Asian immigrants in Britain showed that, in 1961, the Indian and Pakistani men and women were on average better educated than the British-born population as a whole, or the West Indian immigrants. (Davison, 1966). Later cohorts of Asian immigrants were not as highly educated as the earlier settlers but they were generally better qualified than those from the Caribbean. These differences in parental background may account, in part, for variations in the achievement of children from West Indian, Indian, Pakistani and Bangladeshi families.

Considerable attention has been paid to the apparent 'under-achievement' of West Indian children in British schools. Those born in the Caribbean sometimes experienced long periods of separation from their families and subsequent difficulties in adjusting to the British educational system. Later, the proportion of British-born Black children increased but, measured by conventional standards such as GCE examination results, there appeared to be fewer children of West Indian background among those passing the exami-

24   *Introduction: Ethnic Conflict and Post-Industrialism*

nations with grades at the higher levels. The question was investigated by a government appointed 'Committee of Inquiry into the Education of Children from Ethnic Minority Groups'. An interim report was published (Rampton, 1981). It was followed by further investigations and a final report *Education For All* (Swann, 1985). Although there was evidence of some improvement between 1978–9 and 1981–2, British-born children of West Indian parentage still lagged behind Asian and other school leavers in the number of higher graded examination passes. Nevertheless, when the educational achievement of the younger generation of West Indian children is compared with the older generation, largely Caribbean-born, a substantial degree of educational mobility is evident.

Notwithstanding the development of 'comprehensive schools', and the expansion of post-secondary educational opportunities from the 1960s onward, the British educational system has tended to be elitist. Entry into post-secondary education is predicated upon good examination results at the 'Advanced' level, sometimes supplemented by College entrance and scholarship examinations, and interviews. Employers also regard these examination results as a basis for selection, particularly when the number of job applicants far exceeds the positions available. In the circumstances, obtaining the necessary credentials is a *sine-qua-non* for improving the status of ethnic minorities.

The Rampton/Swann Commission identified a number of factors which were impeding the opportunities of ethnic minority children. They included evidence of racism among some teachers and the need for improved teacher training; the importance of better pre-school facilities for West Indian children; and a 'multicultural' approach to the curriculum with particular attention to the needs of linguistic minorities. It recognised that Britain was 'faced with a dual problem: eradicating the discriminatory attitudes of the white majority on the one hand, and on the other, evolving an educational system in which *all* pupils achieve their full potential' (Swann, 1985:768).

FUTURE PROSPECTS

It has been noted that academic social scientists have not been very successful in forecasting the outcome of economic and social changes associated with post-industrial developments. There are dangers in assuming an overly optimistic view of the future but it would be equally inappropriate to insist that revolution is imminent, or that a

Introduction: Ethnic Conflict and Post-Industrialism 25

collapse of the global polity, economy or society is inevitable. The contradictions inherent in contemporary social systems are real and could lead to disaster. They may also serve as a stimulus to positive and corrective action, which must take long-term consequences rather than short-term expedient effects into account.

'Racial harmony' may be bought, in the short term, by exclusionary or repressive measures but only at the cost of greater conflict at a later date. Bargaining, rational concessions and negotiated compromise may also create a temporary state in which overt manifestations of conflict are avoided (Banton, 1985). But such expedients are no substitute for measures that ensure true equality of opportunity and condition for all, and the full integration of ethnic minorities into the political, economic and social systems of a modernised, multicultural, post-industrial society. Britain and other post-industrial societies have yet to achieve the necessary technological and economic transitions that such a society requires, much less the social transformations induced by demographic pressures and racial diversification. The British people in their attitudes and values, successive Labour and Conservative governments in the policies they have adopted, and the institutions of British society by their resistance to change, have failed to come to terms with the changing realities of a global society, and the conflicts and contradictions that this entails. So far, Canada and Australia have avoided the more violent manifestations of these latent conflicts but any significant increase in unemployment levels could precipitate a crisis.

Britain, Canada and Australia are not the only advanced industrial countries facing conflicts arising from immigration. France, Germany and Switzerland have all experienced reactionary political movements, a resurgence of racism and anti-semitism, and have adopted policies designed to restrict immigration and encourage 'repatriation'. As Castles *et al.* (1984:229) put it 'The citizens of western Europe no longer have the choice of whether they wish to live in multi-ethnic and multi-cultural societies. They already do. The issue yet to be decided is whether the ethnic minorities are going to be pushed to the margins of society by racism and discrimination, or whether they can succeed in their struggle for equality without loss of identity'. The dilemma is characteristic of all post-industrial societies today.

Part I

Immigration

Part I.

Introduction

2 Structural Change and the Sociology of Migration

Migration is an interdisciplinary field of study. Important contributions have been made by archaeologists and anthropologists who traced the great migrations of *homo sapiens* before the dawn of civilization. Historians took up the story depicting the influence of trade, war and empire-building in the distribution of population and contact between cultures. Social geographers and demographers used quantitative techniques to measure spatial relations of migrants and ethnic groups in selected regions and metropolitan areas. Economists examined the influence of income levels and employment opportunities on internal and external migration, the effects of immigration on consumer demand and inflation, as well as the consequences of remittance payments to former countries. Social psychologists considered motivation questions, such as why some people move and others do not. Lawyers and political scientists have been concerned with policy issues and the administrative regulation of international migration.

Can the phenomenon of international migration as it exists today, in both its economically and politically induced forms, be understood within the framework of contemporary sociological theory? It would be easier to answer this question if there were consensus among sociologists concerning the essential components of sociological explanation. Clearly, no such agreement exists. Sociologists are divided between those who operate at the micro and macro-levels of analysis, those who adopt 'functionalist' or 'conflict' models, and those who focus on subjective, phenomenological meaning and social linguistics, against those who use traditional quantitative, empirical methods. Some work within a deterministic or positivist tradition, while others emphasise the voluntaristic nature of human action and the probabilistic basis of any social explanation. Each of these schools of thought is likely to focus on a different aspect of the phenomenon of migration and to offer, at best, partial explanations or selective interpretations.

30   *Immigration*

The most important contribution by sociologists has been to our understanding of the processes of absorption and adaptation of immigrants in receiving societies although, in recent years, there has also been research on the multi-way movements of population and the factors associated with return migration. The theoretical perspectives adopted by sociologists have generally been implicit, rather than explicit, and often of an eclectic nature, borrowing heavily from other disciplines such as social biology, economics and psychology. A distinctive sociological paradigm of international and internal migration has not yet emerged (Kubat and Hoffman-Nowotny, 1982). Migration was not a central concern of the 'grand theorists' of sociology, in either the nineteenth or twentieth century. Most saw it as one aspect of industrialisation associated with the rise of capitalism in the eighteenth century. It manifested itself as part of the process of urbanisation and metropolitanisation. It involved the decline of rural communities and the creation of culturally heterogeneous and cosmopolitan populations, competing for employment and struggling to survive in an often alien city environment.

EARLY THEORISTS

Malthus regarded migration as an inevitable consequence of over-population. He saw the great open spaces of the New World as providing a temporary escape from the cycle of poverty and misery which kept death rates high and prevented improvements in living standards for the majority. However, he believed that population increased in a geometric ratio while resources increased only in arithmetic proportions. Consequently, an equilibrium would eventually emerge, in North America, that would be no less harsh than that already evident in eighteenth-century Europe. In contrast, Marx condemned Malthus for his reactionary views on the inevitability of poverty, plague and warfare as population restraints. Marx placed the blame for poverty squarely on the greed of capitalist employers who deliberately kept wages down, in order to maximise their profits. In examining the effects of economic and political changes in France, Ireland and Scotland, Marx highlighted the complicity of governments and the military in coercing peasants and small farmers into migration, through enclosure movements, clearances and state-assisted emigration movements.

Durkheim clearly regarded migration as one of the factors which led to the breakdown of traditional communities held together by

Structural Change and the Sociology of Migration   31

'mechanical solidarity'. The transition to 'organic solidarity' based upon a social division of labour and economic inter-dependence was often accompanied by 'anomie', or the collapse of a common value system binding people together.

The resulting confusion and lack of social integration could lead to pathological consequences, including crime, suicide and group conflict. The anomic causes and consequences of migration were further explored in the more recent work of Hoffmann-Nowotny (1979; 1981).

Max Weber's views of migration are less clearly defined. Like Marx and Durkheim, he was concerned with the consequences of industrialisation and the rise of capitalism. He was less impressed by its disintegrating effects and noted the importance of religion, particularly the so-called 'protestant ethic', which he regarded as a necessary condition for capital accumulation and the disciplinary code imposed on the workforce, under capitalism. He saw migration as an incidental factor creating new social classes and ethnic status groups.

The Chicago School

It was not until sociologists in the United States began to study the mass movement of population into the cities, at the turn of the century, that the sociology of migration began to establish itself as a distinct sub-field within the discipline. Beginning with the work of W. I. Thomas and F. Zaniecki (1918) on the *Polish Peasant in Europe and America* and proceeding through the many studies of immigration and race relations conducted by Robert Park and his colleagues in Chicago, the foundations were laid for the sociology of migration as it is today. Few studies have failed to be influenced by the conceptual framework and vocabulary used, between the First and Second World Wars, by writers such as Park himself, together with E. W. Burgess, Louis Wirth, E. V. Stonequist, Franklin Frazier and others in Chicago (Bulmer, 1984).

Influenced by the evolutionary theories of Herbert Spencer and others, the Chicago sociologists adopted an organic model of society in which conflict and competition for scarce resources, within a particular ecological environment, led to the eventual asimilation of immigrants and ethnic minorities. 'Assimilation' was understood as a progressive tendency to be more like members of the receiving society, particularly the social systems and culture of the dominant strata, which were perceived as a relatively homogeneous 'Anglo-American' majority. Park's 'race relations cycle' was seen as applying also to linguistic and religious minorities, who arrived in successive waves from Europe. Beginning with a stage of open conflict between immigrants and the more established populations, and moving through institutionalised competition for land, housing and employment, the new arrivals accommodated themselves to their environment, learning a new language and adopting, with varying degrees of compliance and resistance, new customs in place of old. Eventually, it was believed that complete structural and cultural assimilation would occur, although it was not altogether clear whether this would involve the adoption of Anglo-American values and life-styles completely, or whether some new amalgam would emerge out of the so-called 'melting pot'.

Two fundamental assumptions underlie the Chicago sociologists' theoretical analyses. Firstly, that the immigration process involved a transition from an essentially close-knit mono-cultural rural community, in the former country, to a more heterogeneous, segmented and often disorganized urban environment, in the new country. Secondly, it was assumed that immigrants entered the society at the bottom of a pyramid of economic and social status. They would eventually improve their position, and be dispersed geographically and socially, depending on the degree to which they acquired the appropriate linguistic and other skills, needed by the burgeoning new industrial society.

The American 'dream' was implicit in the analysis of the Chicago school, to the extent that they saw upward social mobility as predicated upon acculturation, combined with the necessary virtues of hard work and enterprise. The intermediate stages might lead to ethnic conflict, social disintegration, zones of transition and psychological stress. The process of assimilation might take more than one generation and, meanwhile, the phenomenon of the 'marginal man', torn between two or more cultures, was typical. The influence of Durkheim, Weber and other European theorists in the writings of these American sociologists was limited. Nevertheless, the model of immigrant adaptation adopted by the Chicago School can be described as 'functionalist', to the extent that the receiving society was treated as an on-going system whose partial equilibrium was disturbed by the influx of immigrants bringing 'old-world traits'.

It was not until after the Second World War, following the immigration of new waves of refugees and others to the United

Structural Change and the Sociology of Migration 33

States, Israel, Canada and Australia, that the ideas of the Chicago sociologists came under critical scrutiny. There was a growing awareness that immigrant adaptation was a more complex process than the earlier writers had assumed. Gordon (1964) examined the American experience and concluded that a clear distinction between the cultural, structural and psychological aspects was required. He recognised that the United States was, in reality, a pluralistic society, although he believed that immigrant minorities would be eventually absorbed. He did not expect that the complete assimilation of ethnic minorities would occur until identification, acculturation and structural dispersion had been achieved. This idea was further developed by Australian social psychologists, Taft (1966) and Richardson (1967) who argued, on the basis of learning theory, that assimilation occurred following rewarding experiences in the new society. They considered that satisfaction with the migration experience would precede identification with it, which in turn would lead to acculturation and social integration.

Eisenstadt's study of immigrants in the early years of the new state of Israel led him to formulate the conditions under which a stable pluralistic society might be established. It is notable that immigrants to Israel were often well educated, and of high occupational status in their former country and were more urbanised than the indigenous Jewish and Arab communities. He argued that cultural and structural pluralism, including a substantial degree of ethnic stratification, could persist indefinitely, as long as there was consensus concerning the legitimacy of the distribution of power and economic benefits, together with a toleration of linguistic and cultural differences (Eisenstadt, 1955).

Further criticism of the classical Chicago model of immigrant adaptation and of the idea of the 'race relations cycle' came from those who recognised that it was no longer appropriate to treat migration without reference to the phenomenon of imperialism and colonial domination. Lieberson (1961) pointed out that Park's ideas could not be applied to the colonial administrators, traders and missionaries in Africa and Asia, or to the white settler populations in these colonial territories. The latter constituted a migratory elite who exercised a dominating influence on the economic and political systems of the receiving societies. They showed no signs of either structural or cultural assimilation.

Furnivall's work in south-east Asia further explored the idea of a plural society. Members of different ethnic groups interacted only in the 'market place', retaining their separate identities and primary social groupings, within the colonial power structure (Furnivall, 1939; 1956). In the post-colonial period attention was paid to the continuing economic domination of dependent societies through exploitation by external investors and multinational companies. Latin American countries, and even Canada, experienced what Clement (1975) calls 'comprador' elites. These are the representatives of the imperial country who assume positions of economic power and influence in the dependent area, forming a migratory elite. Cultural imperialism may also occur when such immigrants acquire undue influence on the education system or control over the mass media.

Neo-Marxian Models

An even more radical critique of the classical Chicago theories is derived from the application of a conflict perspective derived from Marx and Lenin. The increasing use of temporary workers in post-war European countries such as France, Germany, and Switzerland, led to revived interest in the idea of 'a reserve army' of labour that the capitalist system could mobilise when needed. The indigenous workers in advanced industrial societies were able to benefit from trade union organization, welfare state provisions and the exploitation of cheap energy and other resources from abroad. They formed a 'labour aristocracy' who were not prepared to undertake the low paid, dirty jobs that required heavy manual labour and long hours, night shifts etc. Employers, therefore, encouraged the immigration of workers from less developed countries to undertake these menial tasks, at minimum wage rates. However, such workers were not encouraged to become permanent residents and were deprived of most of the benefits of citizenship in the receiving countries. When recession occurred they could be compelled to return to their former countries. Castles and Kosak (1973) applied this neo-Marxian model to the European case, while other writers such as Portes (1981) applied a similar analysis to illegal Mexican and other migrant workers in the United States.

A combination of Marxian ideas concerning class conflict and Weberian views on market relations in the allocation of housing and other resources was used by John Rex and others in an interpretation of the British situation. Immigrants from so-called 'New Commonwealth' countries constituted a racial minority that established permanent residence and is now entering a second and third generation.

Structural Change and the Sociology of Migration 35

They argued that the Black population in England was forming a permanent underclass, which identified closely with Third World anti-colonial liberation movements, and had potentially revolutionary consequences for British society. Without necessarily agreeing with this conclusion, it is evident that Rex's analysis is more sophisticated than the simple Marxian view, particularly when applied to a situation in which immigrants have settled permanently, their children are fully acculturated to the new society, but where they still constitute a highly visible minority subjected to racial discrimination (Rex and Moore, 1967; Rex and Tomlinson, 1979)

Other contributions to the theoretical understanding of immigration have come from sociological and economic studies in the United States. These have highlighted the stratified and 'split', or segmented, nature of labour markets in advanced industrial societies (Bonacich 1973; Edwards *et al.*, 1975). Immigrants, ethnic minorities and women tend to find themselves in marginal industries and secondary labour markets, unable to penetrate the higher-paid occupational positions that are protected by credentialism, professional organizations, trade unions, licensing requirements and the internal labour markets generated by large corporations. Social networks and institutional discrimination serve to exclude immigrants from all but temporary employment and low paid occupations. Undocumented (illegal) migrants tend to be particularly vulnerable in this respect. Women and racial minorities may suffer a double or triple jeopardy, facing discrimination even within the secondary labour market. The model of immigration that emphasises ethnic stratification and labour market segmentation combines some features of the class conflict and structural pluralism models.

Post-Industrialism

By the 1960s it was evident that technological developments were generating rapid social changes in advanced industrial societies. The advent of computers, robotics, satellite communication systems, supersonic jet aircraft and space exploration, was having a profound influence on many aspects of economic and social life, including migration. There was a growing demand for highly qualified manpower and a 'brain drain' from the less developed to the more technologically advanced societies. Rather than the earlier mass movements from rural to urban areas, migration in advanced industrial societies involved a large-scale exchange of population between

36 *Immigration*

metropolitan areas. Some migrants entered the receiving societies at the middle and higher levels of socio-economic status. These elite migrants had an innovative and stimulating impact on the receiving society. Rather than assimilating to the norms of the majority, they were more urbanised and often better educated than the indigenous population. They had a catalytic influence which effected significant transformation of the social structure, modernising pre-industrial economies and facilitating the transition to post-industrialism in more advanced ones.

In later studies Richmond and others, using the Canadian experience as a basis for comparative studies with other countries, further developed the view that immigrant adaptation in advanced industrial societies could not be properly understood either in terms of the 'functionalist' theories of the Chicago School and its later adherents, nor in terms of class conflict alone. A multivariate approach to immigrant adaptation in receiving societies was required, which distinguished the factors influencing economic integration from those determing acculturation, social integration, identification and satisfaction. These were not necessarily correlated with each other, nor could they be represented as a linear process leading to eventual assimilation, dependent only on length of residence (Goldlust and Richmond, 1974; 1978). Linguistic and instrumental, or 'cognitive', acculturation was a pre-condition for the effective utilisation of skills and qualifications, but did not necessarily lead to high levels of satisfaction or identification with the receiving society.

The implications of this multivariate approach to immigrant adaptation, in the context of technologically advanced sending and receiving societies, was further developed in terms of education, occupational status, acculturation, ethnic identity and social conflict, in a series of comparative studies of Australia and Canada (Rao Richmond and Zubrzycki, 1984; Richmond and Zubrzycki, 1984; Burnley and Kalbach, 1985). They concluded that no single theoretical model could account for the complex realities of immigrant absorption in these countries. There was some evidence to support the 'colonial' model in Canada because of the role which highly qualified immigrants from Britain and the United States had played. The 'stable pluralistic' model also fitted the Canadian case more closely than the Australian, where the evidence for ethnic stratification and class conflict was stronger. When the situation of immigrant women was considered the 'labour market segmentation' theory had some explanatory value in both countries. Above all, structural

Structural Change and the Sociology of Migration 37

changes attributable to post-industrial developments, influenced the situation of immigrants who were generally located in metropolitan areas. They and their children were taking advantage of educational opportunities and exhibited residential, demographic and occupational characteristics that were closer to those typical of 'post-modern' societies than the 'third-plus' generation.

Political Controls

Advanced industrial countries experienced economic and technological changes which have brought about an unprecedented combination of low growth, inflation and high unemployment in the last decade. A coincidence of structural and cyclical factors has reduced the demand for labour and hence the need for immigrants. There has been an increasing pre-occupation with the question of immigration control. Governments in traditional receiving areas have moved from positive or permissive policies to negative restrictions. Legal and administrative controls have been instituted to exclude certain categories of international migrant and discourage others from permanent settlement. There has been growing concern over questions of undocumented migrants, illegal entrants, overstayers and temporary workers. Many net receiving countries have endeavoured to encourage return migration and to reduce dependency on imported labour (Kubat, 1979; 1984).

Economically the world is a complex system of economic production and exchange. All countries are inter-dependent and influenced by an international division of labour. Even the Soviet Union, China and other socialist countries enter into economic exchange relations with the capitalist world. All are constrained by an international monetary system, in which vast capital sums are instantaneously transferred from one market to another, by electronic means. Multinational companies transcend the boundaries of particular states as do various international agencies, such as the IMF and the World Bank. Military alliances and economic treaties, such as NATO, the Warsaw pact and the EEC, further limit the powers of previously independent states. No country today has absolute autonomy or complete soveriengty. Conflicting superpowers dominate the world economy and polity creating client-states in varying degrees of economic and military dependency.

Despite global economic interdependency, superpowers are locked into ideological confrontation, and an arms race, which threatens the

38   *Immigration*

precarious 'balance of terror' that has prevailed since World War II. Within the superpowers and some of their client-states, there is growing political dissidence, sometimes taking the form of terrorist violence. Furthermore, client-states in peripheral areas experience direct and indirect intervention in their economic and political affairs, de-stabilising governments and giving rise to internal political dissent and civil strife. Ethnic nationalism, subversion, political liberation movements, class wars, wars between neighbouring states, revolutions and counter-revolutions, all create new sources of international migration and refugee movements.

An outstanding characteristic of the last two decades has been the declining importance of economically motivated 'voluntary' migration and the growing numbers of politically induced 'involuntary' population movements represented by expellees, escapees, deportees, refugees and those displaced by war and avoidable famine. It is hardly an exaggeration to say that politics have taken over from economics as the major determinant of international population movements.

CRITICAL THEORETICAL ISSUES

It is evident from this review that no one paradigm will suffice to explain the many different aspects of international migration and its consequences for sending and receiving societies. Empirical evidence lends only partial support to the various theories put forward and the hypotheses derived from them. No one model will explain such differing situations as undocumented migrants in the United States, highly qualified professionals in Canada, 'guestworkers' in Germany, Black and Asian immigrants in Britain or Indochinese refugees in Italy. However, it is possible to identify certain key developments in social theory which, at least potentially, may contribute to a better understanding of the changing character of international migration. The critical theoretical questions involved are:

1. The nature of *power* and the processes of legitimation.
2. The meaning of structure and the processes of change.
3. The nature of conflict, contradiction and opposition in social systems.
4. The question of social action and human agency.

Structural Change and the Sociology of Migration 39

Power, Authority and Legitimation

International migration cannot be understood without reference to the concept of *power*. This is particularly true where governments insist upon regulating the flow of population within or across borders. Totalitarian societies exercise more rigid controls than democratic ones over internal migration and over emigration. However, even democratic countries continue to legislate conditions of admission for temporary or permanent residents, notwithstanding international agreements designed to facilitate the free flow of people within economic communites.

Power is also a vital question when considering the relationship between immigrant/ethnic minorities in receiving countries and the dominant groups. Access to education, housing, employment and 'welfare state' services may depend upon the power of the minority relative to the majority. The ability of the immigrant population to mobilise its resources, to produce leaders and to organize itself, will determine the extent to which languages are retained, cultural maintenance occurs and separate ethnic identities are forged. In situations of conflict and competition, relative power will determine the allocation of resources among immigrants and between the immigrant and indigeneous populations.

Whether examined in terms of individual or collective behaviour, power is always a relative concept involving degrees of autonomy and dependence (Giddens, 1979:93). Although the relationship is an unequal one, there is a sense in which the ruler is dependent upon his/her subjects. Thus immigrants depend upon the receiving society in many ways, but the latter also depends upon immigrants. It is a two-way relationship. Coercive measures include the direct use of force to deal with violent opposition, the threat of punishment (including deportation), and the withdrawal of economic and social services, hitherto available to immigrants. Power may also be exercised through the offer of rewards for conformity, or compensation for forced repatriation. Immigrants and the receiving society may benefit from (generally unequal) exchange of relationships. Low status in the receiving society may be accompanied by educational and occupational opportunities for children, or rates of pay that offer relative gratification, compared with those available in the former country.

Inequality of power may be translated into *authority* when the subordinated individual or immigrant group is persuaded of the legitimacy of the structures of dominance. Prevailing ideologies emphasise the 'rights' of original peoples or charter groups, at the expense of newcomers. However, consensual forms of power arise when cooperative activities permit the pursuit of goals that could not be achieved, without an appropriate division of labour and hierarchical organization. When considering the power of subordinate groups, such as immigrants or ethnic minorities seeking to organize politically, objective and subjective factors are involved. The relative power of a collectivity will be determined by numbers, access to resources and knowledge of how to use these resources, including factors such as education and technology. However, these must be combined with organizational capacity, leadership and collective consciousness (e.g. ethnic group identity or class awareness), before the outcome of an interactive relationship can be explained or predicted.

At an international level there is clearly an imbalance in the structure of economic and political power which is exacerbating the existing uneven development of various regions. Pressure of population and limited resources in 'Third World' countries continue to generate a high propensity to emigrate, which is resisted by the wealthier countries' experiencing their own internal economic difficulties. Punitive and deterrent measures have been taken by some countries, designed to exclude potential immigrants, to impede the movement of others (such as close relatives of earlier migrants)who have legitimate rights of entry, and to compel the remigration of those who have not established a legal claim to permanent settlement (CRE, 1985).

In order to justify these more stringent controls, immigrant receiving countries have resorted to nationalistic slogans, and sometimes explicitly racist ideologies. Even when formally rejecting the more extreme claims of neo-fascist movements (such as the 'National Front' in Britain and France), governments have tended to respond to the fears of some of their electorate by adopting anti-immigration policies. These trends have coincided with a distinct change, in a more right-wing and authoritarian direction, in the political and social systems of some advanced industrial societies (CCCS, 1982).

Social Structure and Change

Terms such as 'social structure', 'system' and 'social order' are widely used in sociology often without clear definition. Since the 19th

Structural Change and the Sociology of Migration 41

century, there has been a tendency to distinguish between 'social statics' and 'social dynamics'. Structures have often been treated as coherently functioning systems undergoing slow, evolutionary change or sudden transformations. Changes may arise from endogenous factors already 'built into' the system, or from exogenous sources such as culture contact. Those adopting a 'functionalist' perspective are more likely to perceive change as a slow developmental process, while neo-Marxist writers emphasise the inherent contradictions within fedual and capitalist societies, that are likely to generate revolutionary change (Smith, 1973; 1976).

Recent attempts to bridge the gulf between 'consensus' and 'conflict' theories, on the one hand, and between 'functionalism' and 'structuralism', on the other, have led to a new approach to a theory of social action (Giddens, 1976; 1979). This involves the concept of *structuration*, i.e. the generation of structure through the intended and unintended consequence of social action and the 'time-space relations inherent in the constitution of all social interaction' (Giddens, 1979:3). Structure consists of rules and resources organized as properties of social systems, which are routinised as regular social practices. 'Structuration' involves the conditions governing the continuity or transformation of structures, and therefore the reproduction of social systems (Giddens, 1979:66).

The value of this model is that it allows a more realistic approach to the question of social change than is possible in classical theories. It avoids the trap of 'over-determination', in which the individual becomes a pawn in the inevitable unfolding of historical processes as well as the opposite fallacy of extreme 'voluntarism', in which no regularity in the process of change can be discerned, because it is reduced to random variation. Giddens' model is a 'recursive' one which permits reflexive self-regulation. In this respect it is similar to Etzioni's concept of the 'active society' (Etzioni, 1968).

In examining the processes of social change in modern societies, Giddens emphasises the reality of a world-economy and a world military order. Within these global structures, quasi-sovereign states interact in relations of partial autonomy and dependence. The uneven development of different regions may be understood in terms of *time-space paths*, exhibiting different rates of change in political and economic forms. Critical variables in these processes of change are class divisions, ethnic differentiation and territorial claims (Giddens, 1979:226–7). To these might be added internal and external migrations which epitomise a relation between time and space in

42 *Immigration*

generating demographic, economic and social change.

Finally, Giddens (1979:228) identifies four critical phases in radical social change. they are: i. industrialisation; ii. political revolution; iii. institutional decay or disruption consequent upon the encounter of traditional and modern cultures, especially resulting from imperialism; iv. institutional decay or disruption resulting from war. It is obvious that each of these situations is closely related to, and often concomitant with, international migration, both 'voluntary' and 'involuntary'. As a subset of category (i), should be added the post-industrial revolution that has transformed the technologies of transportation and communication and, consequently, the nature of international migration in the modern world.

Conflict, Contradiction and Opposition

Population movements can arise from conflicting situations in sending areas and can generate conflict in receiving societies, particularly where different ethnic and racial groups are involved. Polyethnic societies emerge out of past or present migration and exhibit varying degrees of cohesion. As noted in a previous paper (Richmond, 1978:6–7),

> Conflict may arise out of competition for scarce resources, the differential distribution of power within the society, fundamental opposition of basic value systems and inherent contradictions in the values held and the institutions serving them. Such conflict may coexist with countervailing forces promoting greater order and stability. These may include economic interdependence and exchange relationships emerging in the market context, the emergence of an underlying consensus on basic values that encourage tolerance of diversity, together with the translation of coercive social controls into legitimated authority.

Competition arises when there is consensus on the value of given objects or goals, both material and symbolic, and when these are in short supply. Some symbolic values, such as 'status', 'prestige', 'honour' etc., are inherently scarce and hierarchical. If the outward symbols that are status-conferring become too widespread they lose their value and other symbolic currencies take their place, maintaining the necessary differential. However, exchange relationships arise when valuations differ and the marginal utility of different goods and

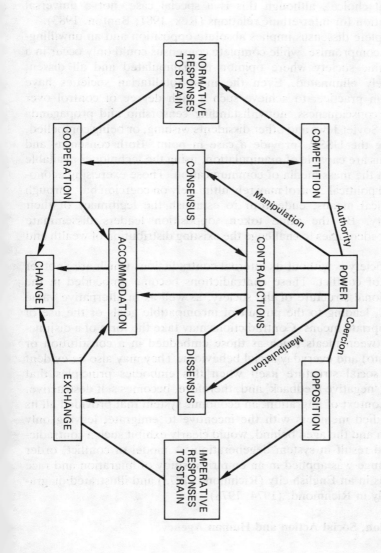

Figure 2.1 Model of conflict, order and change

44 *Immigration*

services permit bargaining to take place. In such situations conflicts may be resolved through market mechanisms, competition and 'rational choice', although this is a special case, not a universal explanation for inter-ethnic relations (Rex, 1981; Banton, 1983).

Complete dissensus implies absolute opposition and an unwillingness to compromise, while complete consensus could only occur in a monolithic society where opinion is manipulated and all dissent coercively eliminated. Even the most totalitarian societies have failed, in practice, to achieve such a high degree of control over human consciousness, notwithstanding censorship and propaganda efforts. Soviet Jews and other dissidents wishing, or being compelled, to leave the USSR, provide a case in point. Both consensus and dissensus are capable of manipulation, using the techniques available through the mass media of communication. Those exercising economic and political control may rely ultimately on coercion but, through ideological means, endeavour to establish the legitimacy of their authority. By the same token, opposition leaders disseminate counter-ideologies to challenge the existing distribution of wealth and power.

No society is without its internal contradictions which are another source of conflict. These contradictions become embedded in the institutional structure of the society, as well as in alternative value systems, leading to the pursuit of incompatible goals or the use of inappropriate means. Contradictions may take the form of a disjunction between ideals (such as those embedded in a constitution or manifesto) and everyday social behaviour. They may also be evident in the social structure itself when this embodies principles that involve 'negative feedback' and, therefore, becomes self destructive. In the context of migration, an economic system that provided all its able-bodied members with the incentive to emigrate, leaving only children and the aged behind, would clearly exhibit such a contradiction and result in system degeneration. A model of conflict, order and change was applied in an empirical study of migration and race relations in an English city (Richmond, 1973) and illustrated diagramatically in Richmond, (1974; 1978).

Migration, Social Action and Human Agency

Sociologists of migration have sometimes distinguished between 'voluntary' and 'involuntary' migration. They have also been inclined to represent migration as fulfilling certain 'system needs' in a

Structural Change and the Sociology of Migration 45

teleological fashion. Thus functionalists have treated migrants as 'necessary' to the economic growth and demographic expansion of advanced societies, while Marxists have argued that capitalism 'needs' a reserve army of labour, which is supplied by immigrants from less developed areas. These formulations raise complex issues of epistomology. They involve questions of freedom and determinism, as well as issues concerning the way in which individual and collective social actions are articulated. What are the constraints placed on individual choice through membership of a group and participation in a system?

One view, recently argued by Banton (1983), emphasises methodological individualism and rational choice. Starting from the premise that people try to maximise net advantage, it is argued that past choices constrain future options, and that competition determines group boundaries. Applied to questions of migration, such a model fits well with traditional 'push-pull' theories. The latter envisage migrants weighing costs and benefits (both material and psychic), in deciding whether to move and where to locate, including the question of re-migration and return. Banton also applies 'rational choice' theory, and a model of competition for scarce resources, to the experience of immigrants in receiving countries. According to the degree of attraction of receiving and sending societies, he distinguishes between 'conformist', 'isolationist', 'colonial' and 'transilient' migrants (Banton, 1983:149).

However, there are serious deficiencies in a model of social behaviour which postulates 'rational choice' as the primary motivating factor. It treats motivation as a purely cognitive and conscious process, ignoring the influence of emotions and unconscious factors. Rather than assuming that individuals habitually seek to maximise net advantage through rational calculation, it would be more appropriate to treat this as only one possibility. Equally likely is the possibility that individuals will be influenced by deep-seated feelings of which they may not be fully aware. Love and hate, fear and bravado, ambition, greed and envy, together with other emotions, are powerful motivating drives for migration, as for other behaviour. The emulation of and identification with leaders, or other 'role-models', also play a powerful part in motivating human actions. Rioting, lynching, looting, and other forms of crowd behaviour, together with advertising, 'brainwashing' and indoctrination, frequently involve the suspension of rational and critical faculties, and the subordination of individual wills to external control.

46 *Immigration*

It is unnecessary to go to the opposite extreme and assume that unreason always prevails over reason and the unconscious over the conscious. In everyday behaviour rationality may prevail in the choice of means to given ends, although the ends – i.e. the preferences themselves – may not be rationally explicable. Furthermore, the human capacity of rationalisation comes into play, after the event, to supply plausible explanations for non-rational behaviour, thereby reducing cognitive dissonance. Such dissonance may occur when initial or return migration does not generate an expected level of gratification (Richmond, 1967). However, to the extent that individuals are 'free agents', their choices are constrained, not merely by past choices, but also by the structure of power in the sending and receiving societies. *Power involves the capacity to influence beliefs and values as well as to provide rewards and punishment.* Hence the importance of multicultural education and the ethnic media, such as multilingual radio and television, in influencing the social integration of immigrants (Richmond, 1981; Banks and Lynch, 1986).

CONCLUSION

What are the implications of this view of structural change and the nature of social action for the sociology of migration? Firstly, the recursive model of structuration requires that attention is paid to the two-way nature of immigrant adaptation, in which the receiving society, as well as the social systems of immigrants themselves undergoes profound changes. Immigrant adaptation must be understood as an active rather than a passive process, and one which has significant repercussions on the structures of receiving and sending societies alike. In post-industrial societies particularly, migration implies a process of *active mobilisation*. This means a 'dynamic interaction between motile individuals and collectivities, giving rise to information flow and feed-back, effecting greater control over material and human resources' (Richmond, 1969:281). Even when immigrants are not selected for their special skills or qualifications, their impact on the political, economic and social systems of the receiving society is considerable. Immigrants are agents of change even when conservative or reactionary forces resist the consequences, such as greater ethnic or racial diversity.

Secondly, international migration occurs in the context of a global economy and polity exhibiting extremes of inequality in the distribution of economic resources, political power and social status. Within

Structural Change and the Sociology of Migration 47

and between geographic areas at approximately the same level of development, 'time-space' paths balance, i.e. migration is of the exchange type with little net gain or loss of population. However, pressure to emigrate from poorer to richer areas continues in the face of resistance from those in wealthier countries, whose inhabitants are determined to protect privilege and maintain status differentials. Advanced industrial countries, facing the consequences of structural changes and internal contradictions, endeavour to exclude migrants and will continue to support restrictive legislation, until immigrants are again seen as economic assets.

Thirdly, there must be a recognition of the *political* context in which migration takes place. Governments can influence people in the decision to move or to stay in one place. Policy decisions concerning economic investment in certain industries or localities can determine the nature of the cost-benefit equation, considered by each individual or family. At the same time, governments may use their formidable powers of persuasion, through the mass media, to generate a climate of opinion that is favourable or unfavourable to migration. In this they may be aided and abetted by private corporations seeking to influence the supply of labour. A government that wishes to induce the migration of an ethnic minority it perceives as a threat to the majority, may adopt a variety of coercive measures to induce emigration or force people into flight. Opposition movements may also stir up hostility to certain groups. External and internal warfare induce migration on an increasing scale. Some immigrants and refugee groups may remain politically active and involved in irredentist or subversive movements, relative to the former country.

Receiving societies also influence the mode of adaptation of immigrants through political action or inaction. Policies which determine the admissibility of certain categories of immigrants and not others, together with those which encourage or discourage permanent settlement, facilitate or impede citizenship participation, and either offer or withold the benefits of the 'welfare state', all have a profound influence on the role and status of immigrant populations. When ethnic or racial minorities are involved in immigration, government actions designed to combat prejudice and discrimination, to promote multicultural education and smooth social integration, are critical. Failure to take such action or, in some cases, the deliberate condoning or encouragement of racist policies, will exacerbate conflict and generate opposition.

48 *Immigration*

Finally, the global political order is an unstable one in which superpowers confront each other in ideological opposition and military stalemate. At the same time, war and revolution are ubiquitous in the economically and politically peripheral areas of Africa, Asia, Central and South America, where the superpowers are themselves implicated. The problem of refugees from these turbulent areas has become an overwhelming one. Even more than economic inequality, political conflicts compel international migration and generate further structural change. Advanced industrial societies resist these changes and are reluctant to provide even temporary asylum, much less permanent homes, for the victims of war, persecution and famine. It is almost certain that the displaced persons of today, and their children born in limbo, will be among tomorrow's political revolutionaries, terrorists and self-styled 'liberators'.

3 Socio-Cultural Adaptation and Conflict in Immigrant-Receiving Countries

The process of acculturation and social integration of immigrants are as complex as the societies involved in the international movements of people. Such migrations include the free movement of labour between countries belonging to the European Economic Community, the 'brain drain' from developing countries in the Third World, the continued movement of people within and between old and new countries of the British Commonwealth to the employment of *Gastarbeiter* in Europe, as well as the flight of refugees and expellees from countries subject to internal warfare or political upheaval. Care must be taken in generalising from any of these varied situations, some of which exhibit unique characteristics. Furthermore, the processes of socio-cultural adaptation may occur without undue conflict when the receiving society is experiencing economic growth and relative affluence, but give rise to problems when unemployment is high or there is competition for other scarce resources, such as affordable housing, access to higher education or the benefits of a welfare state.

Earlier sociological studies of the assimilation of immigrants were often based upon an over-simplified misrepresentation of the characteristics of the migrants themselves and the conditions in sending and receiving societies. In the nineteenth and early parts of the twentieth century, waves of immigration to North America and other areas of the New World largely consisted of poorly educated peasants who entered countries that were themselves experiencing all the upheavals associated with the early stages of urbanisation and industrialisation. The problems of socio-cultural adaptation experienced by such immigrants were quite different from those whose international movements have taken place in the age of jet aircraft, radios, telephones, television and computers. Even in the earlier era it was not appropriate to treat the migrants as uniformly of peasant

50   *Immigration*

origin. At the same time the receiving societies themselves were not always culturally homogeneous or monistic.

Today more than ever it is important to recognize the polyethnic and culturally diversified character of both sending and receiving countries.[1] There is no single 'American way of life' into which immigrants arriving in the United States must eventually be assimilated. The United States is ethnically stratified, culturally pluralistic and exhibits a diversity of life-styles. The same applies to other countries such as Australia, Canada, France, the United Kingdom, and many others who have experienced large-scale immigration in the last three decades. Almost all these countries have indigenous racial and ethnic minorities who have retained distinctive languages, religions and sub-cultures for several generations. To these already heterogeneous populations have been added the more recent immigrants and their children who have increased still further the ethnic diversity of the countries concerned.

It is important also to recognise variations among the immigrants, even those arriving from the same country. Politicians, public officials, teachers, welfare workers and others who come into contact with immigrants often speak of ethnic 'communities' as if the new arrivals were a closely knit people sharing a single set of values and united by a common language and cultural background. This is rarely the case. Immigrant populations exhibit their own class structure and are divided by various dialects, differing religions and opposing political beliefs. Ethnic 'leaders' often represent only particular factions, though they may claim to speak for the immigrant community as a whole. To the extent that immigrants from particular countries eventually exhibit some degree of social cohesion and develop their own separate institutions and organizations it is often in response to discriminatory treatment in the receiving society. Immigrants need to develop a power base in order to protect their interests. Out of this situation new definitions of 'ethnic' identity evolve that are unique to the receiving society.

Sending and receiving countries alike are exposed today to rapid social changes that influence everyone, even those who remain all their life in one place. The technological consequences of space exploration, satellite communications, computerisation and robotics are already evident in industry and in domestic life. The full economic and social impact of these changes has yet to be experienced. However, the processes of acculturation and social integration of immigrants as well as the situation of those re-migrating or

Socio-Cultural Adaptation and Conflict 51

returning to their former country have already been profoundly influenced by this 'post-industrial revolution'.

Some Determinants of Immigrant Adaptation

The immigrant adaptation process is influenced by pre-migration conditions, the transitional experience in moving from one country to another, the characteristics of the migrants themselves and conditions in the receiving country, including government policies and economic factors.[2] Other important determinants include: age on arrival in the new country; the education and qualifications of the immigrants concerned; their degree of exposure to the mass media, including ethnic newspapers, radio and television; and the types of social network entered into in the receiving country. The process of adaptation is a multidimensional one in which acculturation interacts with economic adaptation, social integration, satisfaction and degree of identification with the new country. More empirical research is needed to establish the precise way in which these variables interact. Multivariate models of the immigrant adaptation process developed for specific countries or cities, at a certain point in time, may require modification when situational factors change (Goldlust and Richmond, 1974).

Among the most important pre-migration factors are those concerning the motives and intentions of the migrants. In some cases migration is seen as a temporary expedient. Motives may be strictly economic or related to a desire for travel and adventure. The migrant, whether male or female, may go alone with the intention of returning to family and friends after a sojourn of a few months or, at most, a year or two. Such temporary migration is not limited to those countries that have encouraged 'guest-workers'. It is also characteristic of some arriving in countries whose policies have been to encourage permanent settlement. Original intentions may not always be fulfilled. It is the experience of most immigrant-receiving countries that many so-called temporary migrants settle permanently whereas some original intentions to settle are reversed. Nevertheless, original motives and intentions do influence the propensity of the migrant to learn the language of the receiving society, the types of social network developed, the degree of participation in the formal organization of the receiving society and the commitment to that country, including attitudes toward citizenship and political involvement. the latter, in turn, is influenced by the policies of the receiving country. Some countries have accorded voting privileges to immigrants after comparatively short periods of residence, while others have made citizenship, and its accompanying rights and privileges very difficult to obtain, even for those with long residence. In some cases even the citizenship status of children born of foreign parentage in the receiving country may be uncertain (Kubat, 1979; Tomasi, 1981).

An important distinction exists between voluntary and involuntary migration. Economic conditions in sending countries may be so harsh that migration becomes the only resort. In this case it may be as coercive a situation as political or religious persecution, or displacement by the ravages of war. However, most economic migration is of a voluntary nature, motivated by the desire to improve the migrant's economic status or the prospects for his children. In contrast, political instability in the sending country, or a deliberate policy of expulsion of ethnic minorities or political opponents, gives rise to involuntary migration. In turn this influences the socio-cultural adaptation of immigrants. Although the prospects of return are generally poor for such people, political refugees frequently maintain a strong attachment to the home country and an aspiration to return, should political conditions change. In turn this may lead to more active participation in ethnic organisations and in some cases even to support for subversive activity against the political regime in the home country.

Political upheaval often means that the actual process of migration, and the transition from one country to another, is accompanied by unusual trauma. All migration leads to the severing of social ties and some anxiety in connection with the adjustment to an unfamiliar environment. The transition and early stages of migration frequently give rise to mild neuroses, psychosomatic illness and sometimes more serious reactions to the stresses involved. In the case of political refugees the stress is often much more serious. Migration may have been preceded by periods in prison or concentration camps. Wealth and possessions may have been lost or confiscated and loved ones may have died or disappeared. As in the case of the 'boat people' from Cuba or Viet Nam, the actual journey to the country of first asylum may have been extremely hazardous, and followed by long periods of waiting in camps under conditions of severe deprivation. Under these circumstances it is not surprising if the first few months and even years of adjustment for refugees and displaced persons are accompanied by social and psychological problems. Family reunion

Socio-Cultural Adaptation and Conflict

becomes a central concern and survival the only immediate objective (Haines *et al.*, 1981).

The auspices of migration constitute another factor to be taken into account. Independent, economically motivated migrants may travel alone or with their immediate family only. If they do not have pre-arranged employment they may be compelled to depend on their own initiative and resources in order to establish themselves at first. Others in this category may be assisted by government or employers in these early stages. Subsequently, migrants may sponsor family members and eventually more formal arrangements may evolve through ethnic organisations, to assist migrants during the early stages of adjustment. In the case of refugees, various countries have adopted different systems of sponsorship and aid by government or voluntary associations. Further research is needed to ascertain the long-term effects of these varying reception conditions. Prima facie hypotheses would suggest that the greater involvement of the voluntary sector would encourage more complete acculturation and social integration, in the long run (Neuwirth and Clark, 1981).

Education

Age on arrival in the new country is understandably an important factor in socio-cultural adaptation. Immigration involves some degree of desocialisation from previously learned attitudes, values and behaviour patterns. In many cases, as in the learning of a new language, children have less to unlearn and are also able to adapt more quickly to new conditions. This is assisted by their involvement in the formal school system of the receiving country, which acts as a primary socialising agent. There is considerable variation within and between countries in the nature and extent to which schools adapt to the presence of immigrant children. The provision of second-language courses, or instruction in the mother tongue, together with special orientation classes and multicultural education programmes are some of the ways in which countries with large numbers of immigrants have responded to ethnic diversity in the classroom. Such programmes tend to be expensive and are often controversial. The precise aims of multicultural education are not always clearly defined and the resources available are often insufficient (Bullivant, 1982).

For older immigrants learning a new language and other aspects of acculturation may present more formidable obstacles. Receiving societies may offer classes in the majority language and other kinds of

54   *Immigration*

initial orientation programme for adults. Sometimes such classes are open only to government-sponsored migrants or to the chief wage-earner in a family. Classes must often be attended after the fatigue of a full day's work and so drop-out rates may be high. The response of immigrants themselves depends a great deal on their own level of education and previous training. Probably, education, more than any other single factor, explains the degree and extent of subsequent socio-cultural adaptation, and the precise form that the adaptation takes (Smolicz, 1979; Goldlust and Richmond, 1978).

In terms of prior educational achievement, immigrants reflect a broad cross-section of the populations of sending countries. It is a mistake to think of immigrants as necessarily having little education. Depending, in part, on the policies and selection criteria used by the receiving countries, the educational level of immigrants may even exceed that of the indigenous population, as in the case of Canada in the post-war period (Richmond and Kalbach, 1980). Refugee movements frequently include people with professional qualifications or managerial and entrepreneurial experience. Even in those countries that have depended on immigrants to provide unskilled labour or to perform more menial service tasks, the level of education of the migrants may be above the average for the sending country as a whole.

Ease of access to educational opportunities in the receiving country has an important influence on the socio-cultural adaptation of immigrants. Those with technical or professional training frequently need to re-qualify or up-grade their qualifications in the new country, in order to be able to practise their trade or profession. Failure to provide such facilities or to assist in the cost of further education by governments or employers leads to the under-utilisation of immigrant skills and abilities as well as frustration and disillusionment on the part of immigrants themselves. Traditionally, second-language classes in receiving countries have emphasised oral teaching and endeavoured to accelerate the speed with which an immigrant learns to understand and speak the official language. Unfortunately, in modern societies, a high degree of literacy, as well as oral fluency, is needed by all those seeking employment in other than unskilled work. Although many immigrants are literate in their own language and bring with them skills and qualifications from their country of origin, they are often prevented from obtaining commensurate employment in the new society. Degree and professional examinations may have to be taken in the unfamiliar language. More

Socio-Cultural Adaptation and Conflict 55

attention needs to be paid to the need to read and write a second language if full use is to be made of an immigrant's previous training and experience (Richmond, 1981*a*).

Education is also an important determinant of the pattern, mode and sequence of socio-cultural adaptation. A distinction may be made between the obligatory level of acculturation necessary for the economic and social survival of the migrant in the new environment and those aspects of acculturation that are optional from the receiving society's perspective. However, this distinction in turn depends upon the type of occupation pursued by the immigrant and the nature of the social interaction with others that this requires. An unskilled labourer on a construction site may not need to be literate in his own language or even be able to communicate orally in the majority language in order to function effectively. In contrast, a doctor, lawyer or teacher must have a high degree of oral fluency and literacy in the majority language before adapting at a level appropriate to his previous education and qualifications.

Some studies have suggested a sequence in the acculturation process in which initially rewarding experiences in the new society give rise to satisfaction. This in turn contributes to the immigrant's identification with the new country which facilitates learning and eventual acculturation, to a point where the newcomer is fully assimilated (Richardson, 1974; Rogers, 1978). Such a sequence seems to be applicable only to less well-educated immigrants who are able to achieve an interim adjustment within an institutionally complete ethnic enclave. In order for skilled manual, clerical, technical and professional workers to maintain or improve upon their occupational status in the receiving country obligatory acculturation must include linguistic, cognitive and behavioural levels of adaptation of a more substantial nature. Such a high level of acculturation is likely to precede the achievement of satisfaction, identification or even significant social integration (Goldlust and Richmond, 1978).

Although the formal education institutions within the receiving society must play an important role in the acculturation of children and adults alike, the mass media also have a strong influence. Newspapers, radio and television are important instruments in facilitating the adaptation of immigrants, whether or not they also attend formal classes. For many immigrants television is the most important socialising agent and influence on their acculturation. However, given the pluralistic nature of many receiving countries, the mass media do not necessarily contribute to the rapid linguistic or cultural

56 *Immigration*

assimilation of immigrants towards the characteristics of the majority population. Ethnic newspapers have always played an important part in providing channels of communication between immigrants from particular countries. Increasingly, radio and television perform similar functions. Through such media immigrants keep in touch with social and political developments in the country of origin, as well as with activities and events among others from the same country or region living in the new society.

Governments in immigrant-receiving countries have sometimes been suspicious of the ethnic press as a potentially subversive influence and have felt obliged to monitor its activities. At the same time, recognizing the tremendous power and influence of the media, governments in some countries have endeavoured to encourage and promote ethnic newspapers, radio and television. By directly or indirectly providing financial support (for example by government advertising) and by using the ethnic media as a means of transmitting ideas and information about the new country, the governments concerned hope to facilitate acculturation and encourage the commitment and identification of ethnic minorities with the majority groups in the society, even before complete fluency in the official language(s) has been achieved. Empirical studies have shown that, even after level of education and length of residence are taken into account, exposure to ethnic media still has a direct influence on the mode of adaptation of immigrants (Richmond, 1981*b*).

Popular Culture and Consumer Behaviour

Most contemporary forms of recreation, sport, entertainment, and popular culture are independent of language, nationality or cultural boundaries. Modern mass communications have enabled millions of people throughout the world to enjoy leisure-time activities that have universal appeal. Some regional preferences may remain for soccer over other kinds of football, for cricket over baseball, or for ice hockey over other kinds of mass-spectator winter sports, but these same activities unite participants and spectators alike, whatever their ethnic origin or nationality. Even though the teams may symbolise ancient rivalries between cities, counties, provinces and countries, the players themselves cross political boundaries with impunity, if the financial incentives to do so are high enough. International migrants have no difficulty following their favourite team's successes in the competitive leagues. The miracle of modern satellite communications

Socio-Cultural Adaptation and Conflict

may even enable them to watch the game live from several thousand miles away!

Much the same considerations apply to other areas of mass entertainment, whether of the 'popular' or the more 'élite' varieties. Language is no impediment to the enjoyment of all forms of music from Rock to Rachmaninoff, Bach to Bacherach or the Beatles to ballet. The cinema and television have overcome language barriers with convincing voice-dubbing. The most successful box-office hits and Oscar winners are seen by millions from the United States to India, from Sweden to South America. Again, technological advances in video-cassettes, cable television, and in satellite communications, facilitate the continued exposure of immigrants to more specialised programmes in their own language. Foreign films are also shown in 'ethnic' cinemas in the receiving countries. The latest advances in home entertainment, in the form of computer games and videographic toys, are even less dependent upon language than their predecessors. Space-Invaders speak a universal language!

Similar considerations apply to almost all aspects of consumer behaviour, and markets, in advanced industrial societies where immigrants have settled. Modern techniques, such as refrigeration, combined with rapid air transportation, make supermarkets and local ethnic shops capable of providing a wide range of produce from all parts of the world. International trade under contemporary conditions has diversified the range of consumer goods available to immigrants and indigenous populations alike. It is not just in ethnic restaurants that formerly exotic foods are available. They have changed the life-styles and consumer habits of people throughout the more affluent countries of the developed world, where immigrants have contributed to a significant diversification of cultures in the receiving countries. Such diversification extends from the culinary sphere into many other aspects of consumer behaviour, including more expensive durable goods and appliances. Such international trade can occur in the absence of immigrants from the countries concerned but the latter act as a catalytic factor. Some immigrants may be directly involved in the entrepreneurial initiatives that promote such import-and-export trade (Kallen and Kelner, 1983).

Modern methods of marketing and distribution facilitate the initial adjustment of immigrants who do not speak the language of the receiving society. Open shelving and self-service facilities enable new arrivals to purchase their requirements with a minimum of verbal exchange. Supermarkets frequently exhibit familiar brand names as

58   *Immigration*

well as introducing the possibility of experimentation with new and unfamiliar products. For those who prefer the more social atmosphere of the corner shop the immigrant communities generally provide enough small retail outlets where the proprietor speaks the language of the immigrants in question. Housewives, who are often the last members of a family to acquire a fluent knowledge of the majority language in the receiving country can, nevertheless, perform traditional domestic roles without serious difficulty.

It is evident that in the realms of consumer behaviour, and of popular culture, there is a process of mutual adaptation on the part of immigrants and members of the receiving society. Extensive cultural borrowing and exchange takes place, facilitated by modern technologies, the effects of which have penetrated sending and receiving countries alike.

Ethnic Nationalism

It is important to recognize that, particularly in a society with its own indigenous linguistic and cultural minorities, complete cultural assimilation into the majority group or dominant strata is not a necessary condition of successful adaptation. Emergent 'nationalist' movements in various advanced industrial countries have demonstrated the persistence of linguistic, religious and other ethnic differences in certain regions. Increasingly, provision is being made, through schools and universities and through media such as television, for the preservation and encouragement of such minority subcultures. Immigrants have added their voices to those of indigenous minorities in claiming the 'right of difference' and the legitimacy of their claims to preserve their cultural heritage. In some cases this has led to government concessions towards greater self-determination, regional devolution or political independence for established minorities and special multicultural policies for immigrants (Hawkins, 1982; Richmond, 1982*a*).

The nineteenth and early twentieth centuries in most advanced industrial countries were associated with the disruptive effects of massive urbanisation and industrialisation, and with the political instability induced by revolution and war. The unity of the emergent nation-state became a major preoccupation. Frequently, this was achieved by bureaucratic centralisation, by the economic domination of core over peripheral areas, and by the creation of a myth of a homogeneous 'nation' coinciding with the often artificial boundaries

Socio-Cultural Adaptation and Conflict

of the state. Sometimes ruthless attempts were made to stamp out minority languages and other 'alien' influences that might appear to threaten unity, or undermine the domination of existing ruling classes. In only a few cases were such countries successful in translating the myth into reality. Countries such as the United Kingdom, France and the Federal Republic of Germany on one side of the Atlantic, and the United States, Canada and Latin American states on the other, remained polyethnic, multinational, pluralistic societies. Post-war immigration further added to their diversity. Within such ethnically stratified, regionally diversified, multicultural societies, more recently arrived immigrants were able to develop their own enclaves[3] with varying degrees of institutional completeness. Particularly for refugees from political and religious persecution, this freedom of expression and liberty to maintain their own particular values and life-styles became their most cherished goal. When contrasted with the persecution they had formerly experienced, this freedom of cultural expression became one of the principal sources of gratification and the basis on which loyalty to the new country was forged. In the present post-industrial era it is increasingly recognised that multicultural policies are not only more realistic but also contribute to the greater unity of societies which might, otherwise, face more violent opposition, if the needs and interests of ethnic minorities were ignored. Despite rhetorical assertions of past imperial glories, and resistance to the idea of decentralisation, modernisation has not led to the disappearance of ethnic diversity (Smith, 1981; Reitz, 1980).

Social Integration

It is in this pluralistic context that the social integration of immigrants must be examined. At the level of primary groups, networks including family and friends of the same ethnic background play an important part. It has been noted how important family reunion is for political refugees, but similar considerations apply to economically motivated migrants who may be separated from spouse or children. In some cases, three-generation families and extended-kinship networks are also evident. Although economic success and upward social mobility make an important contribution to the immigrant's level of satisfaction, close ties with family and friends may be even more important. In lower income groups, families not only provide moral support but are also sources of economic security and mutual

60 *Immigration*

aid. However, ethnically homogeneous social networks can have a retarding effect on occupational mobility and acculturation, if they channel communication into truncated channels or dead-ends rather than being open, supportive and facilitating. (Richmond and Goldlust, 1977; Anderson and Christie, 1982).

Earlier waves of immigration to North America and elsewhere tended to give rise to ethnic residential concentrations in urban centres and fairly high degrees of social segregation. When combined with low socio-economic status this led to ghetto formation and social pathology associated with poor housing and a sense of deprivation. More recent immigrants to the cities of the United Kingdom and Western Europe have sometimes repeated this pattern (Castles and Kosak, 1973; Rex and Tomlinson, 1979). However, territorially based and geographically bounded communities are increasingly being replaced in modern societies by looser social networks. In the absence of direct discrimination in the housing market, and with greater ease of transportation and communication, ethnic links can be maintained even when an immigrant population is more widely dispersed. Larger ethnic populations in cities can maintain their own internal labour markets, retail stores, professional services, recreational facilities, old people's homes and ethnic organisations, without necessarily suffering a high degree of geographical segregation from the rest of the population (Kalbach, 1981).

Although immigrant associations may play an important role in facilitating the initial adjustment of immigrants, and may continue to exert influence through acting in a representational capacity in negotiation with government authorities, actual membership and participation in such organisations is typical of only a small minority of immigrants and their descendants. Active participation, and particularly the assumption of leadership roles, is generally confined to the better-educated, longer-term residents. Even contact as a client with either voluntary agencies or government departments specifically catering for the needs of immigrants is generally infrequent. Personal networks and the mass media are more often the sources used by immigrants for information and assistance when needed.

The social cohesion of an immigrant group will depend upon a number of factors among which size is clearly significant. Institutional completeness and a complex organisational structure are only possible when numbers are large. By the same token, the response of municipal or central government authorities, school boards and the

Socio-Cultural Adaptation and Conflict

like, to the special needs and interests of immigrants will depend on the numbers involved and the effectiveness of their organisations in mobilising support for certain actions. There are obvious economic constraints and logistical problems involved in providing language classes or other special services, for small numbers spread over many different ethnic groups. However, the same number of people concentrated in a single linguistic or religious category in a certain area, may be in a position to exert more pressure and to obtain special facilities or concessions. Even where numbers warrant, it may still require articulate leaders and sympathetic political support from others in the majority group, before resources are allocated for such special purposes (Martin, 1978).

Racial and ethnic prejudice among the indigenous population may lead to complaints about 'foreign' customs with regard to clothing, food consumption, religious rituals, recreational pursuits or personal habits of immigrants that are regarded as offensive. However, it is in the economic and political arena that serious conflict between first-generation immigrants and the majority population are most likely to occur. Most critical is perceived competition for jobs, housing and opportunities for social mobility through the educational system. In some cases immigrants face explicit discrimination in these spheres. In others the discrimination may be more covert. Immigrant women may experience a double threat, facing discrimination on the basis of sex as well as race or national origin. Conflicts of this kind may persist into the second and subsequent generations even after socio-cultural adaptation has proceeded to a point where only such ascriptive factors as race, sex or religious affiliation remain as diacritical indicators. Extremist movements may endeavour to maintain an ideology of racial or cultural purity, advocating strict immigration controls and even the expulsion of 'alien' people. Although such extreme racist or ethnocentric views may be held by only a small minority, leaders of such movements may be able to mobilise popular sympathy, particularly at times of economic crises. Demonstrations and violent clashes may ensue. In turn, immigrant minorities who are victims of such collective violence or individual attacks may feel obliged to protect themselves, sometimes leading to an escalation of fear and violence in the process (Scarman, 1981).

It has been noted that, whatever their original intensions or the policies of the governments concerned, 'temporary' migrants often settle permanently and return migration is not uncommon among those expected to settle. Among the latter, return migration is

62   *Immigration*

sometimes seen as failure but this is not necessarily the case. The motives for return migration are varied. They may be related to family responsibilities, retirement, or a stage in a migrant's occupational career. When not expelled by the country concerned as a consequence of a deliberate policy to discourage permanent settlement, most returning migrants are satisfied with their experience abroad; some may even consider emigrating again at a later date. Some countries have actively encouraged the return of their own nationals when economic conditions are favourable, in preference to becoming dependent on immigrant workers. Receiving countries have also offered incentives to return (Rogers, 1981). Sending countries have had difficulty ensuring the satisfactory employment of returnees and the effective utilisation of the skills or experience gained abroad. Returning migrants face the necessity of re-establishing social ties and of finding their place in an economic and social system which has itself undergone change in their absence. This is particularly true for those whose absence has been prolonged and whose children have been brought up in the country of immigration.

Length of Residence and the Second Generation

After age on arrival and education, length of residence in the new country is the single most important determinant of the degree and pattern of socio-cultural adaptation exhibited by immigrants. Learning a new language, modifying attitudes, values and behaviour patterns, acquiring a knowledge of the new society's institutions and developing new social networks, all take time. If the immigrant is unmarried on arrival it may be a while before marriage takes place, a family is established and new kinship connections built up. For those married before migration there may be a delay in achieving family reunion, especially if this is not encouraged by the authorities in the receiving country. Marriage to a person of the same ethnic origin will lead to a more homogeneous social network and a different pattern of acculturation and social adaptation than marriage outside the group. The longer immigrants are away from the country of origin the more their own sense of personal identity will change. If the receiving country encourages permanent settlement and facilitates early acquisition of citizenship, a dual sense of ethnic identity may occur. This is rendered more likely when holiday visits to the home country, exposure to ethnic media and the maintenance of a homogeneous

Socio-Cultural Adaptation and Conflict

social network lead to the retention, over a longer period, of attachments to the home country. However, in a pluralistic society adopting multiculturalism as an official policy, separate or dual ethnic identity is not incompatible with a commitment to permanent residence and a feeling of loyalty to the new country. Only in wartime, or in the event of direct political conflict between the home and adopted countries, is such loyalty likely to be put to a crucial test. Even then, the historical record shows that immigrant-receiving countries have often over-reacted to fears concerning 'enemy aliens' and their descendants. (Both the American and Canadian governments have recently recognised the injustices perpetrated towards Japanese immigrants and their second-generation descendants during the Second World War.)

The strength of ethnic identity and use of a non-official language among the second and subsequent generations varies greatly according to circumstances. Languages have both instrumental and expressive significance. Children born in the new country are more likely to retain the language of the parents if there are practical advantages in doing so. This may be the case where a parent or grandparent has not acquired a knowledge of the majority language in the new society or where return visits are frequent. Other practical considerations include the availability of instruction in the mother tongue and its usefulness for business purposes or professional communication. Where new waves of immigrants are arriving, or where strong trade or other links with the former country are maintained, the incentive for bilingualism is greater (de Vries and Vallee, 1980; Isajiw, 1981).

In the absence of instrumental reasons for language maintenance, those relating to its symbolic and emotional significance come into play. Such considerations generally appeal more to the better-educated immigrants who wish to pass on to their children an appreciation of the history, literature and 'high' culture of the home country, including its music, art and drama. Such expresive considerations are further re-inforced when language is associated with religion. The Church or religious community often becomes the principal agency for instruction in the parental language, when religious services and rituals are still conducted in that form. Minority religious groups in North America, including Protestant sects fleeing from persecution, as well as others such as Jews, Greek and Ukranian Orthodox and, more recently, various Asian communities, have a sense of ethnic identity which is closely linked to both language and religion. In contrast, the majority Catholic and mainline Protestant churches may contribute to language loss, through encouraging assimilation to the majority group.

Conflicts between parents and children are not confined to immigrant families. However, the particular form taken by inter-generational conflict may be related to the question of immigrant status and ethnic identity. Much depends on the attitudes prevailing in the wider society. The views of teachers and the status accorded to the minority group are important. If a child is made to feel inferior at school, or is ridiculed in the neighbourhood, he may wish to rebel against his parents and repudiate the language or cultural group from which they are descended. In the early stages of migration children may learn the majority language more quickly than the parents. They may be called upon to serve as translators or interpreters, which reverses the traditional status and authority relationship, which in turn is resented by the parents and can lead to conflict.

Early socialisation plays an important part in determining whether a person retains a distinctive sense of identity in later life. A popular hypothesis has it that the second generation rejects its parents' values and endeavours to become fully accepted by the new society, while the third and subsequent generations have more positive and sympathetic interest in their cultural roots. Empirical evidence is lacking for this interpretation. Recent studies in Canada suggest that there is a more progressive loss of ethnic mother-tongue knowledge and use by generation and considerable variation by origin group in the extent of ethnic identity retention. In any case the substantive meaning and practical significance of ethnic identity is generally quite different for third and subsequent generations, than for the first and second (Isajiw and Makabe, 1982).

Religion provides an important reinforcement for ethnic identity and the sanctions associated with it may give rise to conflict. This is particularly the case in areas of sexual behaviour and marriage. The beliefs and values of particular immigrant groups may be at variance with the norms and practice of the receiving society. Courtship, pre-marital sex, contraception, abortion, age at marriage and the question of religious endogamy are all issues over which the younger generation may disagree with the views of parents or religious leaders. Arranged marriages and curbs on the freedom of young people to choose their own friends and partners, or to attend dances and other places of entertainment or recreation, are all potent sources of conflict and tension between generations. Understanding

Socio-Cultural Adaptation and Conflict

and counselling on both sides is needed if such disputes are to be avoided. Other conflicts may occur in connection with the observance of religious rituals, fasting, food taboos and other distinctive customs (Watson, 1977).

Although racial differences are not necessarily linked to either linguistic or religious factors, they are salient as identifying the second generation and subsequent descendants of earlier immigrants. 'Visible' minorities, even more than linguistic or religious ones, are likely to experience social and economic discrimination. Even when all their education has been received in the country concerned, and their qualifications are the same, members of black or Asian minorities in predominantly white societies face discrimination in employment, housing and access to other services. The basis of conflict is normally not socio-cultural but strictly economic. Nevertheless, some young people in these circumstances may adopt a distinctive lifestyle or join certain religious or political movements, as a form of socio-psychological defence against the feeling of oppression experienced in the wider society (Pryce, 1979). When such feelings of alienation are accompanied by high rates of youth unemployment and squalid housing conditions it is not surprising that they sometimes lead to violent protest, rioting, looting, gang warfare and other forms of deviance. When racism is deeply embedded in the attitudes and institutions of the receiving society, coercive measures may be taken by the authorities to suppress violent crime or demonstrations, rather than recognising the need to change the attitudes and behaviour of the majority group (Miles and Phizacklea, 1979; Scarman, 1981).

Conclusion

Global economic crises in the last decade have aggravated the problems of adaptation facing immigrants and their children while at the same time, increasing hostility towards them by those who feel threatened by 'foreigners.' Despite a short-lived sympathy for the plight of refugees in the 1970s, the political climate in recent years has not been favourable to the absorption of immigrants, who tend to become the scapegoats for various economic problems. At a time of high inflation, escalating unemployment and pressure to curb government expenditure, social services, special educational programmes and multi-cultural policies tend to fall victim to governmental fiscal restraints (Richmond, 1982a). Major structural shifts are taking place in employment markets as a consequence of both demographic and technological changes. The socio-cultural adaptation of immigrants and their children cannot be considered independently of their socio-economic status in the receiving countries. Whatever restrictions those countries may place on immigration in the future, they have a responsibility to ensure just and equitable treatment for those who are now living there. Although some voluntary repatriation may take place, this is not a practical solution. Social, cultural and educational policies are needed that will ensure successful integration within the context of a genuinely polyethnic and multicultural society.

A number of alternative modes of adaptation by immigrants to the varying conditions of different receiving societies are possible. Only misplaced value-judgements would lead to the conclusion that one form of adaptation is necessarily superior to another. It is no longer reasonable to argue that only the disappearance of an ethnic group through cultural assimilation, geographical dispersion, intermarriage and complete identification with the dominant stratum of the majority group, constitutes a proper goal of social policy. At the same time, receiving countries have an obligation to combat racial and ethnic discrimination against immigrants and other minority groups, while ensuring equality of opportunity in educational institutions and the job market. Where racism has been a historical reality and discrimination is institutionalised, bold measures may be needed in the form of human rights legislation and affirmative action programmes to overcome the handicaps otherwise facing immigrants and their children. This is particularly true where visible minorities are concerned.

4 Immigration and Unemployment in Canada and Australia

Since the end of World War II, Canada and Australia have both pursued positive immigration policies designed to augment natural increase through net migration and to meet specific manpower shortages. However, Canada much more than Australia has been faced with a dilemma in trying to reconcile the continuing flow of immigration with significant fluctuations in the economy and comparatively high levels of unemployment. In both countries, sympathy for the plight of refugees has been tempered by concern for their effective economic integration and the fear that immigrants will be competing with new entrants to the labour force, particularly young people.

Until the 1970s, unemployment in Australia remained at a level which, in Canada, would be regarded as full employment, (See figures 1, 2 and 3). Australian unemployment rates remained below 2 per cent throughout the 1950s and 1960s. In contrast, unemployment in Canada rose from 2.4 per cent in 1951 to 7.1 per cent a decade later. However, in the 1970s Australian unemployment rates rose to over 6 per cent by the end of the decade, while in Canada the rates fluctuated between 6 per cent and 8 per cent until a steep rise, after 1980, to a peak of 12.1 per cent. In both countries unemployment rates are higher for women than for men and for the young inexperienced workers. Furthermore, there is considerable variation within the immigrant labour force in unemployment rates depending on nationality, education and qualifications (Ford, 1977; Denton, Robb and Spencer, 1980; Young, 1980; Fisher, 1982).

Although the absolute and relative numbers of unemployed in Australia have been lower than in Canada, the question of maintaining immigration during periods of recession has been a politically sensitive issue in both countries. In 1949 the Australian Immigration Planning Council was established with representatives from employers, labour unions, academics and government officials. This Council met regularly with political representatives and recommended an annual level of immigration that they believed to be compatible with the anticipated economic conditions in the following year and the expected absorptive capacity of the labour force. Although both political and economic conditions entered into Canadian immigration policy formation, it was not until the new Immigration Act, of 1978, that any comparable machinery for consultation was established there. The government is now obliged to inform Parliament annually of the proposed levels of immigration. Under the new legislation it is necessary for the Minister of Employment and Immigration to consult with the Provinces and with other interested parties and experts, before determining an appropriate level of immigration for the coming year. A report is now laid before Parliament indicating the recommended levels of immigration for the following year and the demographic, economic and humanitarian considerations that have entered into the formulation of these proposals (Department of Employment and Immigration, 1980).

Immigration Levels and Unemployment

Macro-economic models and simulations suggest that even very substantial increases in the level of immigration have only a marginal impact on gross unemployment levels. There appears to be some consensus among economists using simulation techniques that the unemployment rate rises about a quarter of a percentage point for every 40 000 gross immigration increase (Davies, 1973; Demers, 1974; Marr, 1976). Current levels of immigration are around 100 000 annually and less than half of these intend to enter the labour force (Department of Employment and Immigration, 1980). The evidence shows that there has been a consistently strong negative association between levels of annual (gross) immigration and the overall unemployment rate in both Canada and Australia (Salter, 1978; Parai, 1974). Figures 4.1 and 4.2 show that during periods of high unemployment in the post-war Canadian economy the level of labour force immigration has tended to fall, whereas in periods of low unemployment it has tended to rise. The only exception to this trend occurred in 1957 and was largely a function of the international situation. The Suez Crisis and the Hungarian Revolution created a political climate in which it seemed inappropriate to close doors to immigrants altogether. Some economists have argued that the inverse relationship between unemployment and immigration is more evident when the unemployment rate is 'lagged' one year. It is argued

Immigration and Unemployment in Canada and Australia 69

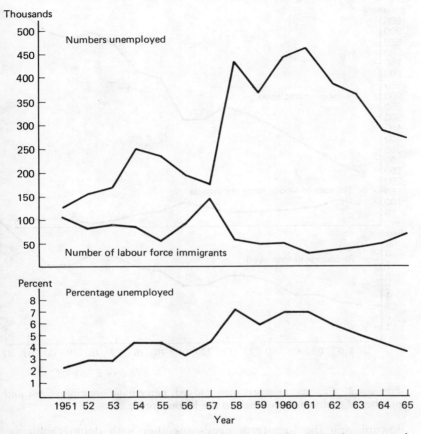

Figure 4.1 Canada: numbers unemployed, percentage unemployment and number of immigrants destined to the labour force, 1951–65

that there will be a time delay between the availability of information concerning unemployment levels and the decision to depart that will be made by potential emigrants. This is predicated on the assumption that 'natural' market forces govern the flow of immigrants and tends to ignore the efficacy of direct government intervention (Green, 1976). However, immigration officials themselves, following directives from Ottawa, are more directly responsible for slowing down the rate of admissions when the economic climate appears unfavourable. Hawkins (1972:111) calls this the 'tap on and tap off' policy. She is critical of it because it creates administrative problems and constitutes a short-term response to the needs of the labour market,

70   *Immigration*

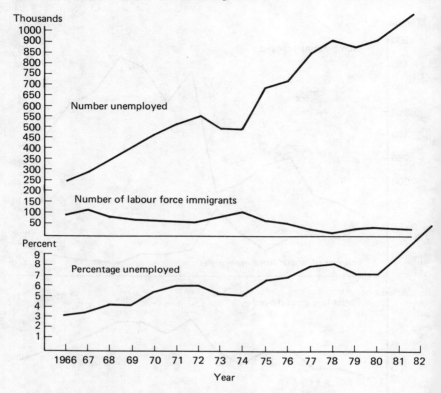

Figure 4.2   Canada: numbers unemployed, percentage unemployment and number of immigrants destined to the labour force, 1966–82

downplaying the long-term needs together with demographic or humanitarian objectives of Canadian immigration policy. It is notable that in recent years the government has deliberately increased the proportion of sponsored immigrants and dependents while restricting the number of labour force immigrants. However, this has been compensated for in Canada by an increasing use of temporary employment visas to meet short-term manpower requirements (Richmond, 1978:116).

The Australian experience is shown in Figure 4.3. The much lower rate of unemployment in Australia, compared with Canada, is evident until the mid 1970s. Despite a smaller total population, the absolute numbers of labour force immigrants admitted annually was very close to the numbers admitted to Canada. The number of labour force immigrants admitted in 1975 and 1976 was substantially reduced

Immigration and Unemployment in Canada and Australia 71

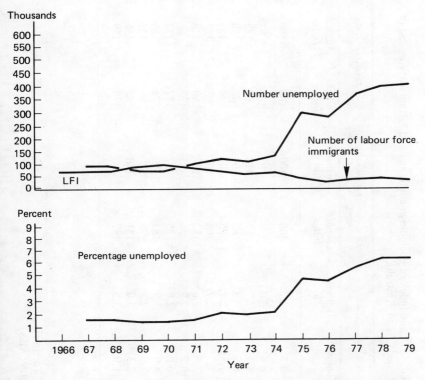

Figure 4.3 Australia: numbers unemployed, percentage unemployment and number of immigrants destined to the labour force, 1966–79

but there has been some recovery in immigration levels since. There is an inverse association between the numbers unemployed and the number of labour force immigrants admitted annually in both countries and the negative correlation is about the same in both countries.

Rates of Unemployment by Birthplace

Having established a negative association between labour force immigration and unemployment levels, it remains to consider whether immigrants are more or less likely to be unemployed than the native-born. Davis and Gupta (1968) examined the unemployment rates for post-war immigrants in Canada and compared them with rates for the native-born derived from monthly labour force surveys up to 1967. Between 1956 and 1962 the rates for immigrants

Table 4.1   Percentage of labour force unemployed, 1971 and index of unemployment by sex and birthplace, for 'rest of Canada'* and Australia

Birthplace	Males		Females		Males		Females	
	Canada %	Australia %	Canada %	Australia %	Canada Index	Australia Index	Canada Index	Australia Index
Total	6.5	1.5	8.3	2.2	100	100	100	100
Native-Born	6.7	1.4	8.4	2.0	103	93	101	91
Foreign-Born	5.5	1.7	8.1	2.7	85	113	98	123
USA/NZ	5.5	2.4	6.2	3.3	85	160	75	150
UK and Eire	5.5	1.6	7.8	2.7	85	107	94	123
Germany	4.4	1.6	7.7	2.7	68	107	93	123
Greece	7.3	1.9	7.5	2.6	112	127	90	118
Italy	5.6	1.1	10.2	1.9	86	73	123	86
Netherlands	2.3	1.3	6.0	2.8	35	87	72	127
Poland	5.4	1.2	5.9	1.9	83	80	71	86
Other Europe	5.1	1.8	7.9	2.8	78	120	95	127
Asia	8.5	2.1	7.3	3.0	131	140	88	136
Others	8.9	2.4	11.0	3.5	137	160	133	159

Base for index: Rest of Canada, Males   = 6.5
                 Rest of Canada, Females = 8.3
                 Australia, Males   = 1.5
                 Australia, Females   = 2.2
*excluding Quebec, Prince Edward Island and NW Territories
Source: 1% PUST 1971 Census of Canada; Table 106 (ABS)

were higher than those for the Canadian-born. However, following the increased selectivity in terms of education and occupational qualifications that marked Canadian immigration policy in the 1960s, the reverse was true in the later period. The authors noted that the lower rates for immigrants were a function of the industrial and regional distribution of immigrants as compared with the rest of the population. They estimated that, in 1967, the unemployment rate of native-born Canadians would have been one percentage point lower than it actually was, if they had had the same (favourable) regional distribution as post-war immigrants. This would have eliminated any significant difference between the two categories (Davis and Gupta, 1968:28). Unfortunately, monthly labour force data for the foreign-born population are not available for the last decade in Canada.

Census data for Canada and Australia provide a means for systematically comparing the experience of immigrants. Table 4.1 compares unemployment rates by birthplace in 1971. In view of the very different levels of unemployment in Canada and Australia, the raw percentages have been standardised and converted into an index for purposes of comparison. In order to increase comparability between the Canadian and Australian experience of immigration, Quebec has been omitted from these calculations.

In 1971, immigrants in Canada had lower unemployment rates than the native-born but the opposite was the case in Australia. There were some differences in the experiences of men and women. Male immigrants in Canada generally had lower than average unemployment rates with the exceptions of those born in Greece, Asia and 'other' countries. The latter category consists mainly of immigrants from the Caribbean and Latin America. Foreign-born women in this country also had lower unemployment rates with the exception of those born in Italy and the residual 'other' category. Although absolute unemployment levels were lower for both native and foreign-born in Australia, the foreign-born had proportionately higher unemployment rates with the exception of males born in Italy, the Netherlands and Poland. Non-European males had particularly high unemployment rates compared with native-born Australian males. Women in Australia had slightly higher unemployment rates than men but were still below the Canadian level. Immigrant women from Italy and Poland were the only ones with below-average rates.

In 1971, regional variations in the level of unemployment and the concentration of immigrants in the Metropolitan areas of Central and

Table 4.2 Percentage and index of unemployment by sex and birthplace, for Metropolitan Toronto and Melbourne, 1971

Birthplace	*Males* Toronto %	*Males* Melbourne %	*Females* Toronto %	*Females* Melbourne %	*Males* Toronto Index	*Males* Melbourne Index	*Females* Toronto Index	*Females* Melbourne Index
Total	6.0	1.4	7.4	1.9	100	100	100	100
Native-Born	5.9	1.4	7.2	1.7	98	100	97	89
Foreign-Born	6.1	1.6	7.8	2.3	102	114	105	121
USA/NZ	4.7	2.2	4.8	2.4	78	157	65	126
UK and Eire	5.0	1.5	5.5	2.1	83	107	74	111
Germany	5.6	1.4	6.9	2.4	93	100	93	126
Greece	6.7	2.1	5.7	2.7	112	150	77	142
Italy	4.3	1.2	11.8	1.5	72	86	159	79
Netherlands	0.0	1.3	0.0**	2.3	0	93	0**	121
Poland	5.1	1.3	9.6	1.7	85	93	130	89
Other Europe	7.5	1.9	9.4	2.5	125	136	127	132
Asia	9.9	2.1	11.5	2.8	165	150	155	147
Others	11.2	1.9	7.3	3.0	187	136	99	158

Index: Base for Toronto Males = 6.0 Females = 7.4
       Base for Melbourne Males = 1.4 Females = 1.9
Note: ** -n is less than 50
Source: 1% P.U.S.T. 1971 Census of Canada
        Table 106 (ABS)

Immigration and Unemployment in Canada and Australia 75

Western Canada accounted for their more favourable levels of employment at a national level. The advantage is reversed in the urban areas. Table 4.2 compares the Metropolitan areas of Toronto, Canada and Melbourne, Australia which are both areas of substantial immigrant concentration. The Toronto data show that the unemployment levels for males were slightly lower for the native-born but, overall, the differences were comparatively small. Again, it is immigrants from Greece, 'other European countries', Asia and the Caribbean who experienced the highest rates of unemployment in 1971. Immigrant males in Melbourne were more seriously disadvantaged, in relative terms. Although immigrants from Italy, the Netherlands and Poland had below-average unemployment rates, other immigrants had rates that were higher than those of the native-born. Immigrant women in both cities had higher unemployment rates although the relative difference was greater in Melbourne. Again, non-European women in both countries appeared to have higher unemployment rates, with the exception of those in the residual 'other' category in Toronto. Given the composition of this group it would appear that West Indian women were not over-represented among the unemployed at that time.

Length of residence in the receiving country has an important influence upon unemployment rates in both Canada and Australia. Table 4.3 shows the rates and indexes of unemployment for the foreign-born by sex and period of immigration, at the time of the 1971 census. It is evident that, in Canada, unemployment rates for immigrant males were below average in all cohorts up to 1965. However, prior to the 1971 census, rates were above average for those who had arrived since 1966. Despite the comparatively low levels of unemployment in Australia, immigrant males were relatively more disadvantaged. The index shows an above average rate for those arriving 1961 or later and a very much higher index for those who had arrived in the five years previous to the census. The index for immigrant males in this cohort was 187 for years previous to the census. The index for immigrant males in this cohort is 187 for Australia compared with 114 for Canada. The experience of female immigrants in the two countries differed somewhat from those of males. In Canada, women who arrived after 1955 had above average rates of unemployment with an index of 108 while those arriving after 1961 had an index of 116. In Australia, immigrant women had below average rates up to 1960, and an index close to the Canadian for 1961–65, but those who arrived 1967–71 were more vulnerable, with

Table 4.3 Indexes of unemployment for foreign born by sex and period of immigration for 'rest of Canada'*
and Australia

Period of Immigration**	Males		Females		Males		Females	
	Canada %	Australia %	Canada %	Australia %	Canada Index	Australia Index	Canada Index	Australia Index
Pre 1946	5.3	1.0	6.3	1.4	82	67	76	64
1946–55	4.4	1.1	6.7	1.7	68	73	81	77
1956–60	5.7	1.4	9.0	2.1	88	93	108	95
1961–65	5.7	1.6	9.6	2.6	88	107	116	118
1966–71	7.4	2.8	9.6	4.3	114	187	116	195

**Periods of immigration for Australia differ by one year.
 *excluding Quebec, Price Edward Island and N.W. Territories

Source: 1% P.U.S.T. 1971 Census of Canada
   Table 106 (ABS)

Base for Index: Rest of Canada, Males   = 6.5
            Rest of Canada, Females = 8.3
            Australia, Males   = 1.5
            Australia, Females   = 2.2

Immigration and Unemployment in Canada and Australia 77

an index of 195. It is clear that, in both countries and for both sexes, there was a significant adjustment period in which immigrants were more likely to be unemployed than the native-born population.

Trends since 1971

Systematic comparisons between the two countries are more difficult for more recent periods because there was no question on birthplace in the 1976 Census of Canada. The Australian census in 1976 showed that, for both men and women born in Australia, unemployment rates were inversely related to age. For the foreign-born the relationship was not quite so consistent. Rates tended to be lowest in the middle age groups. Unemployment rates in most age groups were considerably below average for Italian males and above average for those born in the Lebanon. Youth unemployment was serious for both sexes and all nationalities, but most acute for those born in New Zealand, the Lebanon and Turkey. Among Australian males 25–44 years of age, unemployment rates were 2.5 per cent for native-born and ranged between 3.2 per cent for those born in the UK to 10.5 per cent for the Lebanese (Young, 1980).

Evidence from the monthly labour force data for Australia in the month of May, 1979, shows that average unemployment rates were 5.1 per cent for Australian-born males and 5.0 per cent for immigrant males (Australian Year Book, No. 64, 1980). The rates for women were 7.9 per cent and 8.4 per cent respectively. There was a clear relation to length of residence for the foreign-born with unemployment rates ranging from 3.9 per cent among those who arrived before 1961 and up to 15.6 per cent for those who arrived in Australia between 1978 and 1979. The highest unemployment rates were recorded for New Zealand immigrants (8.7 per cent) and the lowest for Italian (4.7 per cent).

Neither Census nor monthly labour force sample data are available for the foreign-born in Canada after 1971. However, some comparisons can be made using the government's longitudinal surveys of immigrants (CIPS 1974 and special tapes). The 1969, 1970 and 1971 cohorts were samples over a three-year period and a 1976 cohort over a one-year period. Table 4.4 shows the percentage unemployed after the first six months, one year, two years and three years, respectively. Unemployment rates were considerably above the national average for both men and women during the first year in Canada. The information which is available for the first three cohorts

78   *Immigration*

indicates that the rates declined in the second and third years until
they were at or below the national average. However, it should be
kept in mind that the immigrant population had a favourable age and
regional distribution compared with the native-born as a whole. The
longitudinal survey data confirm the evidence of the 1971 Census to
the effect that Third World immigrants tend to have above average
unemployment rates (Saunders, 1978). The 1981 census showed that
unemployment for Caribbean immigrants in Montreal was double the
rate for the Canadian-born. In Toronto it was 50 per cent higher.[1]

Table 4.4   Longitudinal survey data re-analysis: percentage unemployed
by length of residence in Canada

Cohort	6 Months %	1 Year %	2 Years %	3 Years %
		Males		
1969	11.8	9.3	6.8	5.6
1970	17.1	10.2	7.4	5.4
1971	11.7	9.2	6.1	3.1
1976	11.3	9.3	—	—
		Females		
1969	7.9	8.3	7.0	5.5
1970	13.2	8.2	7.5	5.3
1971	14.5	13.0	8.3	7.1
1976*	23.6	12.9	—	—

*The 1976 cohort of women sampled all labour force participants including
married women.
Earlier cohorts were reported for single women only.
Source: Special tabulations from longitudinal survey data tapes (Manpower
and Immigration).

Conclusion

This comparison between immigrants in Canada and Australia, in
terms of unemployment experience, raises a number of important
policy questions. There are those, in both countries, who would
argue that there is no justification for permitting any immigration at
all when unemployment rises above a certain minimum level. Even if
one accepts this view, it is difficult to determine what the critical level
of unemployment should be before the tap is completely turned off.
Australian evidence suggests that there was an over-reaction in the

early 1970s when unemployment first began to rise. Immigration levels were cut back so severely that in 1975 Australia actually experienced negative net migration as a consequence of more people leaving the country than entering it (Price, 1975; 1980). This was certainly not the effect that the government intended and it moved quickly to rectify the situation by permitting higher levels of immigration in subsequent years, despite a continuing rise in unemployment levels among young people. Canada also came close to experiencing negative net migration in 1978 although, in the absence of reliable data on the outward movement, precise estimates are not available (Statistics Canada, 1979).

Regional disparities are much greater in Canada than in Australia. High unemployment rates in the Atlantic Provinces tend to inflate the national average but these are not traditionally areas of immigrant settlement. Government policy combines with self-selection to ensure that immigrants tend to gravitate toward the areas of relatively full employment and economic growth. Thus, for a time, Alberta attracted more immigrants than in the past.

The situation becomes more complicated when specific manpower shortages are taken into account. In recent years, Australia has followed the example of Canada in introducing a system of immigrant selection that places emphasis on occupational skills and qualifications (Price, 1980). In both countries, additional consideration is given to those occupations considered to be in short supply. From a long-term point of view there are clearly advantages in improving manpower training programs and increasing the supply of native-born workers with the requisite qualifications. Unfortunately, manpower planning is still not a precise science. The education and training of highly skilled and professional workers can take anything from one to ten years beyond high school. Anticipating the needs of employers several years ahead is difficult and unreliable estimates can lead to severe over- or undersupply at a time when employers need to move quickly to satisfy immediate needs. Most advanced industrial societies have come to depend upon immigration as a means of overcoming short-term requirements as well as chronic shortages (Bryce-Laport, 1980).

The comparatively low levels of labour force immigration to Canada in recent years will have had a negligible effect on the overall level of unemployment. Unemployment levels are a consequence of economic factors that are global in origin and international in their impact (Barber and McCallum, 1980). Recently arrived immigrants

80   *Immigration*

tend to be the victims of unemployment rather than its cause. Despite high levels of education, Third World immigrants appear to be particularly vulnerable in this respect. Youth unemployment is currently a serious problem in both Canada and Australia (Young, 1980; Denton, Robb and Spencer, 1980). It affects the native-born of native parentage, the native-born of foreign parentage as well as foreign-born youth. So far, both contries have avoided the kinds of violent confrontation that have taken place in Britain between members of different racial and ethnic groups. Youth unemployment does not necessarily cause racial violence but it does generate a climate in which other precipitating events may be more likely to create conflict. Cutting back on immigration, or closing the doors completely, would not solve the problem of unemployment and it would not necessarily reduce ethnic tension. The best antidote would be policies designed to promote economic growth and to achieve the effective integration of all new entrants to the labour force, irrespective of age, nationality or ethnic origin.

5 Third World Immigrants in Canada

Since the end of World War II Canada has pursued a positive immigration policy encouraging the permanent settlement of immigrants from many countries. After 1974, there has also been extensive use of temporary employment visas which enable people to work in Canada for periods up to one year, with the possibility of renewal for a longer period in certain cases. Third World immigrants have become an increasingly important source of temporary and permanent workers. In the latter case, the immigration of a spouse and other dependents has also been encouraged. In addition, refugees have been accepted from various countries in Asia and Latin America. Again, 'family reunion' has been a component of this movement. However, temporary workers have not been allowed to bring family or dependents.

Prior to 1962, regulations restricted immigration from Third World countries to Canada. Only 'token' numbers were admitted from India, Pakistan and Sri Lanka, together with a small number of domestic workers from Caribbean countries. From 1968 onwards, selection for permanent settlement was on the basis of education, skills and qualifications deemed to be in demand in Canada. As the proportion of Third World immigrants increased the movement assumed the character of a 'brain drain' from these countries. In addition there has been a significant movement of students from Third World countries, some of whom have remained in Canada after completing their studies. Temporary employment visas were issued to less skilled workers, largely for seasonal employment in agriculture and domestic work in hospitals, institutions or private homes. The former were mainly male and the latter predominantly female.

The scale of the permanent (landed) immigrant movement in recent years is shown in Figure 5.1, for the period 1971–1982. The statistics include the refugee component. Permanent immigration from all countries averaged 141 000 annually over this period. The proportion from Third World countries rose from 36 per cent in 1971 to a peak of 63 per cent in 1980, declining to 54 per cent in 1982. In absolute numbers, 1974 was a peak year with over 107 000 coming

81

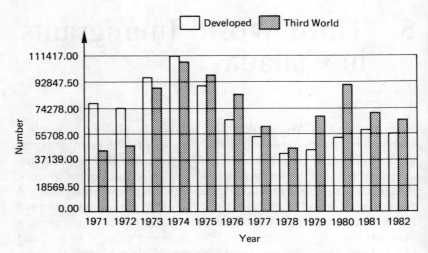

Figure 5.1   Immigration to Canada by region, 1971–82

from Third World countries, mainly those in Asia, the Caribbean and Latin America. A declining proportion of these immigrants intend to enter the labour force and only 45 per cent did so in 1982. The government has restricted selected worker immigration in favour of dependents in the face of poor economic conditions, although it continued to utilise temporary employment authorisations (Wong, 1984).

The refugee movement has been a significant component of the permanent immigration, constituting some 140 000 of the total immigration over a twelve-year period. The Indochinese were the largest single component or 40 per cent of all 'refugees and designated classes' admitted (Lanphier, 1981). The government's assisted refugee allocation for 1983 was 12 000 of whom 70 per cent were from Third World countries. Figure 5.2 shows a more detailed break-down of immigration to Canada by regions of the world, for 1983. Almost two-thirds of the 'landed immigrants' that year were from Third World countries, of which the Asian and Pacific component was the largest (38 per cent of a total of 89 157).

Approximately 165 000 short-term employment authorisations have been issued annually, and a further 45 000 extended for more than one year. Of these 40 per cent are from Third World countries, mainly Central America and the Caribbean. About 100 000 student authorisations are issued annually, about half of which are renewals, and more than half the students are from Third World countries.

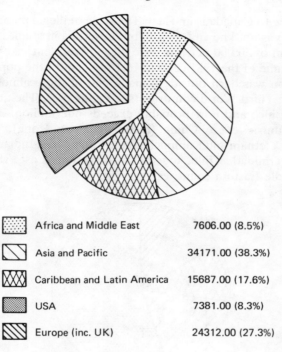

	Africa and Middle East	7606.00 (8.5%)
	Asia and Pacific	34171.00 (38.3%)
	Caribbean and Latin America	15687.00 (17.6%)
	USA	7381.00 (8.3%)
	Europe (inc. UK)	24312.00 (27.3%)

Total: 89157.00 (100%)

Figure 5.2 Immigration to Canada by world area, 1983

The movement of people from the Third World to Canada has given rise to some re-migration and a return movement. Unfortunately, Canada does not maintain records of emigration and no reliable data are available on the scale of return migration. An analysis of 1981 census data compared with annual immigration figures for the decade 1971–81, would permit some estimates for 'settler loss' to be calculated by the residual method but, given the problem of census under-enumeration and some inaccuracy in admission records, such estimates are not very reliable. Preliminary analysis suggests that the return migration of Third World immigrants is less than that of others who have been admitted as 'landed immigrants', but is, of course, much higher among those only having temporary employment authorisation and student or visitors' visas. Nevertheless, overstaying a visitor's visa or temporary employment authorisation has given rise to some illegal immigration and 'clandestine' movements, although border controls are such that actual illegal entry to Canada is unusual. The scale of illegal immigration to the country is not known for sure, but government studies estimated a maximum of 50 000 persons were illegally resident in 1983.

At the time of the 1981 census, 16.1 per cent of the population of 24.3 million was born outside Canada and of these almost 978 575 came from Third World countries (see Figure 5.3). The number has increased since and now probably exceeds one million. The major source countries were China (including Hong Kong), Indochina (including Vietnam and Kampuchea) the Philippines, India, Pakistan, Jamaica, Trinidad, Chile, together with various East African and some Middle Eastern countries.

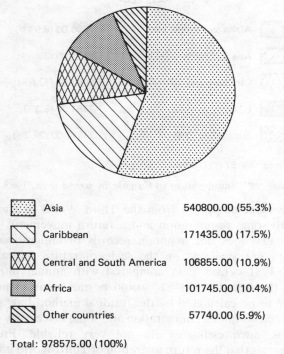

Figure 5.3 Third World immigrants in Canada, 1981

Immigration Trends

A study of the trends in Third World immigration to Canada, 1961–1977, showed that the proportion of permanent immigration

Third World Immigrants in Canada

from these countries had increased from 8 per cent in the early 1960s to more than 50 per cent by the end of the 1970s (Lanphier, 1979). The demographic characteristics indicated a predominance of young adults and intended occupations which reflected their comparatively high level of education. The study reviewed research which had been undertaken by government agencies and academics concerning the economic and social integration of Third World immigrants and concluded that they experienced greater problems of adjustment than other immigrants, largely due to prejudice and discrimination against 'visible minorities'.

Lanphier also examined trends in the issue of temporary employment authorisations, a question which has been further investigated by Wong (1984). The evidence suggests a growing dependence by Canada on temporary workers to meet certain labour shortages, including those arising from seasonal employment demands and socially 'undesirable' employment such as fruit harvesting and domestic service. These shortages persist, despite high unemployment among Canadians, who are able to take advantage of unemployment insurance or welfare assistance and are, therefore, reluctant to accept these unskilled jobs.

Studies of the refugee movements to Canada and reviews of the policies governing them showed that, between 1968 and 1979, 82 448 refugees were admitted, the main Third World sources being Vietnam and Lebanon. Since then, the flow of refugees from South East Asia has declined (Lanphier, 1981; 1983). The refugee determination process in Canada has proved to be a cumbersome one with many delays before full refugee status is awarded. There has been some abuse of the system in which economically-motivated migrants, who would not qualify for admission to Canada by the usual selection criteria, have entered Canada as visitors and then endeavoured to remain in the country by claiming refugee status. By 1986, the numbers involved were more than the system could handle and the government adopted an 'administrative clearance' procedure to remove the backlog, while tightening up on the scrutiny of new applications and entry via the USA.

There were about 65 000 immigrants from Latin American countries to Canada, in the decade 1971–80. Mata (1983; 1985) developed a model to explain the waves of immigration from these countries and the factors influencing them. Specifically, four major immigrant waves from Latin America are evident. Beginning in the post-Second World War period there were many professionals from the

86　　　　　　　　　　　*Immigration*

industrially-advanced areas who had previous links with Europe, being first or second generation re-migrants. In 1973, there was an 'Andecan' wave from Ecuador and Colombia consisting of skilled and unskilled manual workers, mainly temporary and 'illegal' migrants who were able to regularise their status in Canada. This was followed by a migration of the Chilean intelligentsia, following the military coup. Finally, there was a 'Central American' wave following the Sandinista revolution in 1979. the proportion of Latin Americans rose from less than 1 per cent of the total 'landed immigrant' movement in 1957 to 6.7 per cent in 1983. The largest single year was 1975 when more than 10 000 were admitted from that region (Mata, 1985:32).

Economic Adaptation

A report based on the 1971 census analysed data by birthplace and period of immigration and provided a demographic profile of all immigrants, by ethnic origin and generation. It examined the economic adaptation of immigrants in terms of labour force participation, unemployment rates, industrial and occupational distributions, together with income (Richmond and Kalbach, 1980). Generally speaking, post-war immigrants in Canada had benefited from their location in major metropolitan areas and had achieved an economic status, measured by occupation and income, which was actually superior to that of the Canadian-born.

The selective nature of Canadian immigration policy, with its emphasis on education and qualifications, contributed to the higher status of immigrants. However, there were important exceptions. They included recently arrived immigrants, many of them from Third World countries. The latter experienced rates of unemployment and income levels that were not commensurate with their sometimes superior educational qualifications. Employers and licensing bodies did not always recognise overseas qualifications and often insisted upon 'Canadian experience'. Further comparative studies of immigrants in Canada and Australia, using 1971 census data, also indicated that the adjustment problems of Third World immigrants were more serious and emphasised the low earnings of women, who often faced the 'double jeopardy' of being female and members of 'visible minorities' (Richmond and Zubryzycki, 1984).

This conclusion was similar to that of Clodman and Richmond (1981) who reviewed available evidence on the incidence and cause of unemployment among immigrants and by Ornstein (1982) and Orn-

Third World Immigrants in Canada

stein and Sharma (1983), who analysed a series of longitudinal surveys of immigrants in Canada, conducted between 1969 and 1978. Much higher unemployment rates were found among those from Third World countries and incomes were below the average for other countries of origin. Women were particularly vulnerable in this respect. Richmond (1982) also undertook a review of various studies of the economic adaptation of refugees and other immigrants, who had come to Canada in the 1970s. There was a consensus among researchers that deteriorating economic conditions in the 1970s were having deleterious effects on the economic situation of immigrants, and that recent Third World immigrants were the most adversely effected. Nevertheless, some members of 'visible minorities' with longer periods of residence had successfully established small businesses in Canada and were not experiencing difficulties that were substantially greater than any small scale entrepreneurs during a period of economic recession (Rhyne, 1983).

Age, sex, education and period of immigration were important determinants of the economic status of Third World immigrants in Canada, as measured by total income in 1980, reported in the 1981 census. Reflecting the selective nature of Canadian immigration policy, Asian immigrants on average had higher educational qualifications than the Canadian-born population, although the proportion with University degrees was lower among the more recent arrivals, due to the increasing proportion of 'family class' migrants and refugees (Basavarajappa and Verma, 1985). Labour force participation rates were above average as was the proportion of employers and self-employed workers and professionals among the longer term Asian residents. More recent immigrants had lower occupational status and incomes. Before adjusting for age and education, the total income of Asian men and women exceeded that of the Canadian-born but standardised comparisons showed that the incomes of Asian born males ranged from 89 per cent of equivalent Canadian males, in the 1960–69 immigrant cohort to 70 per cent in the 1975–79 cohort. Asian women earned much less than men but when standardised comparisons were made with Canadian-born women they were relatively better off than Asian men. Those in the earlier cohort earning 107 per cent of equivalent Canadian-born women, and the more recent arrivals 83 per cent (ibid: Table 8, adapted). As in the case of other immigrants to Canada, some of the apparent advantage in terms of income is a consequence of the relative concentration of the foreign-born in major metropolitan areas where unemployment is

88 *Immigration*

lower, and average incomes higher, than in other parts of the country.

Social Integration

In addition to examining the economic dimension of immigrant adaptation, the 1971 Census Analytical Study (Richmond and Kalbach 1980) also considered questions of family organisation, fertility, educational achievement, language use and naturalisation. Immigrants from Asian countries (the largest Third World group) were above average in educational achievement, generally spoke at least one official language (English or French) and were like most other immigrants in low fertility rates. Asians had a higher than average propensity to become naturalised Canadians.

Survey data collected in Toronto in 1970 was used to examine the family relationships and social integration of immigrants (Richmond and Goldlust, 1977). The number of Third World immigrants in the sample was small but the evidence showed that other immigrants and native-born Canadians tended to exhibit significant degrees of prejudice and discrimination against Blacks and Asians, and to maintain social distance from them. Subsequent studies by Sharma (1980; 1981a; 1981b) used survey data collected directly from immigrants, including those from Third World countries, confirmed the problems of social adjustment experienced by recent immigrants. Men, women and children all faced problems of one kind or another that were sometimes aggravated by racism. While European immigrants indicated that language barriers were their greatest handicap, those from Third World countries tended to complain most about discrimination and the inadequacy of existing governmental and voluntary social agencies.

Third World Immigrants: Specific Nationalities

Caribbean immigrants in the metropolitan Toronto area were first studied by Ramcharan (1974; 1976; 1982), who examined the history of West Indian immigration to Canada, the economic status of immigrants in Toronto and the extent of perceived discrimination. He showed that this was directly related to skin colour, dark complexioned Blacks reporting more discrimination than light skinned Blacks or Asians. He subsequently compared the experience of Caribbean immigrants with 'visible minorities' from other coun-

Third World Immigrants in Canada 89

tries and concluded that 'multicultural' policies which encouraged pluralistic forms of integration tended, in the long run, to exacerbate adjustment problems for immigrants. This led him to advocate 'the dispersion of members of the racial minorities into the wider society', with a view to becoming part of the power structure and changing the institutions that presently support discrimination, prejudice and bigotry (Ramcharan, 1982:111).

Understandably, because of their francophone origins, Haitian immigrants are mainly found in Quebec, particularly in the Montreal area. In 1981 there were almost 27 000 Haitians in Canada. Although many were well educated and had professional qualifications they had difficulty finding suitable employment and Haitians generally faced prejudice and discrimination. Nevertheless, in 1971 their occupational distribution in Quebec, when compared with anglophone West Indian immigrants, showed a higher proportion in teaching and nursing and fewer in administration, service occupations and manufacturing (Jean-Baptiste, 1977; Piche *et al.*, 1983).

By 1981, the West Indian born population of Canada numbered 211 120 including the Guyanese. Women were in the majority (sex ratio 0.83) and 71 per cent had arrived in the preceding decade. Of those fifteen years and older, more than half had some post-secondary education (compared with 36 per cent of the Canadian population). Labour force participation rates were high (84 per cent male and 82 per cent female). Caribbean-born males were under-represented in managerial occupations but somewhat above average in the professional and technical category. Almost a third were working in manufacturing compared with 19 per cent of the male labour force as a whole. The occupational profile of West Indian women was closer to that of the female labour force as a whole, but they were less likely to be in clerical and sales and more likely to be in manufacturing (15 per cent compared with 8 per cent).

Despite the high level of education, income levels for males were only 91 per cent of the Canadian average, whereas foreign-born males, as a whole, averaged 108 per cent. When controls for age, period of immigration and educational level were applied, Caribbean immigrant men consistently showed incomes lower than the average for equivalent Canadians, or comparable immigrant groups. West Indian women earned less than men but did better, on the whole, when compared with other women, both immigrant and Canadian-born. Incomes were approximately 11 per cent above the average for all women 15 years and over. However, more recently arrived West

90 *Immigration*

Indian women with post-secondary qualifications earned less than similarly qualified immigrant women from other countries (Statistics Canada, unpublished tabulations).

Chinese immigrants can be divided between the 'old' and the 'new' migration from Hong Kong and elsewhere. Whereas the former were the often aged survivors of an earlier period when immigration to Canada from China was restricted and consisted mainly of unskilled workers who remained isolated in 'Chinatown', recent immigrants are young, well-educated, English speaking and enterprising. They rarely remained within the residential confines of 'Chinatown' (Con, 1982; Johnson, 1983; Lai, 1970). Chow (1983) considered the question of Chinese language classes attended by children who came to Canada very young, or who were born there. The extent of interest in Chinese language maintenance depended upon various factors in the family background, including Kinship networks.

Lam (1982; 1983) studied the adjustment problems facing Indochinese refugees from Vietnam, Laos and Campuchia, living in Montreal. In this mainly French-speaking environment the recently arrived immigrants were still recovering from the trauma of their often hazardous escape from war-torn countries. Many were afraid that the separatist movement in Quebec would force them to move yet again. They were having serious difficulties in establishing themselves in steady employment at a time of economic recession. Some were professionals or merchants who had lost all their possessions and had little hope of regaining their former prosperity. Nevertheless, they expressed satisfaction with their experiences in Canada and appeared to be resigned to their present fate. Their overwhelming preoccupation was with the fate of their relatives left behind and with their efforts to reunite families. Some of the psychological dimensions of the refugee adjustment experience typically include a sense of loss and social dislocation. There are significant effects on family relationships (particularly when husbands become economically and socially dependent on spouse or children), and consequent feelings of depression with various psychosomatic disorders (Chan and Lam, 1983).

Immigrants from South Asia (India, Pakistan, Bangladesh and Sri Lanka) together with those of similar ethnic origins from other countries such as Kenya, Uganda, Trinidad and Fiji have formed an increasing proportion of the Third World movement to Canada. The Sikh population has grown, particularly in British Columbia, as has

Third World Immigrants in Canada 91

the Hindu and Muslim population from various parts of the world. In 1981, there were 68 000 Sikhs, nearly 70 000 Hindus and over 98 000 persons who reported Islamic religion in the census. A recent study of the South Asian population in Canada concluded that there has been a 'firm integration' into Canadian life with selective retention of certain aspects of the varied cultural heritage through the maintenance of close networks of family and friends together with the development of critical institutions such as temples, newspapers and business associations (Buchignani *et al.*, 1985). As well as forming a significant proportion of Canada's 'visible minorities', these communities have found themselves involved in controversial political issues arising from the situation in their former countries. The fear of 'terrorism' has been added to that of racial prejudice as a factor inhibiting their full integration into Canadian society.

Conclusion

This brief review of research on Third World Immigration, indicates the multidimensional nature of the problems investigated. There are a number of issues that have not been studied which warrant further research. They include the economic consequences of these migrations for the sending countries. Canada clearly benefits both from the 'brain drain' aspect as well as the utilisation of unskilled and semi-skilled workers, who are admitted only temporarily. The latter contribute to unemployment insurance, health and pension schemes from which they can never benefit. Remittances to Third World countries, by both temporary and permanent migrants, have consequences for those countries that have not been assessed. The Economic Council of Canada has urged a review of Canada's trade relations and bilateral aid to Third World countries in the light of changing industrial strategies and world economic conditions. Recently, the Department of External Affairs issued a 'Green Paper' dealing with Canada' international relations, in which questions of competitiveness and security in the modern world are reviewed. The changing ethnic composition of the population as a consequence of Third World immigration is bound to influence Canada's relations with other countries in the future.

On a purely individual basis, Third World immigrants in Canada probably achieved net economic benefits, even when they faced initial adjustment difficulties that are aggravated at a time of high

92 *Immigration*

unemployment in the receiving country. However, the collective consequences for sending and receiving societies are more difficult to assess, and must be considered in the broad context of 'North/South' disparities in economic development, and the interdependence of a global economy. The demographic and social effects of international migration on sending and receiving countries are also complex. There are significant implications for social integration, political cohesion and cultural pluralism that need further research.

Part II

Racism and Multiculturalism

6 Environmental Conservation and Immigration: A New Racist Ideology?

Immigration policies, like other governmental decisions, are thrashed out in a political arena and are an accommodation to conflicting interest groups and their respective ideologies. Actual legislation and regulations governing the admission of immigrants have tended to swing between the two extremes of a complete 'open door' policy, and one of an almost total exclusion of all but a small number of people with preferred qualifications and national backgrounds. The interest groups most often supporting a larger and more diversified immigration flow have included, firstly, transportation companies and all those associated with the travel industry, which depends for its livelihood on the promotion of large population movements. Secondly, the proponents of immigration generally include large land owners and developers for whom a larger population is a prerequisite for economic growth. The classical example of a combination of these two interests was that of the Canadian Pacific Railway (CPR) which, as part of its contract with the federal government in Ottawa for the development of a railway to the west coast, received large land grants in the prairie provinces of Canada. The CPR became one of the largest promoters of immigration at the turn of this century. Thirdly, capital investors and employers generally tend to favor immigration. Employers and managers in expanding new industries frequently require large numbers of skilled workers which cannot always be supplied domestically; at the same time, employers in declining and marginal industries are interested in immigrant workers when they can be persuaded to work for wages or under conditions that are less attractive to the existing populations of the receiving society. Generally in favour of further immigration are the representatives of immigrant groups themselves and ethnic minorities who, through chain migration and 'family reunion', hope to increase their numbers and strengthen their influence in the new country. These interest

96 *Racism and Multiculturalism*

groups generally espouse a liberal ideology which emphasises freedom of movement as a human right, equality of opportunity and access to resources, cosmopolitan values, cultural pluralism, and the desirability of nondiscrimination in immigration policies.

Those interest groups more often opposed to immigration include both organised and unorganised labour, which frequently see immigration as a potential source of competition for scarce resources, and as undermining labour unions and wage levels. Immigration is seen as particularly threatening at times of economic recession and high unemployment. Secondly, opposition to immigration is very frequently expressed by the socially mobile and less secure sectors of the middle classes, particularly those who have espoused particular moral, religious and nationalistic values which they feel would be threatened by a large influx of 'aliens'. Thirdly, the ranks of those opposed to immigration may sometimes be joined by an older generation of immigrants or their children who perceive further waves of immigration as threatening the precarious *modus vivendi* they have established with the receiving society. The opponents of immigration may be joined by those for whom hostility toward immigrants and ethnic minorities is an expression of a basic authoritarian personality.

The immigration policies of major English-speaking countries such as Great Britain, the United States, Canada and Australia have always been influenced by racism and bigotry, although the economic interests favouring immigration have sometimes been strong enough to overcome these attitudes. At other times, immigration policies have exhibited a compromise whereby a controlled and selective immigration policy was pursued favouring the dominant race or nationalities already established in the new country. In English-speaking countries, the prejudice and discrimination against non-Anglo-Saxon immigrants has been often explicit and outspoken. At other times, its expression has been covert. Today, it is no longer respectable for intellectuals, scientists and politicians to express racist views openly or to advocate explicit discrimination. Theories that attribute genetic inferiority to certain races, nationalities, or classes are no longer popular and command only eccentric support. Furthermore, racial discrimination is not politically expedient when trade and diplomatic relations with the Third World must be promoted. However, even when belief in the racial superiority of the British and some other Western European nationalities was fashionable (and even defended by eminent biologists and social scientists), it was

Environmental Conservation and Immigration

quite comon to provide other arguments for restricting immigration and particularly for excluding certain races and nationalities.

From an academic point of view, there is some dispute whether these alternative defences of exclusionary immigration should, strictly speaking, be described as "racist." Two leading authorities' on race relations and immigration in Britain take opposing views on this question. Looking at it from the point of view of the history of social thought and the influence of Social Darwinism on race relations, Michael Banton had argued that only when genetic inferiority and superiority are ascribed to certain populations as a justification for differential treatment should the theory or argument be defined as an example of 'racism.' (Banton, 1961; 1967; 1969). The alternative view is expressed by John Rex who has stated that, while a race relations situation would always be marked by some appeal to a deterministic theory, that theory might not always be a biological or genetic one but might be based upon religious, cultural, historical, ideological, or sociological grounds. (Rex, 1970; 1973).

Subsequently, Rex elaborated this point. He argued that to confine the term racism to the use of genetic theories would be to 'trivialize the sociology of race relations almost beyond belief.' He suggested that racist ideas must be examined in the context of the sociology of knowledge and the relation between ideas and social structures. He also pointed out that there has been a resurgence in popularity of explicitly racist theories and other Social Darwinistic perspectives among some biologists and psychologists. If Social Darwinism is defined, broadly, as the advocacy of social policies on the basis of false biological analogies, then the use of arguments based upon ecology, conservation, and environmental protection to support exclusionary immigration policies must be regarded as another manifestation of racism in disguise. In effect, the proponents of restrictive immigration policies appear to be saying that if we can no longer ensure that the majority of immigrants will be Caucasian, then let us find some convincing argument for having none at all, or very few! As such, it is the latest in a long line of euphemistic arguments and policies that have been used at various times, in different countries, to justify immigration restriction and, particularly, the exclusion of non-white immigrants from Britain, Canada, Australia, and the United States.

In order to avoid the semantic dispute between Banton and Rex, I shall call these indirect arguments "quasiracist." A key element in all of the arguments used, and devices adopted, to justify exclusion and

98   *Racism and Multiculturalism*

discrimination is the self-interest of the existing inhabitants and
settler communities in the receiving societies. Intrinsically, the various arguments and the laws and regulations had a rational basis.
However, it was the deliberate manipulation and exaggeration of
these considerations which enabled them to be utilised in a highly
restrictive and discriminatory way. Thus, rational considerations
became ideologically distorted.

EXAMPLES OF IDEOLOGICAL DISTORTION

The history of immigration and its control in various countries is
replete with examples of the ideological distortion of otherwise
rational arguments and policies. The misuse of legitimate concerns
regarding conservation, environmental protection, and population
growth is only the latest in a long list of similar cases. For example,
the prevention and control of the spread of infectious and contagious
diseases is a proper concern of any government. The immigration
regulations of almost all countries include provisions for the medical
inspection of potential immigrants and other public health provisions
relating to transportation. However, one of the most frequent
stereotypes promoted by those opposed to immigration, or to the
entry of particular races or nationalities, is that which suggests the
unwanted group may be responsible for spreading loathsome diseases. Charles Price, in his study of restrictive immigration to North
America and Australasia, mentions this as one of the elements in an
inquiry into immigration into Australia in 1854; it was among the
allegations made by those opposed to immigration from Eastern
Europe to Britain and the United States at the turn of the century
(Price, 1974).

In Canada in 1911, a draft order in council would have prohibited
'any immigrant belonging to the Negro race, which race is deemed
unsuitable to the climate and requirements of Canada' from landing
in Canada. However, this order was vetoed. Instead, medical inspec-
tions at the US–Canada border were used to prevent black would-be
migrants from entering the country (Troper, 1972). At about the
same time (in 1908) Canada introduced its notorious 'continuous
journey regulations.' Ostensibly, these were a public health measure
designed to prevent the spread of disease from ships stopping at
intermediate ports. However, their real purpose was to exclude East
Indians from Canada. Unlike the Chinese and Japanese, the East

Environmental Conservation and Immigration

Indians were British subjects and could not legally be excluded. However, the government was aware that there was no shipping line plying directly between India and Canada. The most infamous incident arising from this occurred in 1914 when 375 passengers were anchored off Vancouver, but were refused entry into Canada because of the noncontinuous journey regulation. The ship remained in the harbour for two months and there were violent anti-Oriental demonstrations.

Concern for the external security of the particular country and fear of war and invasion have been the basis for exclusionary immigration policies and for discrimination against racial and national minorities. Australia's white immigration policy was prompted very largely by defence considerations and fear of being surrounded by Asian countries. Even after the Second World War, defence considerations were still being used as grounds for promoting British and European immigration to the exclusion of Asians. In Canada and the United States, the discriminatory treatment of Japanese residents, and their American- and Canadian-born children who were citizens, are further examples of the sometimes hysterical anxieties to which these considerations can give rise. After the Second World War, Canada repatriated a large number of Japanese, although it has since been recognised that the fear of invasion and the security threats were grossly exaggerated.

Internal security and the question of subversion has frequently been used as a ground for excluding particular nationalities. At the turn of the century these fears were frequently expressed in Britain and the United States with regard to eastern European immigration. At that time the bogey men were the so-called 'anarchists.' More recently, the passage of the McCarran Act in the United States in 1952 (despite President Truman's veto) was an example of the use of the fear of communism, and concern with questons of internal security, as a way of excluding potential immigrants from Asia and parts of Eastern Europe. Subsequently, the President's Commission on Immigration and Naturalization criticised the Act of 1952 because it promoted a claim of Nordic supremacy, discriminated in favour of the nations of western and northern Europe and against those of southern and eastern Europe, the Near East, and Asia. In responding to the Commission's report, Senator McCarran claimed that his act 'does not contain one iota of racial or religious discrimination. It is, however, very tough, very tough, on communists, as it is on criminals and other subversives.' (Ziegler, 1953)

100 *Racism and Multiculturalism*

Closely related to questions of internal security were the frequent allegations that immigrants are more likely to exhibit criminal tendencies. Such views had been expressed frequently by opponents of immigration in Britain, Canada, and elsewhere. The chief of police in Toronto is on record as having frequently blamed immigrants for a rise in the crime rate. These assertions are made notwithstanding the fact that all systematic studies support the conclusion that the crime rates of the foreign born are generally lower than those of the native born populations of the countries concerned.

One of the most frequent concerns expressed by those opposed to immigration has been that immigrants will provide a pool of cheap labour, be used as strike breakers, and generally threaten the improvements in wages and working conditions achieved by labour unions. Such fears are often associated with stereotypes of racial minorities whose material standards and dietary habits supposedly enabled them to live 'off the smell of a rag.' Such views provided a rationale for such discriminatory legislation as the requirement that potential immigrants must be in possession of certain sums of money and, in the case of Canada, the imposition of taxes on Chinese immigrants. In 1885, the amount was $50.00 on entry and was gradually increased to $500 in 1903.

The alleged inability of certain races and nationalities to assimilate into the receiving society has been a common basis of exclusion and discrimination. The Canadian Immigration Act of 1952, which was the legislative authority for immigration regulation until 1977, contained clauses which permit regulations to be made that would exclude immigrants on the basis of 'peculiar customs, habits, modes of life or methods of holding property in his country of birth or citizenship;' and 'his probable inability to become readily assimilated.' (These clauses were omitted from the new Act of 1977 now in force.) Studies carried out on behalf of the United States Immigration Commission of 1907 distinguished between the 'new' and old immigrant flows, and alleged that the former exhibited lower rates of naturalisation and other indications of slower assimilation. Subsequent research showed these claims to be unfounded and largely a consequence of not taking into account the different periods of immigration of the immigrant groups concerned. Nevertheless, census monographs in Canada, for the years 1921 and 1931, perpetuated the same myths with regard to the eastern and southern European groups compared with the British and others from northern and western Europe.

Environmental Conservation and Immigration 101

In Australia, Charles Price (1974) has shown that a desire for social homogeneity was a major factor in promoting the white Australia policy. Among the discriminatory measures adopted in various countries to exclude particular nationalities were the notorious 'literacy tests,' such as those incorporated into the Commonwealth Immigration Restriction Act of 1901 in Australia. This prohibited 'the entry into Australia of any person who, when asked to do so fails to write out at dictation, and sign in the presence of an officer, a passage of 50 words in length in a European language.' Similar legislation was introduced in British Columbia in 1900 and repeated annually until 1908, despite some question at the federal level as to the legality of such regulations. In Canada, the alleged unsuitability of the climate for settlement by blacks and Asians had been used as a reason for exclusion as recently as 1955.

Related to the question of social homogeneity is the concern that a racially and ethnically diversified immigration will give rise to religious and ethnic strife. This is often expressed as an exaggerated concern for the welfare of the immigrants and ethnic minorities themselves. Such notorious opponents of black and Asian immigration to Britain as Enoch Powell have argued a case for repatriation on the ground that this would benefit the immigrants themselves as well as white Britishers (Foot, 1969).

All the examples I have given of 'quasiracist' attitudes and policies have one element in common: they all have a superficial plausibility and an element of apparent rationality. Few people would wish to question the desirability of preventing the spread of disease, resisting threats of invasion, taking precautions against the subversion of democratic institutions, preventing crime, racial and ethnic conflict, or undermining the living standards of workers. However, all of these good causes can be used to misrepresent and distort the real situation. And, as with the more or less conscious deceptions and disguises of human interest groups, these plausible arguments must be recognised as ideologically racist (Mannheim, 1936).

ENVIRONMENTAL CONSERVATION AND IMMIGRATION

Since the mid-1960s, most English speaking countries have relaxed to some degree the discrimination that previously existed against black and Asian immigration. Great Britain is an exception in that, as far as

102   *Racism and Multiculturalism*

Initially, Australia adopted attitudes and policies that emphasised door policy was pursued so long as the numbers arriving were comparatively small. When the numbers began to increase, in the late 1950s, the government felt obliged to introduce the first of a series of Commonwealth immigration acts which restricted the admissibility of those from present or former Commonwealth countries, even those carrying British passports. In practice, however, the number actually entering the United Kingdom continued to be quite substantial (Richmond, 1975). In the United States, the major departure from previous regulations came in 1965 when priority was given to reuniting immigrant families and permitting the entry of professional persons and other workers in short supply in the United States. A revised quota system was put into effect in 1968 which tended to reverse the previous priorities, placing severe limitations on Western Hemisphere immigration. In Canada, all formal discrimination by race or national origin was removed from immigration regulations in 1962. Since then the proportion of black and Asian immigrants has risen to almost one-third of the total in recent years. Australia moved more slowly in removing restrictions on Asian immigration, but the numbers admitted for permanent residence did increase during the 1960s and all formal restrictions were removed in 1974 (Richmond and Rao, 1977).

Concurrently with this liberalisation of actual immigration policies, there has been a backlash of opposition from certain groups. The emphasis upon highly qualified immigrants, particularly in Canada and Australia, had led to an increase in opposition to immigration from some professional groups such as medical doctors and university teachers. A new manifestation of Social Darwinism has appeared in recent years and is being used to rationalise exclusionary immigration policies. The underlying premise of the new argument for reducing immigration is as superficially plausible as those offered in earlier years. It is derived from recent developments in our understanding of the delicate balance of ecological forces that sustain our population on earth. Few would deny the reality of a population and resource crisis at the global level. Present rates of population growth, particularly in developing countries, will put serious pressures on food and energy resources. It is generally agreed that mass emigration will not solve the population problem. The solution lies in more effective fertility control, greater productivity, and a more egalitarian distribution of resources. However, arguments based upon the need to reduce urban congestion, prevent further environmental pollution,

Environmental Conservation and Immigration · 103

and reduce energy and resource consumption are now being used to support exclusionary immigration policies.

Indeed, the most outspoken opposition to immigration in Canada and Australia has come from influential lobbyists and spokesmen who argue that, contrary to the traditional view, these countries have reached, or will shortly achieve, an optimal level of population relative to the available productive land, energy resources, and other ecological considerations. Linked with these views are expressions of concern at the level of urbanisation and metropolitanisation of the populations of these countries. These arguments are being put forward by some of the most eminent scientists, including biologists, medical doctors, and demographers.

In Australia, the argument against immigration on environmental grounds was first put forward by Professor Fenner, Director of the School of Medical Research at the Australian National University in 1971. He claimed that, 'Australia is far more vulnerable than the other large centres of Western culture, North America and Europe, to the damaging effects of a large number of people.' He went on to point out that Australia suffers from an arid climate and that, relative to its size, its ecosystems are much more fragile. This led him to conclude that a substantial lowering of the rate of population growth in Australia was desirable, including, among other things, a reduction in immigration (Fenner, 1971).

Very similar views were echoed in Canada, where the large Arctic and sub-Arctic territories are also recognised as ecologically fragile and incapable of supporting large populations. At seminars sponsored by the Conservation Council of Ontario, in 1972 and 1973, biologists argued, 'Canada is already over-populated in terms of its sustainable carrying capacity, and this means that a lot of debate about the action alternatives can be avoided if this point is understood' (O.C.C. 1972). Arguments against immigration were also advanced in Canada on behalf of environmentalists at hearings of a Special Joint Committee of Parliament, in 1975. For example, a spokesman for British Columbia's Wildlife Federation argued that the Greater Vancouver and lower mainland areas of British Columbia should be protected from further immigration 'until we can reconcile the numbers of people that can be accommodated without destroying our liveable regions.' The same view was put forward by the President of the Conservation Council of New Brunswick who suggested that 'immigration into Canada must be reduced drastically and, eventually, almost to zero' (Canada, H of C 1974–5).

104 *Racism and Multiculturalism*

In its report, the Science Council of Canada examines Canada's vailable agricultural land, food supplies, energy and capital needs, labour force, and population options. While recognising that, due to the very low birthrates at the present time. Canada may well be faced with a severe labour shortage from the mid-1980s onwards, the committee came down firmly against increased immigration as a solution to this problem. The principal recommendation of the report is that Canadian population growth should be slow. 'The country should adopt a long-term population policy to achieve this slow growth. An initial target of 28–30 million for the year 2000 seems reasonable, assuming that the fertility rates remain between 1.8 and 2.1. an annual net immigration (immigration minus emigration) of about 50 000 per annum would achieve this goal.' They go on to say that in view of the uncertainty about fertility levels, immigration programs should be reviewed at least every five years. (Science Council, 1976)

It is interesting to note the suggestions made in the course of the report by members of the Science Council as a means of compensating for the possible labour shortages that would follow from slow population growth and a restriction on immigration. They include the following:

(1) Canadians should work harder.
(2) Canadians should give up any idea that the future of society will be leisure oriented;
(3) Increased labour force participation rates by women and youth should be encouraged;
(4) Older members of the labour force should postpone their expected retiring age and remain in work;
(5) Canadians should be prepared to do more of the 'traditionally unpopular jobs,' usually left to immigrants!

It should be emphasized that, both in Canada and Australia, at the official level alternative arguments favouring the maintenancy of moderate levels of immigration have so far prevailed, notwithstanding the influential stature of those opposing immigration on environmentalist grounds. Professor W. D. Borrie, in his report to the Australian government based upon the National Population Inquiry, pointed out:

Environmental Conservation and Immigration

the minority who have advocated zero growth have been very articulate, strongly dominated be elite educational groups, with their argument often backed by deep understanding of the Australian environment and ecology. The associated aspects of conservation, the onset as quickly as possible of the stationary state, and controlled consumption to minimize the wastage of non-renewable resources, are set not only as a goal for Australia, but for humanity at large. (Borrie, 1975: p.711)

Those opposing immigration have generally associated themselves with the zero population growth movement. In Canada, the ZPG propaganda has included the publication of graphs showing the possible consequences of a net immigration in the order of 500 000 per annum. Nowhere is it noted that net immigration to Canada has rarely exceeded 100 000 and, in recent years, has been closer to 75 000 per annum. The same organization published a picture in a number of Canadian newspapers representing Canada as a young woman with an unwanted pregnancy. The context made it clear that opposition was not only to high birthrates, but also to immigration.

The zero population growth movement in the United States has also been vocal in its opposition to immigration. The danger of the ZPG movement diverting attention from the real causes of environmental damage and excessive energy consumption has been noted by Philip Hauser, who pointed out that 'it is ironic that at this point in history, demographers should have to take issue with "angry ecologists" overstating their case and using "the population explosion" as a major enemy in their effort to stem environmental pollution. There are two dangers inherent in this situation. One, the danger that the problems of environmental pollution and the population explosion may be used as a smoke screen to obscure other problems that should have priority, including the problems of slums, racism and the "urban crisis" in general. Second, the overstatements of the case . . . may do great harm if boomerang effects follow' (Hauser, 1970).

Nothing I have said in this paper should be construed to mean that, at a global and a national level, we should not be taking positive steps to achieve fertility control, to reduce excessive consumption and wastage of energy and other resources, and to prevent environmental pollution. However, to argue that the existing levels of immigration to countries such as Britain, Canada, Australia, or the United States should be stopped or substantially reduced, for purely ecological reasons, must be recognised as an ideological proposition serving the

106 *Racism and Multiculturalism*

interests of the more affluent segments of the world's populations. Such an argument could only be sustained if it were considered that the environments presently enjoyed (and often spoiled) by affluent nations must be perpetually protected from habitation by the less advantaged. Not only would such policies be contrary to fundamental human rights, but they would place serious obstacles in the way of those people from developing countries who seek to improve their own material conditions and career opportunities through geographic and social mobility. Completely unrestricted immigration would undoubtedly disrupt the economic and social systems of advanced societies, but moderate levels of immigration are well within the absorptive capacity of these countries. Indeed, in the long run, the declining rates of growth of population in post-industrial societies (and the imminent absolute decline of population in some western European countries) will mean that positive net immigration will be to their own economic advantage. Only through immigration (on a scale large enough to compensate for outward movements of population and the effects of an aging population) will it be possible to sustain the levels of economic productivity necessary to provide adequate health and welfare services, including those directed toward the elimination of environmental pollution. I suggest that the opposite view, now expressed by those who uphold the virtues of a 'steady state,' who urge limits to growth, and who use environmental conservation as an argument against immigration, is new ideology designed to protect the privileges of the affluent. It can appropriately be described as racist, or at least 'quasiracist,' because its implementation would mean a substantial reduction in black and Asian immigration to countries such as Canada and Australia, just as the formal legal barriers to their admissibility have been removed.

7 Canadian Unemployment and the Threat to Multiculturalism

The term 'multiculturalism' has a variety of meanings depending upon the context in which it is used. From a demographic and socio-cultural point of view it simply describes the reality of Canadian society. Close to 6 per cent of the population was born outside Canada. In addition to the two official languages, more than one in ten of the population reports a mother tongue other than English or French and these numerous languages are still frequently in use in the home and the community. The Native Peoples of Canada maintain distinctive life-styles, and religious minorities (such as Mennonites, Hutterites and Doukhobors) have retained largely separate and distinctive communities. The poly-ethnic origins of the Canadian population are still evident into the second and subsequent generations (Kalbach and McVey, 1979, 176–241; O'Bryan, Reitz and Kuplowska, 1976).

However, the idea of 'multiculturalism' conveys more than just a statistical account of the distribution of language, religion and ethnic origin. The concept has philosophical and ideological connotations. It is an expression of certain ideals which are deliberately contrasted with the view that ethnic minorities should eventually assimilate into a culturally homogeneous society. Multiculturalism as a policy postulates a fundamental respect for ethnic differences which are perceived as having intrinsic value. The preservation of a heterogeneous cultural heritage, respect for differing religious beliefs and values, together with a firm commitment to pluralism, are a part of the multicultural ideal. Multiculturalism is an ideology that emphasises freedom of cultural expression, and social justice for all ethnic groups. Whether founding members of a charter group, Native Peoples, or recently arrived immigrants, the philosophy of multiculturalism emphasises equality of opportunity and non-discrimination (Burnet, 1978).

It goes without saying that, in practice, Canadian society falls short of fulfilling these liberal ideals. Economic inequalities persist and there is differential access to political power and influence (Porter, 1965; Clement, 1975). Federal and provincial government policies that explicitly embrace the concept of multiculturalism have made little more than a token contribution to removing ethnic prejudice and discrimination. It has been agued that 'the myth of multicultural-ism is based on high-sounding liberal ideals, not on the empirical reality of Canadian society' (Peter, 1981:65). One view is that multicultural policies have served simply to buy the loyalty of ethnic minorities while maintaining the hegemony of the political and economic elites of Ontario and Quebec. The central problem is one of maintaining national unity and cohesion in the face of the potentially divisive consequences of ethnic and linguistic heterogene-ity (Breton, Reitz and Valentine, 1980). In the struggle for organisa-tional power and constitutional reform the interests of anglophone and francophone elites, together with those of provincial political parties in power, tend to override those of other ethnic groups (Breton and Breton, 1980: 2–3). In the debates over the constitution, secessionist tendencies and provincial devolutionary pressures have largely excluded the influence of Native Peoples, immigrants and other linguistic and religious minorities.

Economic Problems and Multiculturalism

It is not only in the constitutional debates and the political power struggle that the ideals of multiculturalism are compromised. Econo-mic conditions also constitute a threat to multiculturalism as a policy and as an ideal toward which we should be striving. It will be difficult for the federal government to maintain its policy of 'multiculturalism within a bilingual framework' when major economic problems, such as inflation and unemployment, are perceived as having much greater priority. If economic conditions continue to deteriorate there could be a backlash against further immigration of any kind, including the refugee program. Given continuing budgetary constraints, programs designed to provide support services for immigrants and those designed to facilitate the long-term integration of linguistic and cultural minorities into our society may be jeopardised.[1]

Central among the concerns expressed in the mass media has been the relation between immigration and unemployment. Among the questions frequently asked are:

Canadian Unemployment and the Threat to Multiculturalism 109

Why continue with an immigration program when unemployment rates in Canada are so high?

Are immigrants competing for and obtaining jobs that Canadians might otherwise have obtained?

Are immigrants being relegated to the least desirable, lowest paid jobs where employment conditions are so bad that Canadians would not accept the employment?

Are unemployment rates higher or lower among recent immigrants compared with the Canadian-born or immigrants who have been in the country longer?

Will economic insecurity, rising unemployment and other structural inequalities give rise to ethnic and racial tension?

Have incidents of violence against racial minorities that have occurred in recent years been caused by economic insecurity?

Will such violence spread if unemployment remains high and will it result in counter-violence by the minority groups themselves?

What steps must be taken to avoid a backlash against policies of multiculturalism and non-discrimination in the face of economic crises and competition for employment?

I do not pretend that, in this brief chapter, I can provide answers to all these questions. In fact, much of the research that would be needed to provide adequate answers has not been undertaken. The most that I can do is to review some of the available data, compare the often conflicting views of economists and sociologists on the economic consequences of immigration, and draw some cautious lessons for Canada from the experience of other countries.

DEMOGRAPHIC AND ECONOMIC ASPECTS OF IMMIGRATION

Since the end of World War II the Canadian government has carefully regulated the numbers of labour force immigrants admitted to the country in the light of economic conditions. There has been a strong negative correlation between the level of unemployment and the number of immigrants admitted (Parai, 1974; Green, 1976; Clodman and Richmond, 1981). The only exception to this was in 1956–57 when the combined effects of the Hungarian crisis and the Suez crisis brought large numbers of refugees and of British immigrants to this country. For once, political and humanitarian considerations overwhelmed the economic advice given to the government

110 *Racism and Multiculturalism*

by its officials concerning the limited absorptive capacity of the economy at that time (Richmond, 1967: 14–15). In recent years, immigration to Canada, including the so-called 'boat people,' has been approximately 100 000 annually. This number is hardly sufficient to compensate demographically for the number of people who leave Canada each year. Statistics Canada's estimates of the outward movement are unreliable and generally on the low side. However, even by their own figures net migration to Canada in 1978 came close to zero (Statistics Canada, 1979). The immigration target announced for 1981 was increased to 130–140 000. On a net basis this will probably add only about 50 000 persons to the total population. Furthermore, in the last five years the government has deliberately reduced the labour force component of immigration by giving priority to family reunion. The proportion of immigrants intending to enter the labour force on arrival has fallen from approximately half the annual intake to less than 40 per cent. Thus, the gross addition to the labour force through immigration in 1978 and 1979 did not exceed 35 000 per annum.

In recent years, growth in the Canadian population has been attributable mainly to natural increase which, in turn, has been declining. Because there are a large number of women in the child-bearing years the Canadian population will continue to grow, even if birth rates remain at the low level of the last decade. However, the large number of young people who have been entering the labour force in recent years is a consequence of the so-called 'baby boom' of the 1950s and early 1960s. Before the end of this decade the number of young Canadians entering the labour force could be less than the number of pesons retiring or otherwise dropping out of the labour force. Much will depend upon trends with regard to earlier or later retirement and, also, to the level of female labour force participation. If the labour force participation rates of married women do not increase above their present level, immigration will be the only source of growth in the labour force.

Meanwhile, the government has made increasing use of temporary employment visas rather than admitting more permanent immigrants. Between eighty and ninety thousand visas have been issued annually in recent years. Some of the visas are valid for only a few months. This is true for those temporary workers admitted for seasonal employment in agriculture. However, increasingly there has been a tendency to renew temporary visas beyond a twelve-month

Canadian Unemployment and the Threat to Multiculturalism 111

period, particularly for those employed in domestic and other service occupations.[2] Such workers have no right to permanent domicile in Canada and may be required to depart immediately their employment terminates. Permanent immigrants intending to enter the labour force have been subject to more stringent admission criteria which include considerations of occupational demand in Canada. More and more independent immigrants are being admitted to pre-arranged employment or to designated occupations in specific locations where there is a demonstrated shortage of qualified workers. Although further research is needed on the demographic and economic impact of immigration, and of those admitted on temporary employment visas, the available evidence suggests that the net effect on the labour force is presently quite small (Clodman and Richmond, 1981).

Competition for Employment

Are recent immigrants competing with the Canadian-born and other immigrants for the same scarce jobs? Or are recent immigrants taking the less attractive kinds of work that others reject? Unfortunately, it is very difficult to obtain reliable information concerning the employment experience and occupational status of immigrants who have arrived in Canada in the last decade. The 1976 census contained no question on birth-place, period of immigration or occupation. Statistics Canada ceased to ask a question concerning birthplace or period of immigration in its monthly labour force surveys after 1973. The government's longitudinal surveys of immigrants followed cohorts arriving in 1969, 1970 and 1971 for a period of three years, i.e. until 1974. A further longitudinal survey, undertaken in 1976, followed recently arrived immigrants for only one year after arrival. No other national surveys are conducted on a large enough scale to enable definitive conclusions to be reached concerning the occupational characteristics of immigrants.

The evidence from the 1971 census suggested that, in terms of industrial sectors and occupations, the foreign-born were widely dispersed throughout the economic system, although highly concentrated regionally and in those areas that had experienced the most rapid growth in the post-war period. Kalbach's analysis of the experience of those who entered Canada 1946–61, and were still resident in 1971, showed that this immigrant cohort had higher labour

112 *Racism and Multiculturalism*

force participation rates, and higher earnings than the native-born. This was true in most cases even after controlling for sex and age. However, the relative concentration of post-war immigrants in metropolitan areas explained a good deal of this advantage. Immigrants who arrived between 1961 and 1971 also gravitated to the metropolitan areas where they were relatively concentrated in service industries and professional occupations. However, there was also a significant concentration of less occupationally skilled immigrants in manufacturing and construction industries as well as some unskilled service occupations. Thus, the highest indexes of relative concentration by occupation were for American males in university teaching, Asian females in health diagnosing and treating occupations, and Southern European men and women in textile fabricating occupations, and in food and beverage preparation (Richmond and Kalbach, 1980).

Information concerning immigration and unemployment suffers from the same deficiency as the data on industrial and occupational distributions. Reliable up-to-date figures are simply not available. At the time of the 1971 census, unemployment rates for the foreign-born were aproximately one percentage point below those of the native-born population. However, this was partly a function of age and location of residence. In Toronto there was no statistically significant difference, although the rates for the foreign-born were fractionally higher than those for the native-born. However, when the specific place of birth and period of immigration is taken into account, the 1971 census data reveal important qualifications to the overall picture. Although immigrants from Britain, United States and most European countries had average or below average unemployment rates, those from Asia and other non-European countries had substantially higher rates. Overall, the unemployment rates for immigrants from these countries were about one third higher than average, but in Toronto, where average unemployment rates were somewhat lower than for the country as a whole, rates for immigrants from Third World countries were more than 50 per cent above average for that metropolitan area. There was some variation by sex. Thus, the average for all males in Toronto in 1971 was 6 per cent, for Asian males, 10 per cent, and for other Third World countries, 11 per cent. In the case of females the overall average was 7.4 per cent compared with 11.5 per cent for Asian females and an average rate of 7.3 per cent for females from other Third World countries. Immigrants who had been in Canada five years or less, at the time of the

Canadian Unemployment and the Threat to Multiculturalism 113

1971 census, also had above average unemployment rates. Exceptions were immigrants from Great Britain, Italy and the Netherlands. Recent arrivals from other source countries were more vulnerable, particularly males from Asia with a rate of 12 per cent (Clodman and Richmond, 1981; Richmond, 1981).

The findings of the 1971 census were confirmed by the results of longitudinal surveys conducted between 1969 and 1976. A study of the labour market adaptation of Third World immigrants (Saunders, 1978) showed that, at the end of the first six months in Canada, immigrants who arrived between 1969 and 1971 had an average unemployment rate of just over 9 per cent; but those from the Third World countries had an average of over 15 per cent. The latter experienced higher unemployment rates than other immigrants during the next two and a half years in Canada, but by the end of the third year the unemployment rate was approximately the same as that of other immigrants. The same study also showed that the duration of unemployment was higher for Third World immigrants than for others during the first three years in the country. Analyses based upon the 1976 longitudinal survey confirm that immigrants during their first year in Canada experience substantially higher than average unemployment rates and also suffer from underemployment relative to their skills and qualifications (Clodman and Richmond, 1981; Ornstein and Sharma, 1983).

The evidence from surveys carried out in the 1960s (Richmond, 1967; Goldlust and Richmond, 1974) is confirmed by the government's longitudinal surveys. These studies suggest that immigrants do not always pursue their intended occupation on first arrival in Canada. Occupational status dislocation on arrival in Canada was characteristic of 41 per cent of those arriving in 1969, and 46 per cent of those arriving in 1970 and 1971. The proportion for the 1976 cohort was 55 per cent males and 44 per cent females. Three years after arrival in Canada a third of the 1969–71 arrivals were still not in their intended occupation. Some of those whose initial experiences here were disappointing probably returned home. The comparison between Third World immigrants and those from other countries suggests that the former have greater difficulties in obtaining the occupation of their choice. In 1973, up to 40 per cent of the Third World mmigrants, compared with a quarter of those from other countries, were still not in their intended occupation (Economic Council, 1978). We know that immigrants from Third World countries were more highly selected and generally better qualified than

114 *Racism and Multiculturalism*

those from other countries, suggesting that the difficulties were related to the non-recognition of qualifications, the demand for 'Canadian experience' and, in some cases, explicit discrimination.

Although firm evidence is not available it is reasonable to suppose that the experience of recently arrived immigrants today is not any better than it was five to ten years ago. Given the upward trend in unemployment in the last decade we can only assume that the tendencies that were evident then will be prevalent on an even larger scale today. Immigrants are not the cause of our present economic problems nor are they the cure. The demand for skills in some of the expanding sectors of industry, where technological advances are taking place rapidly, is likely to far exceed the numbers that could be induced to come as immigrants to Canada. Whatever may have been the case in the past we cannot expect to solve our skilled manpower problems through immigration in the future. This has been explicitly recognised by former Minister of Employment and Immigration in a speech when he noted that Canada is no longer able to rely heavily on imported workers to alleviate labour shortages. The pools of skilled labour abroad are drying up and it will become increasingly difficult to attract skilled immigrants in the future (Axworthy, 1980).

Meanwhile, immigrants already here continue to experience difficulties particularly during their first three years of residence. This is particularly true of Third World immigrants who, despite high educational levels, continue to earn below the level of other immigrants. Survey data from Toronto suggest that, in 1970, Black and Asian immigrants earned significantly less than the Canadian-born of the same age and education. Although there was no significant difference in occupational status there was a significant gap in earnings. This suggests that, even when employed at a level commensurate with education, immigrants from Third World countries may still experience discrimination in income. Data from the same survey suggest that self-reported experiences of discrimination and employment were three times the average of the population for Asian immigrants, and four times the average for Blacks, reaching 36 per cent of the latter (Richmond, 1975–76). A further study, carried out in Toronto 1977–79, shows that West Indian immigrants earn much lower incomes than would be expected on the basis of their education and job status (Reitz, Calzavara and Dasko. 1981). A later survey in Toronto, carried out in the Fall of 1980, found that one in five immigrants from Third World countries

Canadian Unemployment and the Threat to Multiculturalism 115

reported having some difficulty with ethnic or racial discrimination *in the previous twelve months* (IBR, 1981). Clearly, the persistence of racial and ethnic discrimination as a feature of Canadian life is incompatible with the theory and practice of multiculturalism.

Ethnic Stratification and Inequality

Any discussion of immigration and unemployment must be placed in the broader context of economic and social inequality in Canadian society and its relation to ethnicity. It has been frequently argued that the Canadian ethnic mosaic is a vertical one in which there is a close correlation between ethnicity and social status (Porter, 1965; Forcese, 1975). Porter regarded policies of multiculturalism and language retention as impeding the achievement of equality of opportunity for individuals, irrespective of ethnic origin. With the exception of immigrants from Britain and the United States, he argued that most immigrants entered Canada at a low level of socio-economic status and that this 'entrance status' was likely to be perpetuated if immigrants did not quickly assume the linguistic and cultural characteristics of the majority group (Porter, 1965; 1975). Subsequent studies have challenged the view that there is a strong link between ethnicity and income or occupational status in Canada. Evidence from the 1971 census lends only partial support to the ethnic stratification hypothesis (Richmond and Kalbach, 1980; Richmond and Verma, 1978). The census data do not support the view that low 'entry status' is a handicap to subsequent economic achievement. In fact, irrespective of ethnic origin, the second generation (Canadian-born of foreign parentage) tended to have higher levels of education, occupational status and income than the third and later generations. It is true that income is not equally distributed between all generations and ethnic groups in Canada but it is not the 'charter groups' who are at the top, as classical theories of immigrant assimilation would suggest. In fact, the third plus generation of British ethnic origin ranked 34 out of 56 categories in terms of the rank ordering of median male earnings, after adjusting for age (Richmond and Verma, 1978: 29). British and Jewish immigrants and their Canadian-born children have the highest average earnings. Also to be found among the more affluent are second generation Asians and Southern Europeans. Native Peoples, French Canadians, pre-war Asian immigrants and the most recently arrived foreign-born (other than the

116   *Racism and Multiculturalism*

British) are likely to be found in the lowest income categories.[3] Recent studies have tended to confirm Porter's view that the British are over-represented in the economic and power elites of Canadian society (Clement, 1975). However, this does not mean that there are serious obstacles to upward social mobility for ethnic minorities in general. Darroch (1979) reviewed the evidence on these questions and indicated a number of significant qualifications to the central thesis of the vertical mosaic. Studies of social mobility in Canada also suggest that ethnicity plays a comparatively small part in determining intergenerational occupational mobility (Turrittin, 1974; Ornstein, 1981). The same may not be true for racial minorities.

RACISM, MULTICULTURALISM AND THE THREAT OF VIOLENCE

So far the problems of unemployment and immigration have been discussed in a largely demographic and economic context. Although the rigidity of the ethnic mosaic has been questioned, the evidence does support the view that recently arrived immigrants, particularly those from Third World countries, experience high levels of unemployment, have difficulty finding employment commensurate with their qualifications and, even when they obtain appropriate employment, may still earn less than others in similar occupations. The role which racism plays in creating these problems cannot be ignored.

The problem of racism finds expression at the attitudinal, behavioural and social structural levels. Various studies undertaken in Canada have documented the extent of racial prejudice. Studies of ethnic social distance have generally indicated that 'visible minorities' are at the lowest end of a scale of social acceptance (Richmond, 1976; Berry, Kalin and Taylor, 1977). A survey in Toronto found that 16 per cent of the adult population could be regarded as extremely racist and another 35 per cent were inclined to some degree of racism (Henry, 1978). The evidence from self-reported studies of discrimination show that racial prejudice is often translated into explicit acts of discrimination in employment, housing, and other social situations (Ramcharan, 1974; Head, 1975; 1980). It is unnecessary to rely upon self-reported accounts of discrimination. Studies of employment agencies and real estate brokers support the view that discriminatory practices are built into the institutional structure of our society

Canadian Unemployment and the Threat to Multiculturalism 117

(Borovoy, 1980). Racist attitudes are consciously and unconsciously inculcated through schools and the mass media. They are reflected in everyday behaviour, where they are often overlaid with a superficially polite appearance of tolerance (McDiarmid and Pratt, 1971; Hughes and Kallen, 1974). The most extreme racist and ethnocentric views were expressed by the National Citizens' Coalition in their advertising campaign against admitting refugees in 1978–79 and by journalists such as Collins (1979). Even more moderate newspaper writers such as Westell (1979) have argued against the continued immigration of non-whites because of a fear that this will precipitate racial tension and violence.

An extensive review of the literature on inter-racial conflict, together with some of the policy alternatives open to Canadians, has been undertaken by Patel (1980). He reviews the experience of Britain and the United States in comparison with Canada. He distinguishes three perspectives in the explanations used and solutions offered for racial violence. The first, defined as the "deviant-individual" approach, identifies violence with particular individuals and groups within society who are not representative of the mainstream. The 'social-forces' perspective relates violence to changing social conditions influenced by factors such as migration, urban crowding and alienation. Patel's third perspective, the 'institutional-structural,' he regards as a more fundamental diagnosis and one which will lead to more constructive policy alternatives. It focuses on violence as 'a rational strategy in the struggle for power employed only after non-violence strategies have failed or when societal structures are incapable of accommodating basic demands' (1980:2). Recognition of these factors in racial violence lead to policies designed to modify institutional behaviour and to remove fundamental structural barriers. It should be recognised that these three approaches to the study of interracial conflict, and to the prevention of violence, are not mutually exclusive. Each may throw light on the circumstances of particular events and all three may be present in varying degrees.

Racial violence itself is not simply a mono-typical phenomenon. It may take a variety of forms. Firstly, there are the isolated attacks by one or two members of a dominant ethnic group upon individuals of a visible minority group. Typical are the incidents of 'Paki-bashing' that occurred in Toronto in the mid-1970s (Pitman, 1977). Closely related events occurred in Vancouver when the persons and property of some East Indian (mainly Sikh) families were attacked. Secondly, there are those violent outbreaks that occur when extremist groups

118   *Racism and Multiculturalism*

face each other in the course of a political march or rally. Although frequently declaring their peaceful intentions, such groups often come prepared to instigate or defend themselves against physical violence. Thirdly, there are acts of violence committed by the police, or other representatives of the law, against visible minority groups. The problem of police harassment is a common one as is the occasional excessive use of violence, including firearms, to deal with situations which normally would not require such force. Fourthly, there are the more organized attacks by some members of dominant groups against racial minorities; such actions have the deliberate intention of coercing the minority or punishing its members for an alleged breach of law or custom. Fifthly, there are situations of internal warfare between ethnic and racial minorities that involve the use of terrorist measures on both sides. The more militant members of the groups concerned engage in activities ranging from armed robbery, arson, bombing, assassination and other military-style operations. Sixth, and last, are those violent activities generally described as 'race riots' in which the members of a racial minority group engage in a form of collective behaviour, induced by crowd conditions, that involve the spontaneous destruction of property and attacks on individual members of the dominant group. Frequently, such riots also involve indiscriminate attacks on 'scapegoats' who may be the innocent members of other minority groups. The use of the police and paramilitary forces to suppress such outbreaks often exacerbates the degree of violence and the number of casualties involved. Fortunately, so far, Canada has experienced only the first three of these types of violence and these only on a small scale.

The single common denominator underlying all these manifestations of interracial violence is the degree of pent-up hostility between the groups concerned which is eventually precipitated in acts of violence. Attempts to unravel the more deep-seated conditions, underlying causes and precipitating events reveal a complex interaction between macro-structural factors, intervening institutional variables and socio-psychological conditions. Elsewhere, I have suggested a multivariate model of factors associated with urban ethnic conflict. I argued that:

> Key factors in the generation of urban ethnic conflict are clearly the prevailing socioeconomic conditions including objective inequalities in the distribution of wealth, income, employment, and educational opportunities between ethnic groups. These in turn are

Canadian Unemployment and the Threat to Multiculturalism 119

related to historical conditions that have resulted in the institutionalisation of racism and patterns of discrimination supported by prevailing legal and social sanctions. Patterns of inter-personal and inter-group relations, including degrees of residential segregation and avoidance behaviour in other social contexts, also stem from and are influenced by similar socioeconomic conditions. The major factor perpetuating the conditions of objective inequality is the political and community power differential. (Richmond, 1976:167)

I went on to suggest that, although objective inequality (political, economic, and social) is an important pre-condition of urban ethnic conflict, feelings of *relative* deprivation and *perceived* social injustice are frequently of even greater importance (*ibid.*, p. 167). This assertion has been criticized by Patel (1980:8) who argues for the greater explanatory value of institutional and structural factors. However, the latter should be seen as necessary but not sufficient conditions for the eruption of violence, which often occurs precisely when objective conditions of life are beginning to improve. Such changes in favour of a hitherto oppressed minority group may be perceived as highly threatening to the dominant group, while not improving quickly enough to satisfy the heightened aspirations and expectations of the minority (Gurr, 1970; Vanneman and Pettigrew, 1972; Isaac, Mutran and Stryker, 1980).

The mass media of communication play an important part in generating an awareness of absolute and relative deprivation, creating a consciousness of injustice which might otherwise have remained unrecognised by dominant and subordinated groups alike. To the extent that the reporting is objective and fair, journalists make a constructive contribution to understanding between racial and ethnic groups. However, irresponsible reporting that exaggerates the numbers of newcomers or scale of illegal immigration and the extent of competition for scarce resources, such as jobs and housing, simply serves to increase the probability of violence. Ideological factors play an important role in mobilising protest, on the one hand, or legitimating discrimination and acts of violence by the dominant group, on the other. In the last two decades there has been a polarisation of ideological perspectives. Liberal policies of an ameliorative nature have been criticised by both left and right. The radical view asserts that the problem lies in the very nature of advanced capitalist societies and that only major structural changes will be of

120 *Racism and Multiculturalism*

any use. Related to this view is the argument that violence is a rational response to institutionalised discrimination and that it actually produces results, in terms of governmental welfare and other policies (Kelly and Snyder, 1980; Isaac and Kelly, 1981; Piven and Cloward, 1971). At the other extreme is the ultra-conservative view that 'law and order' must be maintained at all costs. It argues against rewarding insurgency by making concessions or extending welfare services. It seeks to reduce government intervention and expenditures other than in respect of defence and related areas. When such policies are translated into economic terms they frequently include a deliberate trade-off between unemployment and inflation, in which the former is allowed to increase above the levels previously regarded as appropriate.

Unemployment and Ethnic Conflict

The relationship between unemployment and overt manifestations of ethnic conflict is a complex one. Based upon earlier studies in Great Britain I have argued, in the past, that economic insecurity and the fear of unemployment were contributory factors in generating racial disturbances (Richmond, 1950). More specifically, I drew attention to the sudden increases in youth unemployment in those areas in England (Nottingham and the Notting Hill Gate area of London) in which significant violent outbreaks occurred in 1958 (Richmond, 1960). Subsequently, critics questioned whether there was a direct causal relationship, pointing out that there have been other times when unemployment has not given rise to interracial conflict (Hiro, 1973; Patel, 1980). The criticism reflects a failure to recognise the multivariate and probabilistic nature of social causality. Neither chronic unemployment nor sudden increases in unemployment (among minority or majority groups) provide, *by themselves*, a necessary or sufficient basis for predicting outbreaks of violence. However, when jobs are scarce and members of particular ethnic or racial groups perceive themselves to be in competition for the available employment, there is little doubt that this adds to underlying tension and increases the probability that some other precipitating event will spark a violent episode. When governments fail to maintain full employment and equal opportunity for ethnic minorities, even more when they abandon full employment as an explicit goal, they do so at the risk of increasing racial and ethnic tension.[4]

Canadian Unemployment and the Threat to Multiculturalism 121

American experience confirms the view that unemployment rates alone, whether those of the dominant group or racial minorities, do not account for outbreaks of violence. Lieberson and Silverman (1965) hypothesised that riots might occur when either Negroes or Whites had relatively high unemployment rates. They compared 25 cities in which riots had occurred with a control group of comparable cities without a riot history. The available evidence (which did not include unemployment rates for the specific year in which the riots took place) was inconclusive and failed to confirm the hypothesis. However, the investigations of the Kerner Commission, which sought to determine the explanation for the series of race riots that occurred in American cities in the 1960s, drew attention to the chronic unemployment and underemployment of Blacks in the United States. The cumulative effects of economic insecurity and deprivation were, in the Commission's view, contributory factors. The 'revolution of rising expectations' made such persistent differentials increasingly unacceptable (Kerner, 1968). More recent studies have focused on the consequences of stratification and segmentation in labour markets. It seems that Blacks, women, youth and recently arrived immigrants all share the insecurity associated with a marginal position in the labour market (Edwards, 1975; Cummings, 1980; Clodman and Richmond, 1981). There is continuing dispute among sociologists concerning possible gains or losses, by the White population, from the effects of racial discrimination and Black subordination (Szymanski, 1978; Villemez and Wiswell, 1978).

CONCLUSION

Recently, unemployment rates in Canada have fluctuated between 7 and 11 per cent, having declined somewhat from a peak in 1978 and risen again. There is considerable regional variation, with the Atlantic provinces experiencing the most severe problems. Youth unemployment in Canada, as in other advanced industrial countries, remains high but will probably diminish as the effects of declining birthrates reduce the number of new entrants to the labour force. The number of labour force immigrants admitted to Canada in recent years has been comparatively small. Although probably experiencing relatively high unemployment rates during their first three or four years in Canada, they do not represent a serious threat to the indigenous labour force. The absence of reliable data on immigrant

122 *Racism and Multiculturalism*

integration since the early 1970s is regrettable. Much more research on this question is needed.[6]

The philosophical foundation for multi-culturalism is essentially egalitarian. It emphasises respect for cultural differences and is antipathetic toward any manifestations of racism or ethnic discrimination. While not proportionally represented in the power elites, there is growing evidence that European immigrants and their children have been economically successful and upwardly mobile in the post-Second World War period. Although it may be premature to draw firm conclusions, the preliminary evidence concerning immigrants from Third World countries, particularly visible minorities, is not as encouraging. Racial prejudice and discrimination are obstacles to the economic and social integration of non-European immigrants. If policies of multi-culturalism are to be meaningful to these groups, major efforts to eliminate racism will be needed.[5] Probably more serious than unemployment, as a threat to multiculturalism, is the general climate of fiscal conservatism with its emphasis on cutbacks in government expenditures. Programs designed to facilitate the short-term adaptation and long-term integration of immigrants into Canadian society require more than token support.

Federal government policies with regard to assistance for refugees have not been entirely consistent. The original plan to match every sponsored Indo-Chinese refugee with a government-sponsored individual or family has not worked out as originally intended. There is a good deal of confusion concerning the eligibility of privately-sponsored refugees for various government services, including free language classes. Funding for the Adjustment Assistance Program in 1981–82 was only about half the level of 1980–81. Furthermore, funds available for voluntary organisations under the Immigrant Settlement and Adaptation Program (ISAP) have been increased by only 5 per cent which, in view of inflation, represents a significant real cut in available resources. At present, these funds are available only to assist immigrants who have been in the country less than three years. However, studies of immigrant adaptation show that immigrants experience adjustment problems, and many need special services, for more than a decade after arrival. Problems relating to families and children often do not manifest themselves until long after initial employment problems have been resolved.

The government needs to undertake a major review of settlement services, including language training, with a view to designing a more comprehensive program for all recently arrived

Canadian Unemployment and the Threat to Multiculturalism 123

adult immigrants, whether or not they are destined to the labour market. Programs are needed that will assist men, women and children to achieve a satisfactory level of English (or French) language literacy as well as oral fluency. Other programs are needed that will focus on the social and cultural aspects of immigrant integration as well as the economic. Family counselling, children's aid services and assistance for 'battered wives' are among the services where social workers need a knowledge of the language and culture of the families concerned, if they are to provide effective support. Recreational and counselling programs are also needed for immigrant youth. An over-emphasis upon the short run economic integration of adult male immigrants overlooks the need for longer term services designed to facilitate social integration. Failure to implement such programs now will generate greater economic and social costs later. Multi-culturalism cannot be bought cheaply.

8 A Canadian Dilemma: Bilingualism, Multiculturalism or Racism?

In 1981, with the cooperation of the British Parliament, Canada repatriated the British North America Act of 1867 and, in 1982, the *Constitution Act* was proclaimed. Attached to this Act was a Charter of Rights and Freedoms which officially 'commits the Federal, Provincial and Territorial governments to the support of a wide range of rights and freedoms that reflect the traditional values of our society', according a government brochure. There is little doubt that the precise interpretation of the Charter, and its application in particular cases, will provide constitutional lawyers and the Canadian courts with much legal argument in the future. Social scientists will hesitate to trespass upon such controversial issues. However, sociologists may doubt the claim that the new Constitution 'reflects the traditional values' of Canadian society about which it may be difficult to reach a consensus. It is necessary to consider the extent to which implementing the Charter and enforcing the Constitution on sometimes reluctant Provincial authorities, will intensify existing social conflicts and possibly generate new ones.

The issue of 'Canadian unity' is a perennial one, which goes beyond regional inequality and ethnic diversity, to include Federal-Provincial relations and major Constitutional issues relating to Aboriginal land claims and fundamental human rights (Pepin & Robarts, 1979). The Federal government, during the long period of Liberal ascendancy, sought to strengthen national allegiances at the expense of regional and Provincial ones. The amended British North America Act, which became the Constitution of Canada, was seen as an instrument for strengthening these centralist tendencies. But, as a leading Canadian political scientist has pointed out, in 1980–81, there was a 'bitter constitutional conflict in Canada' and the Charter was finally enacted 'against the vigorous opposition of large numbers of powerful interests in the country' (Smiley, 1981:59).

LANGUAGE RIGHTS

Clause sixteen of the Charter affirms that English and French are the official languages of Canada and of the Province of New Brunswick. By 'Canada' in this context is meant 'all institutions of the parliament and government' at the federal level. Other Provinces are not bound by the Charter to provide the same official language rights and services in their Legislative Assemblies, Courts or bureaucracies. Quebec deliberately refrained from endorsing the Constitution Act, or any of its provisions, insisting that French should be the only official language of that province. Since the election of a Conservative government in Ottawa there have been overtures from Quebec designed to achieve a Constitutional accord, but there remain many sensitive issues.

The question of language rights is critical in Quebec, but also in other Provinces of Canada which have a significant francophone population. Such rights have been a controversial issue in Manitoba since its incorporation into the Canadian Confederation, in 1870, and continue to generate acrimonious disputes. The 'official' status accorded to French in that Province by the *Manitoba Act*, 1870 was rescinded by Order-in-Council, in 1888 and by amendments to the rules of the Legislature. The constitutionality of these actions was not challenged until recently, but attempts to settle the dispute through political negotiation failed. Consequently, the issue of the validity of all Manitoba statutes was submitted for determination to the Supreme Court of Canada (Banks, 1985). The Court decided that Manitoba was obliged to ensure that all its statutes were printed in both official languages. However, a later decision (May, 1986) held that such routine documents as parking summonses could be in either language. The Supreme Court also held that a person has the right to use either language in the Courts, but there is no obligation on the part of the judiciary to understand both languages. In other words, from a Constitutional standpoint, interpreters and translators are acceptable. The Court left it to the Federal and Provincial legislatures to take any further action needed to make bi-lingual services a reality, where they do not already exist. Meanwhile, the provincial government of Ontario, while insisting that it will endeavour to provide necessary services to its francophone citizens, has resisted entrenching such rights in its own legislation. Other provinces have not even considered extending them to their francophone minorities.

Canada: Bilingualism, Multiculturalism or Racism?

The Charter goes beyond the question of official languages in government institutions to assert minority language rights in education. Clause 23(3) gives those whose mother tongue is English or French a right to have their children receive primary and secondary school instruction in their own language. The same right is extended to those who received their primary school instruction in Canada in English or French, irrespective of their mother tongue. The right is qualified only by a consideration of the numbers of children for whom such minority language instruction is warranted. Unfortunately, such rights were expressly denied by the language laws of Quebec. Through Law 101, passed in 1977, the *Parti Quebecois* endeavoured to impose French language instruction on all children except those whose parents were themselves educated in English schools in Quebec. This recognised the existence of an indigenous anglophone minority in the Province but did not extend the same rights to English speaking families who moved to Quebec from elsewhere.

The language laws designed to make Quebec a unilingual francophone Province included provisions that all commercial signs and advertisements were to be in French. With the exception of certain multinational companies that were specially exempted, all corporations were required to conduct their business in the French language. In the decade since the legislation came into effect, French has become more widely used than before, even in the predominantly English sections of Montreal. However, the legislation was of doubtful constitutional validity. It was challenged in the courts and found to violate rights to freedom of expression.

To understand the nature of the conflict over official languages it is necessary to appreciate the demographic realities of Canadian society. Although 27 per cent of the population of Canada is of French ethnic origin, only 25 per cent speaks French at home and most of those who do so are resident in Quebec. Outside of that province only ten per cent of the population of Canada understands or speaks French. The majority of francophones, outside Quebec, live in New Brunswick, or on the borders of Quebec and Ontario. Except in these areas, English language assimilation has occurred among both French and other groups. Although one in five of the population is of European ethnic origin, only one in twenty has retained a mother tongue, other than English or French, as the home language. Some of these are first generation immigrants themselves, including the large Italian, Greek, Portuguese and Eastern European populations of large cities, such as Toronto and Montreal. In Montreal, for example, there is a growing population of francophone Haitians. Immigrants in Quebec are encouraged to learn French rather than English, but many prefer to acquire the language of the continental majority.

In Quebec as a whole, only one in three of the population is officially bilingual, sixty per cent speaking French only. Partly as a consequence of language legislation and deliberate unilingual policies in Quebec, French is no longer exclusively the language of the working class. It has become the principal language at work for managers, professionals and clercial workers, as well as for production and manual workers. Various studies have shown that the status of the French language in that province has improved over the last fifteen years but a knowledge of English is still seen by many as a necessary condition for occupational advancement, perhaps because this frequently means a willingness to move to another province, or even to the United States (Laporte, 1983).

It is not surprising that the question of bilingualism should be such a source of continuing controversy. Canadians in Ontario and in the western provinces, many of whom are of neither British nor French ethnic origin, consider that the non-official languages of Canada should be given more consideration. There are increasing efforts to preserve so-called 'heritage languages', both through voluntary measures in the home and community, but also through formal instruction in the regular school system.

MULTICULTURALISM

Clause 27 of the Charter of Rights states that it 'shall be interpreted in a manner consistent with the preservation and enhancement of the multicultural heritage of Canada'. This is consistent with the policy of 'multiculturalism within a bilingual framework' which the Liberal government in Ottawa, under former Prime Minister Trudeau, announced in 1971. This followed the recognition in volume four of the report of the Royal Commission on Bi-lingualism and Bi-culturalism, that a quarter of the population did not have any ancestral link with the so called 'charter groups'. The implementation of multicultural policies since that date has been vested in a Federal Minister under the Secretary of State but the programmes have been subject to widespread criticism. Some sociologists regard so-called multicultural policies as an electoral ploy designed to attract votes,

Canada: Bilingualism, Multiculturalism or Racism? 129

particularly in Ontario and the West, and as a vehicle for patronage. Others have seen it as a divisive policy calculated to preserve the economic dominance and the political hegemony of the British elites. In fact, since its inception, only limited resources have been allocated to multicultural programmes (Burnet, 1983). Attention was focused mainly on language maintenance, music and the arts. Later, questions of racial prejudice came to the forefront and the federal Conservatives, under Prime Minister Mulroney, have indicated a concern for promoting ethnic minority business. Little has been done to remove the fundamental inequalities that are still evident in Canada's 'vertical mosaic'.

Nowhere are these inequalities more evident than among the Native Peoples of Canada. almost as an afterthought, and only after much pressure was brought upon the federal and provincial governments, clause 35 was incorporated into the amended British North America Act, which became the Constitution. The clause states that 'the existing aboriginal and treaty rights of the aboriginal peoples of Canada are hereby recognised and affirmed'. Provision was made for a series of federal–provincial conferences to be held in an attempt to reach agreement concerning the nature of these 'existing' rights. Up to 1986, after three such conferences, no agreement had been reached. Eventually the courts will have to settle the various land claims and other disputes that are already generating opposition by provincial governments, and private interests, including those of national and multinational corporations, seeking to exploit the rich oil and mineral resources of the traditional Indian Reserves and Inuit territories.

Meanwhile, the Native Peoples of Canada are the victims of more than two hundred years of exploitation and neglect. They have the highest rates of mortality, morbidity, alcoholism, suicide, unemployment, poverty and poor housing, of any segment of the population. Native women experience the 'double jeopardy' of discrimination because of race and gender. Women who married a non-Indian were also deprived of the rights of residence on the Reserve and any other privileges, accorded by custom or treaty, both for themselves and their children. Men who inter-marry are not so penalised. Recent Federal legislation removes this source of discrimination in the future but leaves it to each Band to determine whether it will reinstate those women who lost their status in the past. Although there is much pressure from women's groups to change these discriminatory provisions, Native men are afraid that their power in Band councils may be

130 *Racism and Multiculturalism*

usurped by white men if the latter are allowed to live on Reserves (Weaver, 1983).

There are further problems in determining who is a Native person in Canada. There are approximately a quarter of a million registered Indians who have that status by law, but the Charter of Rights refers also to the Metis, the Inuit and others whose designation as a Native person is customary, rather than based on the narrow definition used in the Indian Act. Although the census of 1981 recorded almost half a million Native persons this is believed to be an underestimate because some communities deliberately boycotted the census. Although divided by language, geography, cultural traditions and generational differences, the Native Peoples of Canada are united in a determination to overcome the handicaps imposed by past discrimination and unequal treatment.

The Assembly of First Nations of Canada, representing Native Peoples, is concerned that the new Charter may threaten rather than promote their interests, as a consequence of its formulation in terms of individual rather than collective rights and freedoms. Boldt & Long (1984) pointed out, 'There is a contradiction between Canada's idealistic commitment to individual rights and its seeming disregard and lack of respect for Indian group rights.' There is a clash between western liberal ideas of individual rights and traditional Amerindian views of collective solidarity and community decision-making. The enforcement of individual rights could, under certain conditions, become an instrument for forced integration and assimilation. As these writers point out, 'Indians do not seek protection for their racial characteristics, because being Indian is a cultural and political identity, not a racial one. Indians seek protection for their identity as a distinct nation of peoples' (ibid.:485–87). It is their collective inequality as distinctive peoples, rather than their individual treatment, that is the central problem.

IMMIGRATION

Inequality is also evident among the foreign born population, although it is generally seen as a problem of individual opportunities for achievement, rather than either individual or collective discrimination. Canada has been highly selective in its immigration policies admitting only those who it was felt would make a useful contribution to the country's economy. Exceptions to this are the sponsored,

Canada: Bilingualism, Multiculturalism or Racism? 131

family reunion component of post-war immigration, together with the humanitarian refugee movements, although even in the latter case, there has been some attempt to match skills and qualifications to Canada's perceived labour force requirements. As a consequence, there has been a significant element of 'brain drain' in the movement to Canada, particularly from the Third World. The education level of immigrants generally is higher than the average for the Canadian born population. Asian immigrants have the highest educational and occupational qualifications of all (Richmond and Kalbach, 1980; Basavarajappa and Verma, 1985).

In fact, sixteen per cent of the population of Canada are immigrants, including those from Britain and the United States. Although the absolute numbers admitted annually has declined in recent years, immigration continues to be a significant source of population growth. After reaching a peak of over 200 000 immigrants in 1974, the annual gross intake fell to less than 90 000 in the early 1980s. There is a growing use of temporary employment visas rather than encouragement of permanent settlement. An increasing proportion of all immigrants now come from Third World countries, particularly Asia, the Caribbean and Latin America. The majority reside and work in the larger metropolitan areas.

Unfortunately, immigrants are not always able to translate their education and qualifications into commensurate jobs and incomes. Most immigrants experience a period of transition and adjustment, often being compelled to take any available employment, however unskilled. This is particularly true at a time of recession and high unemployment. Lack of recognition of educational qualifications and employment credentials, combine with language problems and lack of Canadian experience, to prevent some immigrants from obtaining the occupations which they (and the immigration authorities) intended or expected. It is not surprising to find that the incidence of poverty and unemployment among recently arrived immigrants is higher than average. Nevertheless, after five years in Canada most immigrants earn average or above average incomes. Recent studies have shown that Asian immigrants, who have been in the country more than a decade have relatively high incomes, but still not as high as their educational qualifications would lead one to expect, if 'all others things were equal' (Vasavarajappa and Verma, 1985). This raises questions concerning hiring practices and opportunities for promotion and the possibility of discrimination against Asian and other immigrants in employment.

132 *Racism and Multiculturalism*

RACISM IN CANADA

Clause (15) of the Charter defines 'equality rights' and outlaws discrimination based on 'race, national or ethnic origin, colour, religion, sex, age or mental or physical disability'. This clause also provides for the possibility of affirmative action, or positive discrimination, designed to ameliorate conditions of disadvantaged individuals or groups. The equality clause did not officially come into effect until 1985, three years after the promulgation of the new Constitution Act. This is some indication that transforming the reality of Canada in society to satisfy the Charter's ideal was seen by Parliament as a major task, requiring the close co-operation of the Provinces and other agencies. It is doubtful whether a three-year delay was enough to enable the provinces to remove the entrenched sources of inequality and racism. Legislation passed in 1986 (Bill C22) was designed to promote 'pay equity' for women, ethnic minorities and the disabled, in those areas of employment within Federal jurisdiction. It establishes an elaborate reporting procedure, to enable levels of remuneration for comparable employment to be monitored, but does little to ensure that employers will adopt affirmative action or other remedial measures. In this respect, the legislation falls far short of the measures recommended by an earlier Royal Commission on Equality (Abella, 1984).

A report by a Special Committee of the Federal House of Commons on the 'Participation of Visible Minorities in Canadian society', titled *Equality Now*, (Canada, House of Commons, 1984), made it quite clear that racism was endemic in Canada and that major reforms will be required before its institutional and individual manifestations are eradicated. It must be recognised that racism is not a new phenomenon in Canada. Throughout the nineteenth century and, indeed, until 1962, Canada's immigration laws, and the way in which regulations were administered, clearly discriminated against non-Europeans. The Chinese were subject to punitive head taxes; the Japanese were virtually excluded by a 'gentleman's agreement' with the Japanese government, and other Asians by a shipping regulation, which prevented the landing in British Columbia of anyone who had not travelled by a 'single continuous journey'! Ostensibly a health precaution, this regulation effectively prevented immigrants from the Indian sub-continent crossing the Pacific in the nineteenth and early twentieth century (Buchignana, Indra and

Canada: Bilingualism, Multiculturalism or Racism?   133

Srivasatava, 1985). During the same period, when the western provinces were actively recruiting American farmers, the discriminatory application of health regulations and other devices effectively ensured that very few Negroes received land grants (Troper, 1972). Although some Blacks and Asians were able to settle in Canada in small numbers, they were subject to discriminatory treatment, both personal and institutional, and were unable to sponsor relatives to join them until the regulations were changed in 1962 (Richmond, 1981).

Among the most glaring examples of injustice was the treatment of Japanese Canadians during the Second World War. After Pearl Harbour, and following the American example, Canada evacuated all Japanese Canadians from British Columbia, alleging potential dangers from subversion. Whether born in Canada, naturalised citizens, or aliens, Japanese men, women and children were removed to Alberta and other inland destinations, where they were kept for the duration of the war in near concentration camp conditions. Their properties, including homes, businesses and fishing boats, were confiscated and sold at minimal prices. Investigations in Canada and the United States showed that the charges of spying and subversion were completely without foundation. Whereas the American government has paid compensation to the surviving Japanese and their families, no such official recognition of injustice, or offer of compensation, has been made so far by Canada (Kallen, 1982).

Various studies have revealed the extent of racial prejudice among Canadians today. Native Peoples, Blacks and Asians are all low on a social distance scale of preference, compared with Canadians of British, American, French or other European origin. Discrimination in employment, housing, public services and accommodations has been well documented. Notwithstanding the fact that provincial and federal governments have instituted Human Rights Commissions, with powers to consider complaints, the remedies available to an individual who experiences discrimination are limited (Driedger, 1978).

The Parliamentary committee on 'Visible Minorities' documents the evidence of racism in areas such as the social integration of immigrants and ethnic minorities, employment and promotion in the public and private sectors, government policies including immigration control procedures, the administration of justice, the education system and the mass media of communication. It made a total of eighty recommendations designed to assist in the eradication of the

134 *Racism and Multiculturalism*

problem. Some of the key policy recommendations contained in the report are worth highlighting.

1. The Federal government is urged to introduce affirmative action into its own employment and development programmes, as well as contract compliance legislation requiring contractors and sub-contractors with federal departments and agencies to implement hiring programmes for visible minorities. In addition, a five year strategy is proposed during which the government would make subsidies and tax incentives available to the private sector for special hiring and training programmes.
2. The government is urged to make improvements in its immigration procedures to ensure that visible minorities are not singled out for unusual treatment or delays.
3. The report recommended that laws designed to prevent the promotion of racial hatred should be strengthened and Human Rights Commissions given more powers.
4. The mass media and the advertising industry should develop codes of practice that will eradicate racist reporting and reflect the multicultural diversity of Canada.
5. Provincial governments should urge school boards to implement a race relations policy; teaching and resource material should be developed to facilitate more positive attitudes toward visible minorities.
6. The present Department of Multiculturalism under the Secretary of State should be given full Ministry status, greater responsibilities in combating racism and additional funding.

(Canada, House of Commons, 1984: 135–41)

This Parliamentary report was prepared and published under the auspices of the former Liberal government. It remains to be seen whether the Conservative administration will act on some or all of its recommendations. In the meantime, the government of British Columbia has taken steps to dismantle and limit the powers of the Human Rights Commission in that province, clearly indicating its opposition to the federal initiatives.

MORAL DILEMMA OR STRUCTURAL CONFLICT?

The visible minorities in Canada, understood as those of non-white racial origin, are estimatd to be seven per cent of a population which now numbers some 25 million. These racial minorities are not evenly distributed geographically. Those of recent immigrant origin are largely concentrated in the metropolitan areas. Racial minorities make up more than ten per cent of the population of metropolitan Toronto, or about 300 000 people out of three million. Although much smaller in absolute numbers than the Black population of the United States, such a ratio comes close to the proportion which existed in that country when Gunnar Myrdal undertook his monumental study of the race problem in the USA more than forty years ago (Myrdal, 1944). At the time he noted that 'An American Dilemma' arose from the contradiction between the ideals of equality, freedom and justice expressed in the 'American creed' largely entrenched in the Constitution, and its amendments, and the reality of prejudice and discrimination against Blacks in that society.

Myrdal focused on the inconsistency between theory and practice in the American constitution and represented the dilemma as primarily a moral one. He believed that the situation of Negroes in the United States would improve as the white population recognised the contradictions and took appropriate steps to remove institutional racism and to improve understanding between the races. The initiative, he believed, would have to come from those who held the reigns of power in that society – that is to say from the white population. Since then history has shown that Myrdal's critics were right when they argued that the conflicts were deeply rooted in the economic system and in the political structure of American society. Only when the subordinated minorities awoke to a consciousness of their inferior status, and mobilised their own resources in a struggle for freedom, was the system changed. Even today, there remain substantial inequalities and injustices affecting the status of Blacks in American society (Lieberson, 1981).

Canada now faces a dilemma and a problem of inequality at least as intractable as that which faced Blacks in the United States. Slavery did not leave its mark, to the same degree, on Canadian institutions, but a legacy remains from the Royal Proclamation of 1763 and the Canadian Indian Act, 1874, which together determined the fate of Canada's original peoples. Native People were effectively deprived of their lands and prevented from achieving full equality and citizenship

136   *Racism and Multiculturalism*

within the new colonial regime. The consequences of those actions today are no less formidable obstacles to 'equality now', than were the traditions of segregation in the American south, when Myrdal undertook his study.

Furthermore, immigrants and their descendants today are attempting to establish themselves, in employment and in the community, at a time of serious economic crisis. Earlier, Blacks in the United States were able to win concessions for themselves, and immigrants in that country saw their children and grandchildren enjoying the prosperity that America was able to offer. They did so mainly in the 1960s, at a time when the economy was booming and unemployment was relatively low. Canada today is faced with a further dilemma. How can policies be designed to promote equality, and to remove discrimination, at a time when there is increasing competition for scarce employment, a revolt against high taxation and a general move to the right in the prevailing political climate?

A leading Canadian sociologist recently expressed this dilemma in no uncertain terms. Breton (1984) argued that two closely related factors must be taken into account if we are to understand Canada's linguistic and ethnocultural reality. They are the structuring of the symbolic component of the social order, on the one hand, and the distribution of social status and recognition among ethnocultural groups on the other. He noted that 'such processes are quite conflictual and emotionally charged' involving a struggle over the distribution of resources, both material and symbolic. He recognised a growing demand for the state to withdraw from these conflicts and allow *market* forces in the economic sphere, and *laissez-faire* policies in cultural relations, to have full play. Government intervention in both fields is anathema to the ideologues of the 'New Right'. However, Breton viewed such arguments against state intervention as futile and insisted that social scientists should not argue for or against such intervention, but endeavour to understand the underlying forces which give rise to them. Unfortunately, the views of academic economists and sociologists are all too often expressed in polemical and ideological terms. The kind of 'value neutrality' Breton appears to favour is not widely practised today.

ETHNIC CONFLICT

What are the prospects for a peaceful solution to the current Canadian dilemma? Will racism and present inequalities persist and

Canada: Bilingualism, Multiculturalism or Racism?   137

even become more severe, or will the relations of linguistic, ethnic and racial groups in Canada change in a more egalitarian direction? Will changes come about through voluntary action by the dominant white Anglophone majority, or will the subordinated minorities be obliged to mobilise their resources and engage in violent conflict, before the system begins to change in their favour?

The answer depends in part upon the balance of power between the groups concerned. Cross-cutting ties, perceived common interests and the need to present a united front against opppression and discrimination, may bring disparate minorities together. It seems more likely that they will remain divided against one another. The interests of urban based immigrants are not necessarily the same as those of Native Peoples in rural peripheries. The more traditional Indian and Inuit communities may find themselves opposed to certain groups who are eager to take advantage of oil and other resources beneath their land, or to engage in entrepreneurial activities which may bring wealth but destroy cultural traditions in the process.

The outcome also depends upon the extent to which the dominant groups perceive their own enlightened self-interest, in the long run, as necessarily involving a shift of economic resources, political power and social status in favour of the minorities. This may be the only way to avoid overt conflict. Gunnar Myrdal believed that the dominant white population of the United States would recognise the need for such enlightened action. Some members of the liberal establishment in that country were so motivated, but they faced formidable opposition from traditional conservative forces. The struggle has not yet ended in America or in Canada.

It is unlikely that changes favourable to racial and ethnic minorities will occur without strong leadership and clearly articulated protest. This need not necessarily be violent or subversive, but has the potential to become radical if there appears to be little or no response from the dominant groups. The central issue is clearly one of power. But power is an elusive concept in the social sciences. It involves a complex interaction between objective material forces, and subjective symbolic socio-cultural ones. Numbers, access to economic resources and technological competence must be combined with ethnic consciousness, organisational efficiency and strong leadership, if a minority is to overcome conditions of subordination and oppression. Often this occurs only when a third party, external to the conflict, joins forces with the minority to overthrow a dominant regime. Such struggles are evident in the Third World and in other

138   *Racism and Multiculturalism*

countries today. The superpowers may intervene, to support one side or another, when they perceive their own ideological and economic interests are at stake. The result is often civil war, insurgency and terrorism.

Canada must endeavour to solve its internal conflicts without such external interference. American influence on Canadian internal and external affairs can never be ignored. Much of the pressure to develop natural resources in the North comes from American-based multinational companies. Economic and political pressures are ever present. Soviet influence is more remote but the possibility of support for subversive movements cannot be ruled out. Canada must resolve its own internal contradictions on the basis of the ideals expressed in the Charter of Rights and Freedoms, modified by some recognition of the proper balance between individual and collective rights. There must be a clear expression of political will by the majority groups and established political parties, before the noble expressions of intent embodied in the Charter can be translated into reality. Such measures are needed now and cannot wait for a more favourable economic climate. Failure to act will only exacerbate the situation by raising expectations and generating disappointment and frustration. Therein lies the dilemma!

Part III

Ethnic Nationalism

Part III

Ethnic Nationalism

9 Ethnic Nationalism: Social Science Paradigms

The study of ethnic nationalism presents social scientists with certain difficulties which go beyond the inherent complexity of the subject matter. Only in the last decade have sociologists and political scientists paid serious attention to the phenomenon, which most writers confidently believed would decline in importance with the growth of urbanisation, industrialisation and other modernising influences. The apparent resurgence of ethnicity as a major source of conflict in modern societies compelled them to address the issue. Unfortunately, it has not always been easy to distinguish the rhetoric of those who are actively involved in promoting the cause of particular ethnic minorities, or defending the status quo, from serious attempts to understand the social forces at work.

Questions of ethnic nationalism, and related issues of race relations and the status of minority groups, arouse deep-seated emotions. Social scientists, among other intellectuals, have often been leaders in protest movements and themselves active in the struggle of ethnic groups against oppressive conditions. To mobilise support for such a movement it is often necessary to engage in ideological debates which depend upon rhetorical devices, the exaggeration of differences, and the creation of myths. Such symbolic resources play an important part in situations of ethnic conflict and in the generation of social change. However, they should not be mistaken for scientific analysis; nor should they be allowed to obscure the need for independent critical perspectives which are not necessarily those of either the dominant or subordinate groups in a particular conflict situation.

Unfortunately, nationalist ideologies and counter-ideologies frequently give rise to violence by both majority and minority groups. All too often nationalist movements, and those who oppose them, resort to hijacking, bombing, assassination, kidnapping, murder, rioting, and terrorism. This, in turn, leads to counter-measures, to repression by police and military, and to inter-state and civil wars, to genocidal policies and a lust for revenge. Most social scientists would be opposed to political expressions of ethnic minority protest, or majority resistance, which advocate or adopt coercive means.

141

142   *Ethnic Nationalism*

However understandable such strategies may be, when other more peaceful or constitutional avenues to change appear to have failed, such violence is both counter-productive and morally indefensible irrespective of the goals pursued. However, some social scientists may believe that the end can, in some circumstances, justify the means. They will place a different interpretation on the analysis that follows.

Terminological Confusion

Research on ethnic nationalism is further complicated by semantic problems. Not only are rhetorical and ideological assertions often couched in the language of the social sciences, but the latter are not always consistent in their use of concepts. Consider, for example, the term 'ethnic'. One sociologist reviewed 65 studies dealing with aspects of ethnicity (of which only 13 gave explicit definitions), together with 27 different defintions culled from dictionaries and theoretical studies (Isajiw, 1970). He examined the common denominators and found the attributes most often mentioned were common ancestry, and the same culture, religion or language. While race was also mentioned in nine of the definitions, it was on a different level of analysis, referring to physical, rather than social or cultural characteristics. He also suggested that most definitions also asserted the ascriptive, or involuntary nature of the attribution, although some writers, such as Barth (1969) and Nagata (1974) argued that ethnicity can be situationally determined. Another common denominator of most definitions was the factor of mutual recognition and identification.

The term 'nation' is similarly open to varied interpretation. Gellner (1983) virtually equated the term 'nation' with 'shared culture', while limiting the association to those cases where 'standardised, homogeneous, centrally sustained high cultures, pervading entire populations' have come about and become the 'natural repositories of political legitimacy' (ibid.:55). Such a definition immediately begs the question of the relation between ethnic group and nation, and tends to confuse nation with 'state'. Indeed, sociologists and political scientists frequently use the term 'nation-state' as if it was taken for granted that modern states were culturally homogeneous. There is growing recognition that, on the contrary, most contemporary states (economically developed and developing) are multinational in character.

Ethnic Nationalism: Social Science Paradigms

Connor (1978) examined the concepts of 'nation', 'state' and 'ethnic group' and emphasised the need to distinguish between them. He did not offer a formal definition of these terms but drew attention to the variety of usage in the literature. He also discussed the phenomenon of *nationalism* and contrasted it with related terms such as ethnicity, primordalism, pluralism, tribalism, regionalism, communalism, and parochialism. He acknowledges that 'one cannot explain the quintessence of nationalism' but that this need not preclude advances in understanding, if we have a proper appreciation of the complexity of the subject (ibid:397).

It is important to preface the discussion of social science paradigms by some further clarification of terminology. It is central to this critical appraisal of the social science literature in the field that *states* are generally *multinational* and that *nations* are often *polyethnic*. Some elaboration of this view is called for. It has been noted that there is some controversy concerning the ascriptive, or primordial, nature of ethnic group membership and the view that ethnicity is situationally defined, that ethnic group boundaries are malleable and permeable, and that ethnicity may be acquired or divested at will. Those who emphasise the primordial and ascriptive aspects suggest a link between ethnicity and kinship, together with the strong emotional ties which link people who believe in their common ancestry and sometimes, also, their special cosmic destiny. Ethnic identity is seen as a core element in the development of personality, intimately linked with the perception of self, early socialisation, language learning and/or religious and political indoctrination.

The alternative view recognises that an individual may have dual, or multiple, identities depending upon the roles played in particular situations. The varied role-sets characteristic of modern societies call for multiplex, over-lapping and sometimes conflicting definitions of personal identity and group membership. More than one language may be learned in childhood, or later; even religious conversion does not necessarily mean the complete relinquishment of all previous beliefs, practices or group attachments. Ethnic group membership may depend more upon rituals of social acceptance and subjective identification, than upon irreversible criteria of an ascriptive and involuntary nature.

Part of the difficulty in reconciling these two views arises from a too simplistic and unitary a view of culture. It is not surprising that social anthropologists have been generally more ready to accept the situational definition of ethnicity than sociologists. The latter gen-

144 *Ethnic Nationalism*

erally treat culture as given, whereas anthropologists treat it as a variable to be studied in its own right. Consequently, they are more aware of its complexity and diversity. Although actually consisting of abstract symbols (verbal, visual and material), cultures are best understood, by analogy, in terms of an organic system consisting of multiple layers which can be peeled off and lead to new growth. Cultures are in a constant state of flux. Both endogenous and exogenous forces promote change in cultures just as they do in social structures. To the extent that ethnic group membership and identity are closely related to culture, so they are similarly multifaceted and changing. Group boundaries modify over time, sometimes becoming more inclusive or exclusive. This does not mean that the notion of 'ancestral' links must be abandoned altogether. Instead, it suggests that the ancestral links may be putative (i.e. attributed) rather than determined by actual genetic connections or necessarily acquired during early socialisation. Ethnic identities and the linkages they create are symbolic and often mythological.

As has been noted the term 'nation' is difficult to define precisely. It is not sufficient to think in terms of a common culture, particularly if the term 'culture' is itself understood to involve complex layers of shared meanings and experiences. Societies generally include many sub-cultures defined in terms of region, status ethnicity and other factors, such as occupation and gender. A territorial referent is a necessary component of the idea of 'nation' but this does not necessarily coincide with particular state boundaries. The geographic parameters of a given nation may not always be so clearly defined as those of a state. Indeed, given the viscissitudes of war and the consequences of migration, national boundaries may be blurred and can even overlap with those of another actual, or aspiring, national group. Nevertheless, an historical association with a certain place is a *sine qua non*. A further criterion is that of shared institutions, which may be economic, social and/or political. A sense of 'nationhood' emerges out of a concrete historical experience of participation in common institutions. Some degree of political autonomy (past or present) is involved although it may not go so far as independent statehood. Nationalism implies defending, or seeking to increase, that autonomy. Ethnic nationalism is only one particular form of nationalism in general.

A territorial base is not a pre-condition for the existence of ethnic groups. Members of an ethnic group may retain their connections with each other, in a variety of networks and associations, despite the

Ethnic Nationalism: Social Science Paradigms

absence of a shared territory. This is particularly the case for immigrant minorities and some religious groups. However, particular ethnic groups may be defined in terms of a former territorial connection. Some immigrant minorities and their children may engage in a form of 'expatrial' nationalism when they aspire to return to their former country, or politically to 'liberate' it from its present rulers.

The state must be clearly distinguished from the nation. The essence of a state is that it is a system of government exercising supreme authority, having a monopoly over the legitimate use of military and other coercive agencies within a clearly defined territory, and whose sovereignty is recognised by other states. At the same time, it is true that in a global system of economic and political power, some states have voluntarily shared sovereignty in limited areas (such as defence or international trade), with other states, or become dependent on one of the superpowers. States may consist of one or more nations. These nations may also in turn be polyethnic.

The sociological distinctions between 'ethnic group', 'nation' and 'state' are hard to maintain, precisely because they frequently overlap in historical reality. Nevertheless, they are analytically distinct. Concrete examples will help to clarify the differences. The United Kingdom of Great Britain and Northern Ireland is at present a state, with all the sovereign powers that are needed to distinguish it from other independent states in the world. Before 1921, what is now Eire (the Republic of Ireland) was a part of Great Britain – now known as the United Kingdom. A long political battle was fought before Ireland was partitioned and the South achieved its independence. The United Kingdom remains a multinational state, in which England, Wales, Scotland and Northern Ireland have varying degrees of political autonomy and a distinct sense of separate 'nationhood' (Rose, 1971).

However, the English are not a single ethnic group. Nor are the Welsh, the Scots or the Irish. Within each of these nations there are separate ethnic divisions based on language, religion, race and culture. The English 'nation' comprises people of different racial origins; it includes Protestants, Catholics and Jews, as well as people with ancestral links to other countries, although most have been resident in England for several generations. The degree of strength of their various ethnic attachments may vary but the English are by no means homogeneous from an ethnic point of view. The Scots are similarly divided between the Gaelic and the Scots/English speakers,

146

Ethnic Nationalism

as well as between Highlanders and Lowlanders and by the various clans which maintain their ancient pride and rivalry. The Welsh are another example of a nation divided by language, religion and by regional differences. Welsh speakers are a minority but a growing one. They seek to bring the English-speaking Welsh into their nationalist movement (Plaid Cymru) because without that support they will never succeed in establishing a claim to greater political autonomy.

Many other examples could be given of multinational states and polyethnic nations. Canada is a single state, once described as having 'two nations warring in its bosom'. The two nations are the French- and the English-speaking sections of the population. But within the Francophone population it is important also to distinguish the *Acadiens* from the *Quebecois*, and the latter from Franco-Ontarians or Franco-Manitobans, all of whom are distinctive ethnic groups. Within English Canada there are distinctions between Protestants, Catholics and Jews that are clear enough to warrant definition as 'ethnic'. There are also differences between those (such as the Ukranians), who retain distinctive ethnic identities, even after linguistic assimilation has taken place, and those who do not. Furthermore, Native Peoples (Aboriginal Canadians), many of whom have been linguistically assimilated into the English or French-speaking populations, retain a strong sense of their separate ethnic identities and are rapidly moving toward the formation of a nationalist movement. This brings Canadian Indian peoples of many different ethnic origins together. They may form one or more nations (such as the Dene of the Mackenzie River valley), but such a nation will remain polyethnic, whether or not it succeeds in achieving statehood, or some other form of political autonomy.

Nationalism does not always involve aspirations for complete independence or statehood. Even when this is part of the ideology, or a utopian plan, pragmatic considerations may involve accepting lesser degrees of autonomy. Nevertheless, given the territorial element in the definition of 'nation', some devolution of authority, fiscal power and administrative responsibility to a population resident in a certain locality is necessarily involved. The exercise of 'ethnic power', is not necessarily nationalistic, although it may use nationalist rhetoric. An ethnic group, when it is politically mobilised, can have differrent goals. These may include the right to the franchise, the use of the ethnic vote to swing results in marginal constituencies, the achievement of special status for particular languages or religions (particularly in education), the removal of injustices and the enforcement of

Ethnic Nationalism: Social Science Paradigms

human rights codes, affirmative action programmes, compensation for past deprivation, the restitution of property, or the recognition of claims for special treatment such as exemption from military service. 'Nationalist' movements may also establish such claims but go further in wishing to achieve self-government within a given geographic area.

The politicisation of ethnicity is not the same as ethnic nationalism, although one may lead to the other where a historical claim to a particular territory can be established. By the same token, not all nationalist movements aspire to complete independence or statehood. The concept of 'sovereignty association' has been used by Quebec nationalists in relation to the rest of Canada, but it is also applicable elsewhere. It implies a sharing of responsibility for certain governmental functions with one or more other states. Defence treaties, customs unions, common market agreements, the recognition of supra-state parliaments and judicial bodies, all serve to erode the traditional powers of states, albeit voluntarily. In other circumstances, military conquest or economic dependency may give rise to effective limits to sovereignty. Although the exercise of 'supreme coercive power' may still be the definitional criterion of statehood, in practice many states have now become dependent on others, particularly the superpowers, for their survival. They have become client-states within a global system of political economy, dominated by multinational companies and nuclear weaponed states (Grant and Welhofer, 1978). This weakening of central state power is a significant factor in the emergence of ethnic nationalism.

THEORETICAL PARADIGMS

Before proceeding to examine some of the theories of ethnic nationalism it is necessary to clarify the meaning of 'paradigm'. The term is used, in the present context, to mean an abstract model which endeavours to represent a complex social system, the changes which take place within such a system, and the processes of adaptation to the external environment, which generally includes other systems in interaction. Just as a theory is more complex than a hypothesis, so a paradigm is more complex than a theory. A societal model, or paradigm, generally involves the juxtaposition of several theories and various assumptions. It necessarily oversimplifies reality by representing systems as 'ideal types'. As such, the models can be used as measuring devices, or yardsticks against which reality can be com-

148   *Ethnic Nationalism*

pared. They should not be mistaken for reality itself, nor should they be regarded as deterministic, or forecasts of an inevitable outcome. Like a computer simulation, a paradigm can assist in representing complex social processes but it is not a substitute for them. It cannot be proved in any scientific sense and it leaves room for human intervention and alternative outcomes. It may help us to understand how reality works but only to the degree that its assumptions are valid, its deductions correct and its conclusions sound. A paradigm is only as strong as its weakest link. Some of the paradigms examined below have very weak links indeed.

Biosocial Theories

Nineteenth-century social scientists were largely concerned with macrosocial questions of 'statics' and 'dynamics'. They asked how society was possible, how order was created out of potentially conflicting individual and collective interests, and what determined long term processes of social change. The idea of 'social evolution' was widely accepted. Darwin acknowledged his indebtedness to Malthus for the idea of 'survival of the fittest' which was later adopted by Spencer (1874/1967). Social Darwinism became both a scientific doctrine and an ideology. It gave spurious legitimacy to the claims of ruling elites, imperialist countries and dominant racial and ethnic groups who asserted their supposedly 'innate' superiority as justification for the permanent subordination of other peoples. Such racist notions played a large part in the nationalist ideologies of fascist movements and the genocidal policies of Nazi Germany.

Most twentieth-century social scientists, particularly after the Second World War, rejected Social Darwinist views. They emphasised that *homo sapiens* is a single species, that superficial somatic differences are not correlated with intelligence, or any other criterion of 'fitness', and that cultural differences are learned i.e. a product of social environment rather than heredity. However, in recent years there has been a renewed interest in biosocial theories of behaviour. the proponents deny that they are racist, or that the recognition of a biological basis for human behaviour is necessarily deterministic. Genetic and environmental factors interact and humans adapt to survive. However, biology sets limits to possible choices, and establishes certain universal propensities (Wilson, 1975).

Van den Berghe (1975; 1981) applied biosocial theories in examining the place of man in society and the nature of ethnic phenomena.

Ethnic Nationalism: Social Science Paradigms 149

He argued that there are certain universal tendencies in human behaviour, such as preference for kin, aggression, domination, and territoriality, that cannot be explained by learning alone and which must be understood as part of 'human nature'. The latter he linked to culture and social structure through a behaviouralist psychology based on hedonistic assumptions (1975:19).

Van den Berghe treated ethnic groups as a type of extended kinship system within which nepotistic behaviour, favouring those who are seen to be part of the group, is functional because it favours the survival of that particular gene-pool or ethnic group. He defined a nation as a 'politically conscious ethny' and a state as 'a collectivity headed by a group of people who exercise power over others'. He regarded 'nationalism' as an ideology expressed by an ethny that claims the right to statehood by virtue of being an ethny (1981:61). He argued that wars of 'national liberation' were likely to succeed only in the technologically backward areas of multinational empires where the costs of suppression would be too great. Elsewhere, when the 'vital interests of industrial states are at stake' such movements were easily crushed (1975; 146).

Other writers, such as Masters (1983), suggested that there is a biological basis for social and political institutions such as the state, to the extent that the latter facilitates natural selection, promotes 'inclusive fitness' and encourages group cooperation in the face of competition. However, there are very real difficulties with biosocial theories of this kind. They are illustrated in van den Berghe's own work when he addresses particular questions such as cultural and structural pluralism in countries such as Canada or Switzerland (van den Berghe, 1981:185–213). It is not sufficient to recognise the universality of dominance and territoriality. The social scientist must be able to explain the *variations* found in different parts of the world and at different periods of time. Van den Berge himself does this, as do most sociologists, by referring to specific historic circumstances and particular cultural patterns. In other words, biosocial theories may make explicit certain intrinsic *assumptions* about 'human nature' (which not all social scientists would accept), but they contribute very little to our understanding of those questions which are of central concern to sociology, antropology and political science viz., the tremendous diversity of social behaviour, the variability of culture, alternative political institutions, and the complexity of human adaptation.

Human beings create their own environments; they do not merely react passively to ecological conditions over which they have no

150 *Ethnic Nationalism*

control. They are constantly changing the physical, biological and social conditions in which they live. Advances in medicine suggest that they will soon be modifying their own genetic inheritance. So far, technology has created conditions which generally favour reproduction and survival, but there are ominous signs that our environment will no longer be viable if we continue on present paths. A nuclear holocaust, or other damage to the delicate ecological balance between the earth and its atmosphere, may destroy the human race. Biosocial theories that tell us man is aggressive because this promotes survival do not help to explain such self-destructive behaviour.

As with the theories of Social Darwinism, modern biosocial theories are capable of ideological distortion and misrepresentation. They are easily mistaken for a political agenda. They tend toward a conservative view and a defense of the status quo. Van den Berghe himself refers to the 'perils of social engineering' and the 'failure of revolution and reform' (1975:250–278). Sociology, he insists, cannot provide solutions although it may expose non-solutions. Other writers have used biosocial theories to cast doubt on the probable success of programmes dealing with inequality, poverty and deprivation, by educational, social or economic measures. The ideological bias in such interpretations is exposed by Rose, Kamin and Lewontin (1984).

Given the many different forms of ethnic nationalism, and the varying degrees of strength and support such movements have achieved, biosocial theories can only suggest why they appear to have such widespread appeal, in developing and developed countries alike. They provide no explanation for the resurgence of ethnic nationalism in the second half of the twentieth century, or for the variety of factors which have been conducive to their success and failure in different countries. More conventional social and political theories address themselves to these critical questions.

Modernisation Theories

The process of 'modernisation' involves a number of related social changes that often occur concurrently. They include new agricultural technologies, urbanisation, industrialisation, the spread of communications, mass education and literacy, political mobilisation and 'nation building'. The traditional view of social development was that these processes would sever ties with local communities and that 'tribal' affiliations would give way to new attachments at a national

Ethnic Nationalism: Social Science Paradigms 151

level. Urbanisation would promote assimilation and modern technology would lead to a convergence of economic and social systems toward a global pattern, consisting of a comparatively small number of relatively homogeneous 'nation-states'.

Deutsch (1953; 1966) examined the relation between nationalism and social communication. More efficient methods of transportation together with information transmission via telegraph, telephone and the mass media mobilised the population, promoted assimilation and the adoption of a *lingua franca*, facilitated geographic and social mobility and generated the need to identify with the symbols of a wider social system. New forms of consciousness emerged that were 'national' in character. The transition to active nationalism involved social controls and the emergence of a collective will often symbolised abstractly in a charismatic leader. Deutsch considered that social communication was linked to instrumental goals and that 'cultural autonomy' could not be detached from economic and political independence (1966:106).

Although Deutsch recognised that the processes of social mobilisation and assimilation might not proceed at the same speed, and therefore could give rise to conflict, he considered that, in the long run, the spread of communications would have a unifying effect. Others have questioned this view. Connor (1972) agreed on the importance of communication and social mobilisation, but regarded ethnic conflict as a direct consequence of modernisation. The idea of 'self-determination' has spread so widely that the legitimacy of any form of alien rule is questioned. Ethnic strife arises from a divergence of basic identity but its absence does not necessarily signify a single nation (ibid.: 341–2). Other writers have reviewed the link between communications, modernisation and nationalism, pointing out that, when parallel groups exist, the mass media can strengthen ethnic identity at the expense of national awareness. An oppressed group may find itself excluded from regular channels of communication. Access to information is also access to power, and open communication channels facilitate the more egalitarian sharing of resources (Said and Simmons, 1976: 49–61).

The modernisation thesis has been further developed by Gellner (1983). In his view, nationalism is a theory of political legitimacy which holds that the political and the national unit should be congruent. He tied nationalism to the process of industrialisation with its consequent division of labour, and commitment to the spirit of rationality. In turn this gives rise to the need for mass education and

152   *Ethnic Nationalism*

training of a generic type. For the modern state 'the monopoly of legitimate education is now more important, more central than is the monopoly of legitimate violence' (ibid.:34). Nationalism has its roots not in human nature but in the pervasive social order of industrial societies. The functional prerequisites of the latter include universal literacy, numeracy and technical sophistication in an age of universal high culture. The transition to industrialism is bound to be violent and conflict-ridden, with competing nationalistic movements. Not all will prevail and Gellner considered that cultural pluralism ceases to be viable under modern conditions. There is a convergence of life-styles and a diminution of social distance. He developed a typology of nationalism-engendering and nationalism-thwarting situations. 'Ethnicity enters the political sphere as "nationalism" at times when cultural homogeneity or continuity (not classlessness) is required by the economic base of social life' (ibid.:94).

The modernisation theory of nationalism links culture to nation and nation to state. It assumes that the economic and technological processes of industrialisation facilitate communication and promote social mobilisation. While the transition from earlier forms of social organisation to modernity may generate conflict based upon ethnic attachments, the eventual outcome is generally regarded as a few centralized states, each based upon a single culture and a unitary system of education and communication. Although the line of reasoning is different, a somewhat similar conclusion is reached when nationalism is analysed from the perspective of a radical 'materialist' view of history and class struggles.

Marxist-Leninist Theories

The Marxian model of social change is a dialectical one which assumes 'cultural' phenomena are determined by the material, i.e. economic substructure which, in turn, responds to the struggle of opposing classes in a series of developmental stages. Feudal societies give way to capitalism of which imperialism is the most advanced stage. The collapse of an imperialist world system must precede the establishment of an international proletariat and a global socialist system. Marxists have long debated the 'national question', i.e. the right to self-determination among linguistic and religious minorities, in terms of 'progressive' and 'reactionary' forces. Lenin believed nationalism could not be reconciled with Marxism, which advanced internationalism. He opposed 'cultural-national autonomy', but sup-

Ethnic Nationalism: Social Science Paradigms

ported territorial national liberation movements if they aimed to overthrow bourgeois capitalist regimes (Lenin, 1913/1967). Once the Soviet Union had come into being, Lenin continued to distinguish between the nationalism of an oppressor nation and that of an oppressed one, but he adopted a pragmatic attitude toward non-Russians, arguing that concessions might have to be made in order to maintain the trust of linguistic and religious minorities in the interest of proletarian solidarity. He was against adopting 'a formal attitude to the national question' (Lenin, 1922/1967:168).

In fact, the Soviet Union is a polyethnic and multinational state which has not always succeeded in subordinating national distinctions in the interest of class unity. Over one hundred nationalities are officially recognised, 22 of them with populations of over one million. In recent years there has been evidence of growing ethnic nationalism in the Soviet Union and pressure on the leadership to resist further concessions to non-Russians. Lapidus (1984) examined the question of ethnonationalism and political solidarity in the Soviety Union and distinguished between 'national sentiment' and political doctrines or movements that warranted description as 'nationalism' (1984:561). She considered that the Soviet system was capable of satisfying national sentiment and managing nationalist tendencies, without creating a serious threat to stability, despite evidence of unrest in some areas, and the desire for emigration among some minorities.

Outside the Soviet Union, Marxist theorists have continued to distinguish between 'progressive' and 'reactionary' forms of nationalism. A symposium published in the *Australian and New Zealand Journal of Sociology*, October, 1978 examined 'Creative Modes of Nationalism' in New Zealand, Canada and Australia. Nationalist movements in these countries were seen as progressive when they opposed the economic imperialism of the United States, or (in the case of French Canadians) bourgeois capitalist domination of Quebec, by English-Canada.

The major difficulty with the Marxian analysis of nationalist questions is its relegation of ethnicity (and related categories of race, religion and language) to an epiphenomenal status in the causal model. Economic determination and the primacy of the class struggle are dogmatically asserted as a fundamental premise. The evidence of history, and of contemporary developments in advanced industrial societies, suggests that, on the contrary, ethnic factors may have a greater influence than class on the development of political and social systems. They are more salient at the level of consciousness than class

154   *Ethnic Nationalism*

membership and cannot be dismissed as merely manifestations of a 'false consciousness', once the dogma of a 'materialist' view of history is rejected.

Internal Colonialism

More recent attempts to understand the phenomenon of ethnic nationalism have borrowed from Marxist/Leninist analysis the concept of imperialism and applied it to the uneven economic development of intrastate regions. Distinguishing between the economically dominant 'metropolis' and its dependent 'hinterland', the tendency to exploit the material and human resources of the latter for the benefit of a more powerful elite at the centre, gives rise to 'internal colonialism'. Peripheral and semi-peripheral areas become progressively more dependent on the core, which accumulates capital (in the form of 'surplus value') by using the resources of the colonised territory and maintaining its population as a 'reserve army of labour'.

The idea of 'internal colonialism' has also been applied to certain situations where ethnic nationalism has arisen, but without the Marxian assumptions. The relation between centre and periphery may be one of relative rather than absolute deprivation. Weberian concepts of *status* rather than class may be applicable and a 'cultural division of labour' may occur between the centre and hinterland population, when the latter is distinguishable by language, or other ethnic characteristics. Hechter (1975) used such a model in his analysis of ethnic nationalism in the 'Celtic fringes' of Britain, particularly the case of Wales. Although illuminating in many instances, the idea of 'internal colonialism' fails to come to terms with the variety of different economic conditions under which nationalist movements arise. They appear to be as evident among the relatively advantaged populations and regions, as among the relatively disadvantaged. It is not always clear how the boundaries between 'core', 'periphery' and 'semi-periphery' are to be defined, how they are related to ethnic factors and what are the dynamics of change over time. (For a fuller discussion see the special issue of *Ethnic and Racial Studies*, vol. 2. No. 3., July 1979)

The sociological analysis of 'metropolis-hinterland' differences should not be confused with the rhetorical and counter-ideological use of the idea of 'internal colonialism' by subordinated ethnic minorities. The identification of racial and ethnic minorities with

Ethnic Nationalism: Social Science Paradigms 155

Third World independence movements, has led some of the victims of racial discrimination, in western cities, to describe their own situation as one of 'internal colonialism'. This is particularly true of Blacks in the United States but is evident among immigrant minorities in other countries such as Britain, where race prejudice has perpetuated inequalities (Rex and Tomlinson, 1979). Although the situation of racial minorities (immigrant or indigenous) in metropolitan cities may be the legacy of imperialism, the situation is not comparable with that which arises from regional economic disparities. The rhetoric of 'colonialism' may be effective in mobilising political protest, but it obscures sociological understanding of essentially disparate cases.

Ethnic Pluralism

The situation of immigrant minorities and urbanised ethnic groups in advanced industrial societies is analytically distinct from that of nationalist movements *per se*. Ethnic minorities in cities may be politicised, and mobilised to protest against segregation, discrimination, inequality of opportunity and exploitation, but this does not represent 'ethnic nationalism'. It has been noted that a territorial referent is a necessary ingredient for a nationalist movement, even when the ultimate goal stops short of an independent state.

The experience of urbanisation and industrialisation, in the context of a cosmopolitan metropolitan area, is generally to reduce but not altogether to eliminate ethnic differences. Varying degrees of assimilation to the dominant language are necessary, depending upon the instrumental needs of individuals and their occupational adaptation. For second and subsequent generations the educational system generally imposes a knowledge of the majority language, even when some concessions are made to the maintenance of 'heritage' languages. The experience of the United States, Canada and other countries is that a dynamic form of pluralism emerges in which ethnic attachments remain salient. Both vertical and horizontal divisions occur, giving rise to residential concentrations, ethnic stratification, segmented labour markets, and ethnic minority political leaders who sometimes succeed in negotiating affirmative action programmes, or other forms of special treatment, for their constituents.

Racial diversity and multiculturalism are demographic realities in many societies, particularly where there has been substantial immigration in the last fifty years. Deliberate attempts to integrate these

156 *Ethnic Nationalism*

minorities into the wider society and to command their political loyalty (especially in time of war), often led to vigorous measures designed to ensure conformity to the norms, values and behaviour approved by the dominant elites. In recent years, such coercive asimilation has given way to a more positive view of pluralism and even, in some cases, to its institutionalisation. Governments have allocated resources to the teaching of minority languages, the encouragement and preservation of other aspects of an ethnic 'cultural heritage', and the promotion of human rights legislation, including affirmative action and positive discrimination designed to compensate for past deprivations.

The instiutionalisation of cultural pluralism in advanced industrial societies has been criticised by those who see such measures as impeding individual achievement based on 'universalistic' performance criteria. It also appears to undermine the liberal concept of individual autonomy in terms of human rights, substituting a concept of 'group rights' and 'collective freedoms', which may override the claims of individuals seeking self-determination and freedom of choice (Glazer and Moynihan, 1975; Glazer, 1983). These issues also arise when considering political devolution or independence for ethnic groups having a territorial base and pursuing nationalist claims. They are particularly acute when the nationalist movement in question is itself polyethnic, and must deal with the rights of other minorities within its borders, after partial or full autonomy has been achieved, through the efforts of a particular ethnic elite. The latter may be as intolerant of diversity or individual non-conformity as the previous ruling class.

Micro-social Theories

It was noted that van den Berghe's biosocial model of ethnic phenomena in general, and of nationalism in particular, rested upon assumptions concerning genetically determined universal propensities of 'human nature', linked to the macroscopic level of socio-cultural and socio-political systems via a hedonistic type of behaviouralist psychology. Other theories of ethnicity and nationalism involve alternative assumptions concerning the nature of human decision-making and action, at the individual level. Explanations of ethnic nationalism vary according to the assumptions made concerning *Homo Sociologicus*.

Ethnic Nationalism: Social Science Paradigms 157

Firstly, there are theories which assume that behaviour is consicous, reasonable, calculated, goal-oriented and designed to relate means to ends, which are themselves capable of rational choice on the basis of subjective value and marginal utility (Blau, 1964; Heath, 1976; Banton, 1980). Secondly, other theories emphasise the importtance of unconscious motivation, unreasonable or compulsive behaviour, actions that are not necessarily goal-directed, and the influence of deep-seated emotions on human behaviour, individual and collective. Such theories go beyond the recognition that 'rational choice' may be impeded by lack of information or other constraints in social interaction. They assert the primacy of affective over cognitive determinants and the power of unreason over reason, particularly when individuals form part of a larger collectivity, subordinating their will to the direction of fanatical and powerful leaders (Fromm, 1941; 1977; Adorno, 1950).

Using a theory of 'rational choice', Banton (1980) argued that groups must be treated as coalitions of individuals that are in constant change because people calculate the costs and benefits of particular alignments. Europeans in the nineteenth century found it advantageous to adopt 'nationality' as an organising principle. In the twentieth century the same idea was adopted by other people in other countries in order to defend or advance their interests. 'National consciousness was not an inherent feeling, but something taught and cultivated to serve specific ends. The growth of ethnic consciousness has followed similar lines, except that it has brought together people who form only part of a nation State, or people who belong to more than one nation State' (ibid.:477). He emphasised that nations and ethnic groups are based on a voluntary identification of their members with one another. He concluded that, although there are limitations in the applicability of transactional theories, based on the assumptions that individuals will maximise net advantages, nevertheless, 'rational choice' helps to explain some aspects of race and ethnic relations.

It is difficult to reconcile such abstract representations with a real world, which daily sees acts of violence, which may be calculated, but can hardly be called rational. Such non-rational behaviour ranges from suicide missions to political assassination; from random bombing of innocent civilians to carefully planned insurgency and military retaliation; from police brutality and army atrocities to civil disobedience campaigns that degenerate into mass riots, pillaging, murder and retaliatory revenge. Ethnic group relations may sometimes be

158 *Ethnic Nationalism*

conducted by the rules of the market place but, all too often, they are governed by passions and hatreds that have persisted for generations. The phenomonen of ethnic nationalism cannot be understood without some explanation for such deeply felt animosities.

It is not necessary to accept all the assumptions or theories of Freud to recognise that unconscious needs and motivations play an important part in human behaviour. Various writers have put forward explanations for group formation, human aggression and intergroup conflict that are based upon an understanding of such unconscious factors. Adorno (1950) examined the factors associated with race prejudice and anti-semitism and emphasised the importance of early socialisation and authoritarian up-bringing. Fromm (1941) demonstrated the links between feelings of humiliation and defeat, economic and personal insecurity and the 'fear of freedom', which led many Germans to accept the dictates of Nazism and to adopt an aggressive nationalism, leading to the Second World War and the Jewish holocaust. In a later work he analysed the phenomenon of human aggression and destructiveness (Fromm, 1977). He distinguished 'benign aggression', which is purely defensive in nature and an adaptive response to direct threat, from 'malignant aggression' which is cruel, destructive, biologically non-adaptive and derived from particular social conditions. Fromm regarded as *rational* those thoughts feelings and actions that promoted the functioning and growth of the whole system and *irrational* those which tended to weaken or destroy it (1977:352). By 'system' in this context he meant the global society and the whole human species, rather than any particular nation or state.

Fanon (1965), himself a psychiatrist, became the ideological spokesman for the Algerians in their struggle for freedom. He recognised the passionate hatred which the oppressed have toward their oppressors, even when expediency compels them to suffer in silence. Eventually, such passivity may be converted into a disorderly rampage against neighbouring ethnic groups, unless channelled by charismatic leadership into systematic opposition to a coercive regime. Aggression is not the only response to frustration, nor is it just a product of absolute deprivation. Unrealised expectations and relative deprivation may also precipatate outbursts of violence, as will actions that violate 'holy' places, symbolic objects, or venerated leaders.

In developing a paradigm of ethnic nationalism it is necessary to have an understanding of the human capacity for rationally calculating means. At the same time, it must also be recognised that rational

Ethnic Nationalism: Social Science Paradigms 159

transactions such as exchange, bargaining, negotiating, trading, concilitation and compromise, may be abandoned when highly valued goals are threatened or when the people (or things) to which an individual or group has a strong affective attachment, are perceived to be in danger. Passion overrides reason, and fear turns to hate, in situations of ethnic and national conflict, when life, property, religious beliefs, sacred objects or political institutions are believed to be in jeopardy due to the actions of an alleged 'enemy'.

SYSTEMS THEORIES AND MULTIVARIATE MODELS

The theories of ethnicity and nationalism considered so far have been relatively simple, suggesting monocausal relationships between particular biological, economic or psychological variables and manifestations of ethnic group solidarity and aspirations for political independence. There is growing dissatisfaction with such sweeping generalisations and an increasing recognition of the complexity of both the dependent variable (in this case ethnic nationalism) and of the factors correlated with it. Multivariate causal models are replacing the search for universal explanations, particular processes are seen as contingent and outcomes formulated as statements of probability. Whether couched in the formal language of 'systems theory', or in less deliberate terms, such paradigms provide a more realistic basis for understanding complex social phenomena. They also suggest the need for caution in the formulation of social policies designed to modify particular systems, given the interdependence of the many parts.

In a number of important contributions, from a sociological perspective, Anthony D. Smith, (1971; 1979; 1981; 1983) recognises that nationalism has existed in one form or another since pre-industrial times. However, he places the recent revival of ethnicity, as a basis of cultural and political movements, in the context of modernisation. At the same time, he rejects the view that ethnic nationalism is bound to decline as rational universalistic achievement norms take precedence over traditional, particularistic and ascriptive ones as a basis for social order.

Smith (1971) developed a typology of nationalist movements making a distinction between 'territorial' and 'ethnic' varieties, although he recognised the possibility of 'mixed' examples. He

160 *Ethnic Nationalism*

further distinguished between stages of economic development of the countries involved, whether the movement was successful or not, and the pre- and post-independence phases. In a later study (Smith, 1981), he elaborated the typology by differentiating ethnic strategies. In polyethnic states ethnic communities could pursue *isolation, accommodation, communalism, autonomism, separatism or irredentism* although the trend was away from the first two options towards more activist positions. 'Nationalism binds together elites and masses in a single ethnic nation with a single legislative will . . . [and] extends the scope of the ethnic community from purely cultural and social to economic and political spheres' (Smith, 1981:19).

The role of elites in the emergence of nationalist movements is critical in Smith's analysis. He distinguished the *intellectuals* who formulate ideals and definitions and the professional *intelligentsia* who actively pursue the nationalist goals, which they perceive as in their own personal as well as collective interest. A critical concept for Smith is that of 'dual legitimation'. Legitimation involves sources of authority which may originate in traditional communities and 'cosmic images', or in the 'scientific state' with its technocratic structure and ideology of 'progress'. There is an inherent opposition between state and community in the modern world. When 'reformist' and 'assimilationist' solutions fail to reconcile this tension, nationalism provides a solution because it is ultimately both traditionalist and modernist (Smith, 1971:256).

Smith postulated a 'quest for national congruence between an ethnic culture and a scientific state' (1981:196) but doubted whether there will ever be a complete transformation in which the state would *serve* the national community rather than direct it. Consequently, he anticipated frequent ethnic revivals in a world of scientific states. Specifically, in Third World countries he believed that attempts by leaders to create territorial nations with a uniform political culture, exhibiting some degree of fit with existing state boundaries, will provide the intelligentsia of African and Asian countries with an extremely difficult, if not impossible, task (Smith, 1983).

One factor in the formation of ethnic consciousness, which Smith emphasised, was that of *war*. Although not necessarily originating ethnic cleavages, wars in pre-industrial and industrial societies have often contributed to the heightening of ethnic consciousness and to the formation of the very myths that serve later to unite the ethnic category. Warfare may be treated as an independent variable shaping ethnicity. Prolonged or total wars strengthen ethnic self-

Ethnic Nationalism: Social Science Paradigms 161

consciousness but weaken the cohesion of multinational states (Smith, 1981:390). Through mobilisation for war, the use of propaganda and through response to external threats, war promotes greater ethnic cohesion. Other indirect consequences include the centralisation of bureaucratic power and the advancement of a rational-secular outlook, which provides an opportunity for the technocratic intelligentsia to promote revolutionary ideologies. Finally, colonialism prepared the way for ethnic nationalism in the Third World. 'European inter-state antagonism fed the Asian and African ethnic renaissance and its wars through the intermediary of the colonial state, itself a deliberate creation of distant treaties and the seedbed for many new territorial loyalties and ethnic antagonisms among the colonised' (Smith, 1981:393).

As a sociologist, Smith is primarily concerned with questions of social cohesion. His work can be compared with that of Cynthia Enloe whose perspective is that of a political scientist. Consequently, political order and development are the main dependent variables which she examines. Like Smith, she also placed emphasis upon the role of the military in defining ethnic boundaries and sharpening ethnic consciousness. Her approach is in terms of a 'systems analysis' but she warned against looking at political systems entirely from the point of view of a dominant group or political elite (Enloe, 1973:7).

She noted that ethnicity has a communal and a personal dimension, that ethnic groups are generally biologically self-perpetuating, that they share clusters of beliefs and values and are internally differentiated. However, she emphasised the changing nature of ethnicity and, therefore, clearly placed herself among those who recognise the situational determinants of ethnic boundaries. In examining processes of change within societies she argued that development and modernisation were not synonymous and that one can occur without the other (ibid.:9). Political development refers to the interaction of public power and public policy. It is a more general phenomenon than modernisation. The latter implies secularisation, mobilisation, mass participation and bureaucratisation whereas development may occur on only one of these dimensions.

Enloe recognised that many states were multiethnic, although it is only in her later work that she clearly distinguished between nation and state. She noted that in the nineteenth century nationalism and ethnic mobilisation were almost coterminous and often class based, but 'the ideologies that consider ethnicity to be a central factor in

162 *Ethnic Nationalism*

historical development tend to be ambivalent, if not outright hostile, to modern society. Their major objection to modernity is its impersonalization and atomization of society' (Enloe, 1973:67). The unification of a multi-ethnic society may require compromise, such as the granting of territorial identity in return for loyalty, or some form of institutional recognition. Federalism is one such solution but it has severe limitations in practise.

Political development for an ethnic group is not necessarily the same as for a nation or state because the former is more concerned with language, religion and social mores and resisting assimilation into the wider society. This still requires effective political action and the need to raise communal consciousness (ibid.:160). Thus consciousness must then be translated into communal power. At one time military skill was all important in this regard but now access to the mass media may also be crucial. Enloe distinguished between weak groups who are 'beyond the pale', those with enough power with which to negotiate concessions and a third category that, at least potentially, has the capacity to govern. But ethnic groups are not the sole influence on their own development because this takes place in a context which involves others. 'In multi-ethnic states where several communities are undergoing political mobilization, national development may be conceived as the sum of communal development plus the central government's capacity to cope with those separate developments and their accumulated consequences' (ibid.:215).

Enloe examined *revolution* as a particular form of socio-political change which is directed toward modernisation and whose medium is violence. Revolutionaries aim to establish a new form of legitimate power at a time when the existing system is losing its legitimation in the eyes of many. Although strong leaders may be needed they cannot succeed without mass support. Enloe argued that ethnic groups can be an obstacle to revolution because communal ties may be a threat to a class based radical movement. Nevertheless, ethnic grievances may serve as catalysts. Ethnic groups are more likely to engage in riot and rebellion, but even civil wars do not necessarily have a revolutionary outcome. Ethnic grievances alone are not a sufficient cause for revolution as other long term trends and short term precipitating factors are needed. Revolution is most likely to occur where ethnic divisions coincide with class lines. Even when revolutionary conditions are sufficient, internal war may only occur when organisation and ideology combine effectively to achieve five tasks: 'recruit revolutionary soldiers and cadres, channel the energies of groups and

Ethnic Nationalism: Social Science Paradigms   163

the newly politicised, justify leadership and coordinate operations, pacify the groups that reject active opposition to the government, use violence in a way that full exploits the incumbant government's weaknesses' (ibid.:233). In later publications, Enloe (1980a;1980b) examined the relation between the police, military and ethnicity in relation to state power and security. She suggested that the use of the military by the state against an internal threat frequently meant pitting one ethnic group against another. Even in the most industrially advanced states ethnic categories still play a part in military formations, and the use of the police in situations of domestic conflict. At the same time, because the military is closely tied to the question of legitimacy, governing elites cannot afford to allow the military to appear simply as the defenders of sectional group interests (ibid.:68). She further suggested that the police and the military may exacerbate conflict in multiethnic societies, particularly where the ethnic composition of the coercive agencies is skewed, thereby promoting the distrust and eventual alienation of weaker groups (ibid.:153).

In her study of the role of 'ethnic soldiers' she considered the problem of state security in a divided society (Enloe 1980b), and showed how states use ethnicity to maintain political order and the authority of a particular regime, through manipulating ethnic manpower. Even when outwardly deploring discrimination, elites endeavour to optimise their own security by exploiting ethnic divisions. She denied that political interaction simply reflects previous cleavages and demonstrated, from numerous historical examples, that politics are a major influence on an individual's sense of belonging, redefining ethnic group boundaries and the saliency of ethnicity in conflict situations (ibid.: 1–8). In many multiethnic societies 'the military develops such a stake in the maintenance of a particular regime and the promotion of a certain ethnic group's interests as to compromise its supra-communal position. In doing so it may also compromise the authority of the state' (ibid.:232).

The theme of state legitimacy is a key element in any examination of ethnic nationalism in the modern world. Industrialised societies, and those moving into that stage, are characterised by a central secular state whose elites legitimate their position through institutional channels such as the law, mass education and the press. Such states promote a nationalistic ideology, endeavour to assimilate ethnic minorities into the dominant group, and pursue patriotic wars against other similar states.

164   *Ethnic Nationalism*

Post-industrial societies differ from earlier ones not only in terms of their technology but also because of the emergence of supranational states (or superpowers), multinational companies and an ideological confrontation between 'communism' and 'capitalism'. The consequence is a decline in the effective power of existing secular states and growing opposition from previously subordinated ethnic groups (Richmond, 1984).

CONCLUSION

The above review indicates that the phenomenon of 'ethnic nationalism' is complex and does not lend itself to simplistic explanations. Contemporary ethnic nationalism is only one type of nationalistic movement. Other types of nationalism existed in pre-industrial societies and in Europe during the nineteenth century. Ethnic *nationalism* must also be distinguished from other forms of ethnic political mobilisation by its territorial referent. Immigrant minorities, and others linked only by associations and networks, may seek recognition and special treatment through lobbying and other political action, but separate national status and political autonomy are not realistic goals in such cases.

Even in the case of genuine nationalist movements, although the declared objective may be complete independence and state sovereignty, in reality many who support nationalist movements are satisfied with a lesser degree of political autonomy, whatever their rhetoric may be. While popular sentiment may favour nationalist aspirations, the economic sacrifices involved, the cost in terms of loss of life and the disruption of normal social relations, together with the fear of an unknown future, may seem an excessive price to pay by the rank-and-file members of the ethnic group concerned. When given the democratic right to chose, through referendum or other means, they may prefer the status quo, while hoping that the threat of secession, and the possibility of violence, will extract some political concessions from the dominant group.

Ethnic elites play an important part in the formation and preservation of nationalist movements. What Smith (1981:108) calls the 'intellectuals' might better be described as 'ideologues' and his 'intelligentsia' must be extended to include those who are prepared to organise and direct terrorist activities and guerrilla warfare. The outcome of such an ideological and violent struggle will depend upon

Ethnic Nationalism: Social Science Paradigms 165

a combination of factors. On both sides of the conflict, the extent of popular support, the degree of ethnic consciousness and the effectiveness of organisation, must be combined with numbers, level of technology and access to resources. Frequently, the outcome will depend upon outside influences and assistance from other powers.

The so-called 'ethnic revival' may be more evident in the eyes of social scientists than in reality. Ethnic divisions have existed from time immemorial. Conflicts have been present (even when apparently latent), and grievances have been nursed for generations. However, ethnic minorities can assert their claims with greater impunity today because of the condition of the world economy and polity.

Existing states are declining in power within a polarised global system dominated by a few superpowers. States are increasingly entering into alliances, signing treaties, adopting international conventions and delegating sovereignty, by degrees, to suprastate agencies. Such agencies encompass military, economic and judicial functions. Ethnic minorities can apeal beyond the jurisdiction of the state for the vindication of human rights violations and for other forms of protection. By terrorist actions they can threaten and blackmail others into publicising and even directly supporting their cause. Nationalist movements may even receive tacit or overt assistance from external sources identified with one or other of the superpowers. In the last resort, the movement may be directly supported by external military intervention. This could, in turn, provoke counter-measures by an opposing superpower. Ethnic nationalism, in its more extreme manifestation as a 'liberation movement', is capable of becoming the catalyst for inter-state conflict and even world war. Rational calculation by dominant groups would indicate the need for concessions before a conflict escalates to that point, but history suggests that reason does not always prevail when ethnic antagonisms are inflamed.

10 Ethnic Nationalism and Post-Industrialism

The rise of ethnic nationalism in the last two decades is associated with the emergence of the supranational state and a post-industrial global economy. This is not purely coincidental. All three phenomena are closely linked with important structural and technological changes in contemporary societies. By ethnic nationalism, in this context, is meant the struggle for recognition, higher economic and social status, and political power by minorities which had previously been exposed to the assimilatory pressures of industrialisation. The ethnic minorities in question may define themselves in terms of race, religion, language or former country. In some cases their aspirations for greater autonomy have a territorial basis in which case the movements may assume a separatist form. However, in many cases the resurgence of ethnic consciousness has been independent of any geographical boundaries. Nevertheless, there has been a significant emphasis upon ethnicity as a force to be reckoned with both economically and politically (Glazer and Moynihan, 1975; Reitz, 1980).

This resurgence of ethnicity in advanced industrial societies has surprised sociologists and political scientists in the conservative, functionalist tradition, as well as those who espoused more radical, conflict theories derived from Marx. The former assumed that the developmental tendencies inherent in the industrialisation process would ultimately assimilate all ethnic minorities into a single homogeneous culture defined by the boundaries of the nation-state. Marxian theorists, while rejecting the view that industrial societies would achieve harmonious integration through the functional division of labour, nevertheless expected that class conflict would eventually override ethnic divisions. Ethnic differences might be exploited by the capitalist class to weaken the solidarity of labour movements but, eventually, a socialist revolution would render ethnic differences anachronistic through the dictatorship of the proletariat (Lenin, 1970; Cox, 1948).

Neither functionalists nor conflict theorists anticipated the technological consequences of post-industrialism, the economic conse-

168 *Ethnic Nationalism*

quences of the emergence of a global division of labour and the power of multinational companies. In turn, these have given rise to the emergence of supranational states that threaten the sovereignty of older nation-states. The latter were the characteristic political organisation associated with an earlier stage of industrialisation. As both economic and political power shift from the national to the multinational and supranational level, a vacuum is created into which the emerging ethnic elites can move. How successful they will be in mobilising support for their ethnic power and nationalist movements will depend upon a variety of situational determinants that must be examined case by case (Dofny and Akowowo, 1980). The last quarter of the twentieth century is clearly an era of transition in which nation-states that achieved their independence and autonomy in the eighteenth and nineteenth centuries are struggling to come to terms with the new global systems of economic and political hegemony. At the same time 'Third' and 'Fourth' World countries are struggling for survival. The success or failure of ethnic minorities in maintaining their separate identities, institutions and organisations, will depend upon the outcome of that power struggle.

POLITICAL AND SOCIAL INTEGRATION

The central problem facing sociologists and political scientists has always been the problem of integration. Ever since the problem was first stated in Plato's *Republic*, two solutions have been expounded. The first represents societies as being held together by the coercieve power of the dominant groups whose interests are, in the last resort, maintained through military force. This force is used to repel external sources of threat as well as for the maintenance of order within the society. The alternative view emphasises the importance of a common value system which binds people together in a social contract or consensus concerning the necessity for order (Parsons, 1952; Cohen, 1968). In practice, of course, both principles operate simultaneously and with varying degrees of emphasis. Even the most coercive regime must endeavour to translate naked force into legitimated authority, if all its energies and resources are not to be dissipated. Once achieved, a position of power can only be maintained if there is effective control over the agencies that disseminate information and influence human consciousness. The central value system must include legitimating principles that justify the existing differential distribution of economic status and political power. At the same time, varying degrees of economic division of labour and social differentiation give rise to mutual dependency which also contributes to the maintenance of social cohesion (Durkheim, 1947; Weber, 1946).

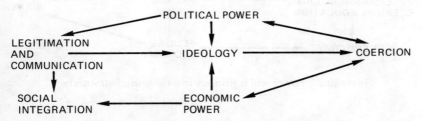

Figure 10.1 Power, legitimacy and social integration

The precise form of this relationship between economic and political power, on the one hand, and types of legitimation and social integration, vary with levels of technological and economic development. The abstract relationship is represented in Figure 10.1. Political power is exercised through control over the coercive forces, including the police and the military. The state is the supreme coercive power and those who control the armed forces ultimately exercise sovereignty. These forces are normally required to protect the territorial boundaries of the state but, in times of crisis, may also be used to quell internal threats to the ruling elites. However, in order to maintain their position, the elites must also exercise control over the agencies that legitimate the power and convert it into authority and the rule of law. The legitimating agencies include the judicial system, the education system and all those organisations concerned with the dissemination of information and the generation of belief systems containing core values. They are responsible for generating dominant ideologies which justify and sustain the existing distribution of political and economic power. These ideologies also rationalise and mobilise support for the use of coercion, for both external and internal purposes. There is a close link between the nature of the economic system, including the division of labour and the distribution of economic status, and the particular forms of social integration characteristic of the society in question. In the last resort the economic elites also rely upon coercive measures to maintain the status quo but, in normal conditions, legitimating agencies such as education and the law are sufficient to maintain social order.

Figure 10.2 illustrates the relationship between economic and political power and the typical mode of social integration character-

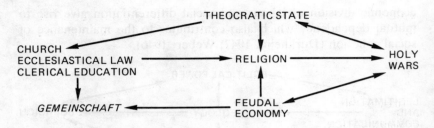

Figure 10.2   Power and legitimacy in a *Gemeinschaft* society

istic of a feudal economy and a theocratic state. Under these conditions there is a close alliance between Church and state in which the agencies of legitimation are dominated by the clergy, who also exercise direct political power. the King or other head of state rules by 'divine right' and is generally autocratic. The Church exercises effective control over both the judicial and the educational system. The dominant ideologies are those of the religion in question which sanctifies the use of military force in holy wars against the infidels. Internal rebellion will be coercively controlled by a ruler who is a 'defender of the faith'. Although such theocratic states have lasted to the present day they have their origins in a feudal type economy in which economic and social roles are essentially ascriptive. The characteristic form of social integration associated with such a system is that of a territorial community or '*Gemeinschaft*' (Tonnies, 1957). Such communities are comparatively small, often involving as extended kinship or tribal system with a restricted division of labour and little social differentiation. The value systems binding such a community together are those of the dominant religion, generally imposed by the priesthood through oral tradition on an often illiterate population. In such a system the law courts are ecclesiastical. Orthodoxy is maintained through inquisitions and harsh punishments. The classical form of the theocratic system was to be found in medieval Europe as it conducted its holy wars against Islam. Today some Islamic countries still exhibit the characteristics of such a theocratic state although their stability under conditions of rapid industrialisation and social change is threatened (Warburg, 1978).

Figure 10.3 illustrates the relationship between political and economic power in the secular states that replaced the theocracies, following the decline of feudalism and the rise of the modern capitalist industrial system. The secular state retained many of the trappings of

Ethnic Nationalism and Post-Industrialism

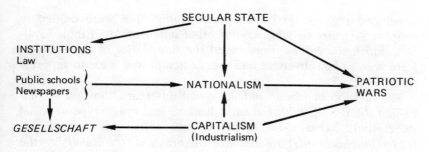

Figure 10.3 Power and legitimacy in a *Gesellschaft* society

its predecessor but effective power shifted from autocratic monarchs to more democratic parliamentary institutions, and a generally independent judiciary. At the same time, control over the education system shifted from the Church to the state. A process of functional differentiation occurred between the various agencies of legitimation. Nevertheless, there was a general consensus on the dominant value system, whose central unifying principle was nationalism. In the industrialised countries the unity of Church and state was replaced by a unit of Nation and state. In fact, those two concepts came to be linked in a way that is critical to our understanding of the emergence of ethnic nationalism in the later post-industrial societies. The nation-state in the industrial era was an assimilating agency. Majority groups and dominant elites were generally intolerant of ethnic variation within its boundaries. The internal cohesion and social integration of the nation-state depended upon an elimination of previous local, tribal or provincial attachments and the inculcation of loyalty to the larger territorial unit dominated by the secular state. Eighteenth- and nineteenth-century nationalism was a unifying force which brought together people of diverse backgrounds at the price of subordinating their ethnic loyalties to the larger entity. The dominant ideology was that of nationalism which idealised the state and deprecated the maintenance of any linguistic, religious or other sentiments that might conflict with loyalty to it (Deutsch, 1953; Smith, 1971; 1976). The holy wars of an earlier era were replaced with the patriotic wars of the nineteenth and twentieth centuries which determined and maintained boundaries of these newly forged nation-states. These countries also engaged in imperialist expansion outside Europe, in competing for access to raw mateials in less

172   *Ethnic Nationalism*

developed regions. The agencies of legitimation were unified in support for patriotic wars against other nation-states. Ethnic loyalties, which sometimes transcended the boundaries of these states, were seen to be subversive and every attempt was made to suppress them.

The division of labour and the social differentiation that accompanied the rise of industrial capitalism created a new type of social integration, based upon economic and social interdependence, formal organisations, bureaucratic structures and *Gesellschaft*. As the economic system became more complex and technologically advanced, the franchise was extended to lesser property holders and eventually the adult population at large. A literate work force and electorate became essential. The public (state) school system became an important instrument of legitimation, an essential assimilating force in polyethnic societies, and the means of inculcating patriotic values. Nationalism in its most extreme forms glorified the state and, in its fascist manifestations, used genocidal policies to eliminate ethnic diversity.

The rise of capitalist industrialism also forged even stronger links between the economy and the military. Even under a feudal system the pursuit of holy wars had important economic and technological consequences. Taxation was never sufficient to pay for the wars in question, thus giving rise to inflationary pressures. However, these also provided an economic stimulus that reduced unemployment and created much profit for the craftsmen who made the armour and weapons used in the crusades and other religious wars. Later, the capitalist economic system became highly dependent upon the growth of an armaments industry whose enormous expenditures not only contributed to many technological advances but were a source of tremendous profit to the companies that manufactured the increasingly sophisticated weaponry. Wars, and the necessary preparation for them, were closely associated with the trade cycles of the nineteenth century. The rearmament that occurred in the mid 1930s provided the necessary anti-deflationary stimulus that brought Europe and America out of the great depression of that period. The capitalist system became increasingly dependent upon the exploitation of nationalism, not only in the advanced industrial countries but also in the Third World. Patriotic support for ever growing defence budgets led to a world-wide industry in new and second hand armaments that has now reached astronomical proportions (Myrdal, 1976; Sampson, 1977).

Post-industrial Developments

The concept of post-industrialism has been used to describe a variety of technological, economic and social changes that are currently taking place in advanced industrial societies, whether they are of the capitalist, free-enterprise type or the socialist, state-controlled form. There is evidence that these advanced industrial states are converging in their increasing interdependence as sub-systems within a global economy (Bell, 1973; Galbraith, 1971; Touraine, 1971). The roots of this global economy go back to the beginning of the industrial revolution and the mercantilism which established trade connections between Europe and the rest of the world (Wallerstein, 1974; Kumar, 1978). The expanding nation-states of Europe established a colonial domination, involving economic exploitation backed by military force, in many parts of Africa, Asia and the New World. What distinguishes the global economy of the post-industrial era is the emergence of multinational companies whose capital investments take advantage of cheap labour supplies outside the already industrialised countries. This has given rise to a designation of the global economy into 'core' regions, 'semi-peripheral' and 'peripheral' areas, with varying degrees of dependency upon the metropolitan centres. In fact, the system is more complex than this trichotomy suggests, as the boundaries between core and periphery are constantly changing. Furthermore, the industrialised countries themselves are undergoing rapid economic change and do not constitute a unitary system. There is a global division of labour even among industrialised countries. However, these post-industrial developments and the emergence of a global economy have threatened the viability of the traditional nation-state. North America and the countries of Western Europe are clearly in transition, but the movement toward supranational states is threatening national sovereignty (Cameron, 1981).

Figure 10.4 illustrates the relationship between the economic and power structures of the emerging supranational states and corresponding forms of social integration. The ultimate coercive power rests with military alliances that transcend the boundaries of nation-states. The world is now divided by the confrontation of superpowers and by a precarious balance of nuclear terror. Each side has the capacity to totally annihilate the other and to destroy much of the rest of the world. Through the genetic damage which the use of nuclear weapons would entail, the destructive capacity extends into future generations of the whole human race. Under these conditions no

Figure 10.4   Power and legitimacy in a *Verbindungsnetz schaft* society

nation-state, not even the largest and most powerful members of these opposing military alliances, can act independently (Kaldor, 1978).

The power of the old nation-states is on the wane as they become more and more dependent upon military, economic, legal and social structures that transcend their territorial boundaries. In the case of Britain, and a growing number of countries in Western Europe, the North Atlantic Treaty Orgainzation (NATO) the Treaty of Rome and the European Common Market place severe restrictions upon their autonomy. New judicial agencies are emerging that restrict the freedom of nation-states and require conformity to international laws and agreements. Agencies such as the International Monetary Fund and the World Bank use powerful economic sanctions to demand conformity to economic and social policies that are against the interests of particular countries but maintain the global economic system. New bureaucratic structures are springing up which will eventually supersede those of the old nation-states. Similar developments are occurring in the Communist dominated countries although the struggle for independence from the Soviet Union continues, just as Western countries resent the growing domination of the United States. War, and the justifaction for military build up and nuclear deterrents, is no longer legitimated in terms of patriotic sentiments of a nationalistic type. Global confrontation is now expressed in terms of the overriding ideologies of Communism and anti-Communism.[1]

Technological Changes

The post-industrial era has been brought about by technological revolution. This revolution has been most evident in the spheres of computerisation and automation, on the one hand, and in communications systems on the other. The full impact of this revolution has

Ethnic Nationalism and Post-Industrialism

yet to be experienced. Previously labour-intensive industries, in both the manufacturing and the service sectors, will come to depend increasingly upon these new technologies. Already, world-wide telecommunications systems link individuals and organisations in complex networks of information exchange. Banks, insurance companies, stock markets and multinational companies, in every industrial sector, are now linked by these systems that permit instantaneous exchanges of information and the rapid movement of currency and capital from one country to another. At the domestic level our lives are being revolutionised by transnational radio and television networks aided by satellite communication systems. The education system is also being transformed by the use of television and various systems of computerised information storage and retrieval. Computer learning systems are beginning to take over from traditional classroom instruction. Interactive computerised communication systems will remove the element of passivity which has characterised listening and viewing in the past.

A new principle of social organisation has been introduced which will transform the social system of post-industrial societies. When the industrial revolution brought with it formal organisations of the *Gesellschaft* type it did not completely replace territorial communities of the *Gemeinschaft* type, but the former diminished in importance as people became more involved in transactional relationships and specialised economic and social roles. By the same token, the complex social and communication networks, the *Verbindungsnetzschaft*,[2] that are characteristic of post-industrial societies will not entirely replace territorial communities or formal organisations. However, relationships based upon interpersonal, interorganisational, international and mass communication networks, will be the characteristic mode of social interaction in the future (Nora and Minc, 1978; Serafini and Andrieu, 1980; Toffler, 1981).

The dominant ideologies of the post-industrial period are those which endeavour to rationalise and justify the activities of multinational companies, on the one hand, and multinational socialist regimes, on the other. In economic terms, the interests of national power elites are no longer aligned with the interests of nationally based economic organisations, whether under private enterprise or state socialism. Instead, the supranational power elites are aligned with the interests of multinational economic organisations, whether these are capitalist or socialist. The military-industrial complex is no longer an instrument of the nation-state for the pursuit of patriotic wars. It has become the instrument of the supranational state for the

176 *Ethnic Nationalism*

pursuit of ideological wars between the capitalist and communist superpowers. Even the civil wars within existing nation-states have become ideological rather than patriotic. They involve economic and military support from external supranational states. Insurgent movements, whether in the advanced industrial countries or the Third World, are linked through complex communication networks with each other and with the dominant suprastate agencies that encourage them. This is true whether the insurgent movements identify with the ideologies of Capitalism or Communism. Terrorism no longer operates within national boundaries but has become an international phenomenon involving bombing, hi-jacking and hostage taking in almost every country of the world.

THE FUTURE OF ETHNIC NATIONALISM

The emergence of post-industrialism has profound implications for the future of ethnic consciousness, ethnic organisations and ethnic nationalist movements. In a theocratic state, variations in language, national identification and ethnic group formation are acceptable as long as all the sources of variation are subordinated to a single religious ideology. The ultimate power structure depends upon a close relationship between the religious, military and economic elites. There can be no religious toleration. Sectarian movements or completing religious faiths, including secular political philosophies, must be ruthlessly suppressed. Ethnic nationalism can survive under the conditons created by theocratic states as long as the ultimate power rests with the religious authorities. This was evident during the Catholic domination of Europe up to the Reformation and, to some extent, is characteristic of Islamic states today.

However, the theocratic structure of power was undermined as feudal economies gave way to industrialisation. New power elites emerged that were no longer identified with the old religious order. The secular state, characteristic of industrialised countries, could afford religious toleration. The vestiges of established religions may have lingered on but religious reformist groups, new sects and widespread agnosticism or atheism were compatible with the new nationalist ideologies. However, the old link between Church and state was replaced by a link between nation and state. The process of industrialisation was a powerful assimilatory force that compelled people to relinquish the *Gemeinschaft* attachments of the rural community in favour of the *Gesellschaft* relationships of the city. No

Ethnic Nationalism and Post-Industrialism   177

matter how heterogeneous the ethnic origins of the city-dwelling industrial workers may have been, new loyalties were generated that ensured the solidarity of the new nation-state. The nineteenth century, and the first half of the twentieth century, in Europe and in North America, was a period during which old ethnic identities gave way to new nationalistic loyalties.[3] Wars of religion were replaced by the Napoleonic era, and two world wars in which the patriotism of the linguistic and ethnic minorities within the nation-states was severely tested. The willingness to be conscripted into the military became a critical issue. Ethnic minorities that resisted conscription, or who were suspected of less than total loyalty to the nation at war, were subjected to severe penalties. In Britain the loyalty of Scottish and Welsh minorities was rarely in question but the Irish were less inclined to fight in the British cause. In Canada, there was a similar disinclination on the part of French-speaking Quebecers. In other parts of Canada, European immigrants and their childrern were often unjustly suspected of unpatriotic sentiments and behaviour. During the Second World War the Canadian treatment of Japanese Canadians is evidence of coercive assimilation and relinquishment of ethnic loyalties that was demanded. The McCarthy era in the United States was probably the last attempt to impose a single nationalistic ideology and to regard any non-conformity as evidence of 'un-American activities'. Already, the ideology of the new supranational state was emerging, that of anti-Communism.

Ethnic Power

Among first-generation immigrants in an industrialised society the maintenance of strong ethnic loyalties was seen as unpatriotic. In Europe, where changing boundaries of nation-states left many linguistic minorities politically isolated from those with whom they had cultural links, the incorporation of minorities into a single unit ready to fight in defence of the country concerned, became a major question in the nineteenth and twentieth centuries. At the same time, in the New World, waves of immigrants were to be incorporated as citizens of their new countries. In both the United States and Canada, the question of inculcating loyalty to the state continued to be an important political issue until after the Second World War. As the second and later generations, of various ethnic origins, established hemselves in the countries concerned, they sought to overcome the

178 *Ethnic Nationalism*

prejudice and discrimination which previous generations had suffered.

The 'Black power' movement in the United States led the way and other ethnic groups followed in their attempt to gain recognition. In many cases, the ethnic minorities in industrialised countries identified closely with the independence movements in formerly colonised territories in the Third World. Political imperialism was replaced by economic imperialism within the framework of the global economy. Ethnic minorities within the industrialised countries began to regard themselves as having been exploited in the interests of dominant groups within the industrialised nation-states. Their situation has been interpreted as one of internal colonialism (Blauner, 1969; Hechter, 1975). The second half of the twentieth century has seen a reaction against the assimilatory pressures of industrialisation and, at least among the elites within the ethnic populations concerned, a struggle for greater autonomy and even independence.

The emerging supranational states can afford to make concessions to the ethnic nationalist movements within industrialised countries as long as one overriding condition is fulfilled. That condition is an unswerving loyalty to the dominant ideology of the supranational state. In Western countries, this means unquestioning support for the economic philosophy of multinationalism, Capitalism and anti-Communism. For countries within the Communist block the reverse is the case. Varying degrees of autonomy can be permitted for the constituent national groups as long as there is unswerving loyalty to the dictates of the Communist party. Any deviation from this is likely to be immediately suppressed, if necessary by military force.[4]

It is not only ethnic groups which are geographically concentrated, and can establish an historical claim to particular territories, who will succeed in promoting their interests within the framework of the supranational state. The very nature of post-industrialism, with its technological advances in communication networks, facilitates the maintenance of language and cultural differences, even in remotely scattered populations. The immigrant minorities in countries such as Canada and Australia are already able to take advantage of multi-lingual radio and television channels. New developments in Pay TV and in satellite communications will further assist and promote the maintenance of linguistic and ethnic diversity. Mass communication networks will be supplemented by interpersonal networks with kith and kin, maintained through rapid transportation and transnational telecommunications systems. Just as the emergence of the industrial

Ethnic Nationalism and Post-Industrialism 179

lised nation-state facilitated religious toleration, so the emergence of the post-industrial supranational state will facilitate the maintenance of ethnic diversity. However, those ethnic nationalist movements that identify themselves with the opposing ideology (multinational capitalism versus multinational communism) will be regarded as subversive and subject to coercive controls.

Ethnic Power Elites

The transition from nationalism to multinationalism, and its associated multiculturalism, will not take place without a struggle between competing power elites. Already, the traditional power elites of the secular states are resisting incorporation into the new structures being created at the supranational level. The growing threat of a nuclear war on a global scale must eventually overcome the resistance of the weaker units who depend for their defence upon larger and more powerful countries. However, encroachments on national sovereignty will continue to be resisted even as independence is undermined by the technological revolution of post-industrialism.[5]

Meanwhile, within the old nation-states both ethnic and regional interests are asserting themselves. The emerging struggle for power has two major dimensions. The first is economic. Generally, it is a struggle for access to and control over natural resources, particularly those relating to energy. In this context, industrial and commercial elites will ally themselves with emerging ethnic or regional movements for autonomy and independence. In some cases, as in Scotland and Western Canada, the economic advantages of greater independence, and even separation, will be emphasised. Questions of mineral rights, export controls and taxation will be controversial. However, the economic elites may fail to gain popular support for their separatist policies which may not be perceived as in the best interests of the population as a whole (Breton and Breton, 1980).

The second dimension of the struggle for power concerns the agencies of communication and legitimation. Specifically, the struggle focuses upon constitutional questions relating to devolution, the judicial system, the education system and the agencies of mass communication. The constitutional issues are fought out in the political arena through the electoral system and by the use of referenda. Again, the interests of regional and ethnic elites may not coincide with those of the electorate. The latter may be suspicious of the motives of the ethnic leaders; they may retain a lingering

180 *Ethnic Nationalism*

attachment to the larger nation-state, or they may consider that their economic interests will continue to be better served by remaining part of the wider society in its federal or other more centralised form. Much will depend upon the ability of the separatist movements to gain control of the socialising agencies that influence attitudes and public opinion. Teachers and journalists play an important part in this respect and are often among the strongest supporters of ethnic nationalism.

Next in importance to the legitimating function of the constitutional debates are those relating to the control of education. Where regional and ethnic interests converge, and are focused on the maintenance of language and culture, the education system becomes a centre of controversy. In the earlier industrialised nation-states a single language of instruction was regarded as imperative and led, in some cases, to the use of coercive measures to eliminate ethnic languages in schools (Khleif, 1980 Brown, 1969). Now newly emerging ethnic elites may adopt equally coercive means to impose their own language requirements. Bilingualism may be imposed upon members of the former dominant group, rather than being a functional prerequisite for an ethnic minority. In some cases the ethnic minority may succeed in imposing monolingual rules upon former majority group members, as in the case of recent Quebec legislation (Guindon, 1978). Where the ethnic minority groups do not have a territorial base they may, nevertheless, succeed in establishing the legitimacy of separate ethnic schools or bilingual instruction.

As the post-industrial revolution transforms the systems of communication in contemporary societies, a struggle for control of the networks also takes place. Access to and control over the instruments of mass communication becomes an important issue. Both child and adult socialisation takes place through exposure to the information and the value systems transmitted through these networks. The school system itself becomes increasingly dependent upon televised and computerised learning systems. Some children actually spend more hours exposed to television viewing or video-terminals than they do in conventional classroom learning. Adults are also exposed increasingly to the flood of verbal and visual communications transmitted through the new technologies. At one time the number of channels was strictly limited. The effect was essentially assimilatory and homogenising. Hence the resistance to American domination of mass communication networks in Canada. However, as the new technologies evolve, a much greater variety of linguistic and cultural

Ethnic Nationalism and Post-Industrialism

information will flow through these channels. Ethnic minorities will seek and generally obtain control over one or more television channels. This will permit the transmission of distinctive educational, informational, cultural and recreational programs in a variety of different languages.

Supranational states of the authoritarian or totalitarian type will have a special interest in controlling the mass communication networks and the education systems. While some linguistic and cultural variation may be permitted, the networks will be the vehicle for transmitting a single dominant political ideology. In more democratically organised societies, there may be greater freedom of expression and more evidence of political discussion and dissent. However, ultimate control over licensing for broadcasting and reception is likely to rest with authorities who will not tolerate the use of the networks for active propaganda in favour of an opposing ideology. Nor will they permit the networks to be dominated by any one foreign source.

As the influence of *Verbindungsnetzschaft* replaces that of *Gemeinschaft,* or *Gesellschaft*, as a characteristic mode of social organisation in post-industrial societies, the maintenance of ethnic identity will become less dependent upon either a territorial base or formal organisations. It will be possible for ethnic links to be maintained with others of similar language and cultural background throughout the world. Interpersonal networks may be sustained through videophones and other telecommunication links that will function much as the 'ham' radio networks have functioned in the past. Mass communication networks will also transcend the boundaries of former nation-states to link people of many different linguistic, cultural and national origins wherever they may be located throughout the world. International migration will still occur but it will no longer be necessary to compel immigrants to assimilate culturally to the majority group in the receiving society.

Ethnic nationalism will merge with the claims of other provincial and regional interest groups seeking greater economic and political influence, wherever numbers and territorial concentration make such an alliance advantageous. Even where ethnic minorities are widely dispersed they will still be able to maintain their links with others of similar ethnicity, wherever they may be. The complex communication networks of post-industrial societies will create the possibility of a new type of society, free of both religious and ethnic intolerance, by permitting great diversity within the structure of a supranational

182 *Ethnic Nationalism*

state. Reactionary movements, endeavouring to reassert national sovereignty and seeking to impose ethnic and cultural uniformity will likely occur. The transition from nationalism to multinationalism and from industrialism to post-industrialism will not take place without conflict. Eventually, a new era of ethnic and cultural diversity may be predicted. Its achievement will depend upon one overriding condition, namely, that the supranational states do not destroy themselves, and the rest of the world with them, in a nuclear conflagration precipitated by the combined forces of militarism and multinationalism.

End-notes

3 Social-Cultural Adaptation and Conflict in Immigrant-Receiving countries

1. Immigration and ethnic origin are not the only sources of cultural variation in modern societies, where diversity, freedom of choice and tolerance for alternative life-styles have been institutionalised. Other sources of such sub-cultural variations include age, gender, sexual orientation, education, occupation, rural suburban city location, religion and recreation. These have all contributed to the multiple choices available.

2. Studies carried out in Toronto, Canada, in 1970 identified five different 'modes of adaptation' by adult male immigrant householders to life in the metropolis at that time (Richmond, 1974). They were differentiated by such critical factors as length of residence, education, knowledge of English and preference for association with their own ethnic group. The five categories were labelled 'urban villager', 'pluralistically integrated'. 'Anglo-Canadian conformist', 'transilent' and 'alienated'. Only the latter category exhibited characteristics that could be regarded as maladjusted or inadequate in terms of socio-cultural or economic adaptation. Had the study inclued women, or been extended to other regions or rural arreas, alternative forms of adaptation would probably have been evident. Other modes of adaptation may be found among more recent immigrants from various ethnic backgrounds or faced with different situational determinants. Further comparative studies are needed in other countries, to identify the full range of possible forms of adaptation.

3. The term 'ethnic enclave' as used here carries no pejorative meaning. It is not the same as 'ghetto' which implies forced segregation, economic deprivation and discrimination. An ethnic enclave may be accompanied by some degree of residential concentration, arising from preference for living close to kith and kin, the provision of mutual support and the emergence of economic and social institutions meeting the special needs of immigrants. In some cases, such enclaves may become relatively self-sufficient and the avenue by which ethnic entrepreneurs and professionals achieve upward mobility.

4 Immigration and Unemployment in Canada and Australia

1. Age-standardised unemployment rates for Canadian-born males were 8 per cent in Montreal and 4 per cent in Toronto at the time of the 1981 census. The rates for Canadian-born women were 10 per cent and 4.5 per cent respectively. Immigrant rates were close to those of the Canadian-

183

184 *End-Notes*

born except among the recent arrivals. For example, comparable rates for Caribbean-born men were 16 per cent and 6 per cent and for women 21 per cent and 6 per cent (Statistics Canada: special unpublished tabulations).

7 Canadian Unemployment and the Threat to Multiculturalism

1. In June 1981, the Minister of Employment and Immigration announced substantial cuts in support for immigrant and refugee services, only partly related to an anticipated decline in the number of refugees to be admitted in 1981–82. Funds for the Adjustment Assistance Program, which were \$32 866 000, were cut to \$17 576 000 in 1981–82. The allocation for the Immigrant Settlement and Adaptation Program in 1980–181 was \$2 330 000 and was projected at \$2 452 000 in 1981–82.

2. The federal government announced in 1981 that domestic workers who had been in Canada for two years or more on temporary employment visas were permitted to apply for landed immigrant status if they showed that they had successfully undertaken courses that upgraded their skills sufficient to enable them to be self-supporting in the Canadian labour market. This measure does not detract from the essentially explosive nature of the temporary employment visa system as applied to female domestic workers.

3. This paper addresses itself mainly to the question of immigrants in relation to unemployment and multiculturalism. However, there is no doubt that the most segregated, educationally deprived and economically disadvantaged groups in Canada are the Native Peoples. A survey carried out by the Native Council of Canada and the Canada Employment and Immigration Commission in 1976 found that, among Metis and non-status Indians, unemployment rates were more than four times that of the rest of the population. The situation on the Reserve is even more serious. As victims of racism the Canadian Indian peoples and Metis have suffered more than any. They are the most likely to respond to their frustration with violence.

4. Recent development in Great Britain, where racial violence has broken out in areas of exceptionally high unemployment and racial heterogeneity, lends further support for the economic insecurity hypothesis I put forward thirty years ago (Richmond, 1950).

5. In June 1981, the Minister of State for Multiculturalism announced programs designed to combat racism which included holding a symposium, establishing a research centre and public education on the question. It remains to be seen whether these programs materialise and whether they make more than a token contribution to removing racism. Little appears to have been achieved so far.

End-Notes

185

6. The 1981 Census of Canada confirms that immigrants who arrived in the preceding decade had higher rates of unemployment and lower incomes than earlier arrivals and that their status was not comparable with their educational qualifications. This was particularly true of those from Third World countries (Statistics Canada: special unpublished tabulations).

10 Ethnic Nationalism and Post-Industrialism

1. This does not mean that there are no divisions between the adherents of these two ideologies. Clearly, there are serious conflicts between the Soviet Communist bloc and the Chinese Communist sphere of influence. Furthermore, there are actual and potential conflicts within the multinational Capitalist countries. This is the theme of Mary Kaldor's study *The Disintegrating West*. A major thesis of her book 'is the passing of the nation-state, or, rather, its struggle for survival in the face of increased interpentration of Western societies and the dissipation of national constituencies. In particular, the multinational corporations are seen to play a key role in changing the rules of the international economy and upsetting the national balance of political forces' (p.10). She does not exclude the prospect of renewed American hegemony but argues that this is conditioned by the rivalry of the United States with Europe and Japan. She anticipates a new division of the world into super-nation states, 'a new global constellation of continental groupings' (Kaldor, 1979:12).

2. I coined this term in Richmond (1969:278). I noted that '*Verbindungsnetzschaft*' is an 'ideal type' concept or abstract representation not necessarily corresponding exactly with the conditions in any actual society, which is likely to contain elements of *Gemeinschaft-* and *Gesellischaft-*like social systems as well. A *Verbindungsnetzschaft-*like social system is one in which the characteristic forms of social interaction take place through networks of communication maintained by means of telephone, teleprinter, television and high speed aircraft and spacecraft, etc. Such relationships are not dependent upon a territorial base or face-to-face contact, nor do they involve participation in formal organisations. Behaviour is governed by a constant feedback from highly efficient information storage and retrieval processes based upon diffuse networks of inter-dependent communication systems.'

3. Reitz (1980:8) quotes Teddy Roosevelt as stating, in 1915, 'the foreignborn population of this country must be an Americanized population – no other kind can fight the battles of America either in war or peace. It must talk the language of its native-born or fellow citizens, it must possess American citizenship and American ideals. It must stand firm by its oath of allegiance in word and deed and must show that in very fact it has renounced allegiance to every prince, potentate or foreign government.'

186   *End-Notes*

4. The situation in Poland is a critical case in point. The greater freedom accorded to the Catholic Church and, for a time, to the Solidarity labour union movement, was only tolerated as long as there was an ultimate conformity to the dictates of the Communist party, which in turn takes its direction from the Soviet Union.

5. In a recent study of *The Information Revolution and its Implications for Canada*, Serafini and Andorieu (1980:28) note that the nation-states have relinquished some of their powers to plurinational or international bodies and that the information revolution may accelerate the erosion of national sovereignty by further increasing the dominance of multinational corporations in the world economy. 'The new advances in computer communications, by significantly reducing the cost of managing large and complex organisations, may tend to increase the optimal size of firms . . . and the new information technology may also help multinationals to increase control by their headquarters over corporate planning and operations by centralising computer resources. Such a step might, indeed, become necessary to co-ordinate the activities of the more specialized branch plants.' Later they emphasise that the information revolution is international and reflects a fundamental structural change causing increasing international interdependence. They note that 'in response to the consequent erosion of national sovereignty, many countries have been experiencing a trend towards economic nationalism' (p.94), but they argue that the effects of the new technologies cannot be stopped at the border.

Glossary of Terms

Authority Power exercised by the consent of the governed as a consequence of legitimation [q.v.].

Citizen A person having a legitimate claim to membership of, protection by, and access to the resources of a given state [q.v.].

Class A socio-economic interest group defined by its relation to the systems of production and distribution in a society; specifically ownership and/or control of capital, versus the sale of labour, services or technical knowledge and skill.

Client-state A state which is dependent upon a super-power [q.v.], for economic and military support and subject to its direct influence.

Competition A form of conflict in which resources, such as economic goods and services, social status or political power, are commonly valued but absolutely or relatively scarce, and therefore are treated in a 'zero-sum' fashion i.e. on the assumption that if one person or collectivity obtains more, there will be less of the valued resource for others.

Conflict A situation of competition [q.v.], opposition [q.v.] or contradiction [q.v.] between individuals or collectivities, which results in the actual (realistic) or assumed (unrealistic), inability to achieve goals.

Consensus A situation of general agreement concerning core values of a society, particularly those relating to the distribution of economic rewards and political power. Consensus may arise from common historical experience and democratic participation, but it may also be manipulated by elites utilising agencies of information dissemination, communication and socialisation, such as the education system and the mass media.

Contradiction A form of system conflict involving opposition of structural principles or one in which the core value system of a society defines certain goals and ideals, but fails to provide the necessary institutional means for their achievement.

Cooperation A process by which common goals are achieved, through mutual support, functional division of labour and social exchange, so that conflict is reduced or resolved.

Dissensus A situation of general disagreement concerning the core values of a society, particularly those relating to the distribution of economic rewards and political power; dissensus may arise from the historical situation of minority groups, experiencing absolute or relative deprivation; also it may be manipulated by dominant elites aiming to 'divide and rule', or by minority group leaders seeking to raise consciousness.

Glossary of Terms

Ethnic Group A people who share certain beliefs, values and cultural characteristics, (such as language or religion), together with a sense of belonging and identity, generally attributed to common ancestry (real or putative).

Ethnic Origin A social categorisation of persons defined by one or more cultural characteristics assumed to be ancestorally determined.

Ethnic Nationalism A movement by a particular ethnic group, expressing aspirations to achieve (or in defence of existing claims to) national status, i.e. relative political autonomy [q.v.]. (The aim of the group may or may not include 'national sovereignty', or 'sovereignty-association' [q.v.])

Ethnonational Group A monoethnic nation i.e. a nation whose members belong to a single ethnic group in contrast with a polyethnic nation [q.v.]

Fascism A totalitarian form of government based upon centralisation of power within a corporate capitalist state, whose elites espouse a nationalistic ideology.

Gemeinschaft A social system based on the principle of a territorial community.

Gesselschaft A social system based on the principles of bureacracy and membership in formal organisations.

Hegemony A near monopoly of economic and political power which facilitates control over communication systems and therefore the manipulation of consensus [q.v.] and legitimation [q.v.].

Ideology A system of ideas and beliefs which oversimplifies complex economic, social and political relations, as a means of legitimating an existing unequal distribution of wealth and power, and diminishing opposition to governing elites. It may give rise to counter-ideologies and/or utopian [q.v.] promises by opposing groups.

Immigration The process of entering a country with the expectation of long-term employment or settlement, as distinct from visitors, students, or temporary workers; an immigrant may be of the 'transilient' [q.v.] type in which case the expectation of settlement may not apply.

Jingoism An ideology that equates the patriotic interests of all social classes, nations and ethnic groups, within a given state, with those of the governing elite, in opposition to the supposed threat of one or more external powers.

Legitimation The translation of power into authority i.e. the exercise of power with the consent and approval of the governed, through the generation of a common value system. Legitimation may occur through traditional beliefs, charismatic leadership, ritualisation, democratic participation, routinisation (bureaucracy), or ideological manipulation.

Migration A movement of population from one defined area to another.

Glossary of Terms

189

Mobilisation The breakdown of traditional, ascriptive, and local community ties through the spread of communications and the exposure of a population to modernising influences, including urbanisation, industrialisation etc.

Multiculturalism A social policy which is designed to achieve a form of pluralistic integration of immigrants and ethnic minorities, without necessarily demanding complete cultural or structural assimilation; or (in some cases) an ideology which perpetuates the domination of one group by encouraging divisions among others.

Multinational State A state whose boundaries encompass two or more nations.

Nation A people associated with a given territory, sharing a history and common social institutions, who now have, or at some time had and wish again to enjoy, a degree of political autonomy [q.v.]. A nation may be ethnically homogeneous or heterogeneous and may or may not have, or aspire to, 'national sovereignty' [q.v.], or 'sovereignty association' [q.v.].

Nation-state A state whose boundaries coincide with those of a single nation, or one where such a coincidence is ideologically asserted by a dominant group.

Nationalism A movement, by a given population, expressing aspirations to achieve (or in defence of existing claims to) national status i.e. a degree of political autonomy [q.v.].

National Sovereignty The achievement and exercise of full state powers i.e. sovereignty [q.v.], by a particular nation, or nations in association with each other.

Opposition A form of conflict arising from value dissensus, i.e. fundamental disagreement concerning societal values and goals, or the appropriate means for their achievement; expression of opposition may be legitimated in a democratic society and suppressed in a totalitarian one.

Political Autonomy Institutions that provide for some degree of self-government, devolution of authority, separate representation, collective rights, cultural or linguistic protection, or entrenched privilege, for particular regions, nationalities or ethnic minorities, within a given state.

Polyethnic Nation A nation which contains within its population two or more ethnic groups.

Post-industrial A society experiencing rapid technological, economic and social change consequent upon developments in automation, communications, control systems and information dissemination.

Power The capacity to achieve individual or collective goals through cooperation and, if necessary, by overcoming internal or external opposition and conflict [q.v.].

Race A social categorisation of a population on the basis of one or more genetically transmitted somatic characteristic, that are used as diacritical

190 *Glossary of Terms*

'markers'. Such a categorisation does not necessarily coincide with any actual 'gene-pool', or 'race' in a biological sense. It may or may not be associated with distinctive cultural characteristics, although these may be acquired as a consequence of, or in a reaction against, segregation and discrimination.

Racism An ideology which asserts the genetic superiority of one population over another; or a set of attitudes, values, behaviours or institutions which directly or indirectly discriminate against or systematically disadvantage, a minority defined in terms of 'race' [q.v.]

Regionalism A subnational (or suprastate) movement designed to promote the devolution of authority to a smaller, or larger, territory than that occupied by a given state. It may give rise to sovereignty-association [q.v.]

Sovereignty The assertion of supreme coercive powers, internal social and political control and the defence of territorial borders, by a state authority, recognised as legitimate and independent by other states.

Sovereignty-association The sharing of certain powers, generally those relating to defence or external economic relations, with another sovereign state.

State A politically sovereign system of government, having defined territorial boundaries recognised by others, within which supreme coercive powers may be exercised by duly constituted authorities.

Status A position in a functionally divided and hierarchical social system i.e. a system of stratification based on a social division of labour.

Structuration The structuring of social relations through time-space paths that incorporate persistence and change.

Super-powers Those sovereign states whose military and economic domination of the world system enables them to exercise effective control over the economic and political conditions of client-states [q.v.].

Transilient An international migrant who moves readily from one country to another because his/her skills are in demand and are readily adaptable to local needs.

Utopia A counter-ideology, or system of ideas and beliefs which over-simplifies complex economic, social and political relations, in order to mobilise opposition to an existing unequal distribution of economic and political power, by promising a new egalitarian social order in the distant future (or in the next life!).

Verbindungsnetzschaft A social system based on extended interpersonal and mass communication networks, including satellite television transmissions, telecommunications, computerised information systems and data bases.

Visible Minority An ethnic minority distinguishable by a readily identifiable characteristic, which may be race [q.v.], or a culturally defined form of dress or special behaviour.

Select Bibliography and References

ABELLA, ROSALIE S. (1984) *Equality in Employment: A Royal Commission Report* (Ottawa: Supply and Services Canada).

ACPEA (Australian Council on Populaton and Ethnic Affairs) (1982) *Multiculturalism for all Australians: Our Developing Nationhood,* (Canberra: Australian Government Publishing Service).

ADORNO, T. W. *et al.* (1950) *The Authoritarian Personality* (New York: Harper).

ALLARDT, ERIK. (1979) *Implications of the Ethnic Revival in Modern Industrialized Society* (Helsinki: Societas Scientiarium Fennica).

ANDERSON, A. B. and J. FRIDERES, (1981) *Ethnicity in Canada: Theoretical Perspectives* (Toronto: Butterworths)

ANDERSON, G. M. and L. T. CHRISTIE (1982) 'Networks: The Impetus for new Research Initiatives', *Research in Race and Ethnic Relations*, 3, 207—25.

AUSTRALIA: *Commonwealth Immigration Restriction Act of 1901,* Act no. 17 (Melbourne: Australia, 1901).

AUSTRALIA YEAR BOOK (1980) Canberra: Australian Government Publishing Service, No. 64.

AXWORTHY, LLOYD (1980) Speech by Minister of Employment and Immigration.

BANKS, J. A. and J. LYNCH (1986) *Multicultural Education in Western Societies* (London: Holt, Rinehart and Winston).

BANKS, MARGARET A. (1985). 'Defining "Constitution of the Province": The Crux of the Manitoba Language Controversy', Paper presented at the meetings of the British Association of Canadian Studies (Edinburgh).

BANTON, MICHAEL P. (ed.) (1961) *Darwinism and the Study of Society* (London: Tavistock).

BANTON, MICHAEL P. (1967) *Race Relations* (London: Tavistock).

BANTON, MICHAEL P. (1969). 'What do we mean by Racism?', *New Society,* 341 (10 April).

BANTON, MICHAEL P. (1980) 'Ethnic Groups and the Theory of Rational Choice', in *Sociological Theories: Race and Colonialism* (Paris, UNESCO).

BANTON, MICHAEL P. (1983) *Race and Ethnic Competition* (Cambridge: Cambridge University Press).

BANTON, MICHAEL P. (1985) *Promoting Racial Harmony* (Cambridge: Cambridge University Press).

BARBER, C. L. and J. C. P. McCALLUM (1980) *Unemployment and Inflation: The Canadian Experience* (Toronto: James Lorimer and Co.).

192   *Select Bibliography and References*

BARTH, F. (1969) *Ethnic Groups and Boundaries* (Boston: Little, Brown).

BASAVARAJAPPA, K. G., and R. B. P. VERMA (1985) 'Asian Immigrants in Canada: Some Findings from the 1981 Census' *International Migration* XXIII:I.

BELL, D. (1973) *The Coming of Post-Industrial Society: A Venture in Social Forecasting* (London: Heinemann Educational Books).

BENYON, JOHN (ed.) (1984) *Scarman and After* (Oxford: Pergamon Press).

BENYON, JOHN (1986) *A Tale of Failure: Race and Policing* (Coventry: Centre for Research on Ethnic Relations, University of Warwick).

BERRY, J. N., R. KALIN and D. M. TAYLOR (1977) *Multiculturalism and Ethnic Attitudes in Canada* (Ottawa: Supply and Services).

BLAINEY, G. (1984) *All for Australia* (North Ryde: Methuen Haynes)

BLAU, PETER (1964) *Exchange and Power in Social Life* (New York: Wiley).

BLAUNER, ROBERTS (1969) 'Internal colonialism and the ghetto revolt', *Social Problems* 16, 4, 393–408.

BOLDT, M. and J. R. LONG (1984) 'Tribal philosophies and the Canadian Charter of Rights and Freedoms', *Ethnic and Racial Studies* 7:4 478–93.

BONACICH, EDNA (1973) 'A Theory of Middleman Minorities', *American Sociological Review* Vol. 38, 583–93.

BOROVOY, A. . (1980) Letter to the Hon. Dr. Robert G. Elgie, Minister of Labour of Ontario, from the Canadian Civil Liberties Association (Toronto).

BORRIE, W. D. (1975) *Population and Australia: A Demographic Analysis and Projection* First Report of the National Population Enquiry, vols. I and II (Canberra: Australian Government Publishing Service).

BOSTOCK, WILLIAM (1984). 'Ethno-cultural control in Australia: the issue of ethnic broadcasting', in James Jupp (ed.) *Ethnic Politics in Australia* (Sydney: George Allen and Unwin) pp.97–113.

BOYLE, A. J. (ed). *Migration and Mobility: Biosocial Aspects of Human Movement* (London: Taylor & Francis).

BRETON, A., and R. BRETON (1980) *Why Disunity? An Analysis of Linguistic and Regional Cleavages in Canada* (Montreal: The Institute for Research on Public Policy).

BRETON, RAYMOND (1983a) 'West Indian, Chinese and European Ethnic Groups in Toronto', in J. L. ELLIOTT (ed.), *Two Nations, Many Cultures: Ethnic Groups in Canada* (rev. ed.) (Scarborough: Prentice-Hall) pp.425–43.

BRETON, RAYMOND, (1983b) *The Ethnic Community as a Resource in Relation to Group Problems: Perceptions and Attitudes* (Toronto: Centre for Urban & Community Studies).

BRETON, RAYMOND (1984) 'The Production and Allocation of Symbolic Resources: An Analysis of the Linguistic and Ethnocultural Fields in Canada', *Canadian Review of Sociology & Anthropology* Vol. 21, No. 2, 123–44.

BRETON, R., J. G. REITZ and V. F. VALENTINE (1980) *Cultural Boundaries and the Cohesion of Canada* (Montreal: The Institute for Research on Public Policy).

Select Bibliography and References

BROWN, COLIN (1984) *Black and White in Britain: The Third PSI Survey* (London: Heineman).

BROWN, CRAIG (ed.) (1969) *Minorities, Schools and Politics* (Toronto: University of Toronto Press).

BRYCE-LAPORTE, R. S. (ed.) (1980) *Sourcebook on the New Immigration* (New Jersey: Transaction Books).

BUCHIGNANI, NORMAN and D. M. INDRA, with R. SRIVASTAVA (1985) *Continuous Journey: A Social History of South Asians in Canada* (Toronto: McClelland and Stewart).

BULLIVANT, BRIAN (1973) *Educating the Immigrant Child: Concepts and Cases* (Sydney: Angus and Robertson).

BULLIVANT, BRIAN (1981) *The Pluralist Dilemma in Education* (Sydney: George Allen & Unwin).

BULLIVANT, BRIAN (1985) 'Multicultural Education in Australia' in J. A. Banks & J. Lynch, *Multicultural Education in Western Societies* (London: Holt, Rinehart & Winston).

BULMER, MARTIN (1984) *The Chicago School of Sociology* (Chicago and London: University of Chicago Press).

BURNET, JEAN (1978) 'The policy of multiculturalism within a bilingual framework: A stock-taking', *Canadian Ethnic Studies* 10, 107–11.

BURNET, JEAN (1983) 'Multiculturalism Ten Years Later' in Jean Elliott (ed.), *Two Nations, Many Cultures: Ethnic Groups in Canada* (Toronto: Prentice-Hall.

BURNLEY, I. H. and W. E. KALBACH (1985) *Immigrants in Canada and Australia: vol. 3.: Urban and Ecological Aspects* (Toronto: Institute for Social Research, York University).

CIPS (1974) *Three Years in Canada: A Report of the Canadian Immigration and Population Study* (Ottawa: Manpower and Immigration).

CAMERON, DAVID (ed.) 1981 *Regionalism and Supranationalism* (Montreal: Institute for Research on Public Policy, 1981).

CANADA (1952) *Immigration Act* RSC 1952, C.325 (Ottawa, Queens' Printer).

CANADA (1974–5–6) Senate/House of Commons, *Proceedings of the Special Joint Committee of the Senate and the House of Commons on Immigration Policy*, 30th Parliament, 1st Session.

CANADA, HOUSE OF COMMONS (1984) *Equality Now* Report of the Special Committee on Visible Minorities in Canadian Society (Bob Daudin, Chairman) (Ottawa: Supply & Services Canada).

CASHMORE, E. and B. TROYNA, (eds) (1982) *Black Youth in Crisis* (London: George Allen & Unwin).

CASTLES, S. and G. KOSAK (1973) *Immigrant Workers and Class Structure in Western Europe* (London: Oxford University Press).

CASTLES, S., H. BOOTH and T. WALLACE (1984) *Here for Good: Western Europe's New Ethnic Minorities* (London: Pluto Press).

C.C.C.S. (Centre for Contemporary Cultural Studies) (1982) *The Empire Strikes Back: Race and Racism in 1970s Britain* (London: Hutchinson).

CHAN, KWOK and L. LAM (1983) 'Resettlement of Vietnamese-Chinese Refugees in Montreal: Some Socio-psychological Problems and Dilemmas' *Canadian Ethnic Studies*, 15:1, 1–57.

CHOW, MARIA (1983) Canadian Chinese Adolescents' Attitudes Towards

194 *Select Bibliography and References*

Ethnic Language Maintenance', unpublished MA thesis (Toronto: York University).

CLAIRMONT, D. H., and D. W. MAGIL (1974) *Africville: The Life and Death of a Canadian Black Community* (Toronto: McClelland & Stewart).

CLEMENT, WALLACE (1975) *The Canadian Corporate Elite: An Analysis of Economic Power* (Toronto: McClelland & Stewart).

CLEMENT, WALLACE (1977) *Continental Corporate Power: Economic Linkages Between Canada and the United States* (Toronto: McClelland & Stewart).

CLEMENTS, K. P. and D. DRACHE (eds) (1978) Special Issue: 'Creative Modes of Nationalism', *Australian and New Zealand Journal of Sociology*, 14, 3.

CLODMAN, J. and A. H. RICHMOND (1981) *Immigration and Unemployment,* (Toronto: Institute for Behavioural Research, York University).

COHEN, P. S. (1968) *Modern Social Theory* (London: Heinemann Educational Books).

COLLINS, D. (1979) *Immigration: The Destruction of English Canada* (Richmond Hill, Ontario: BMG Publishing).

CON, HARRY, E. WICKBERG *et al.* (1982) *From China to Canada: A History of the Chinese Communities* (Toronto: McClelland & Stewart).

CONNOR, WALKER (1972) 'Nation Building or Nation Destroying?' *World Politics*, XXIV, No. 3, 319–55.

CONNOR, WALKER (1978) 'A Nation is a nation, is a state, is an ethnic group, is a . . .' *Ethnic and Racial Studies*, 1, 4, 377–400.

COX, D. and J. MARTIN (1975) *Welfare of Migrants,* Research Report for the Commission of Inquiry into Poverty (Canberra: A.G.P.S.).

COX, O. C., (1948) *Caste, Class and Race: A study in Social Dynamics* (New York: Monthly Review Press).

CRE (Commission for Racial Equality) (1985) *Immigration Control Procedures: Report of a Formal Investigation.* (London: C.R.E.).

CUMMINGS, S. (1980) 'White ethnics, racial prejudice, and labor market segmentation' *American Journal of Sociology* 85: 4938–50.

DARROCH, G. (1979) 'Another look at ethnicity, stratification and social mobility in Canada' *Canadian Journal of Sociology.* 4:11.

DAVEY, ALFRED (1983) *Learning to be Prejudiced: Growing up in Multi-Ethnic Britain,* (London: Edward Arnold).

DAVIES, G. W. (1973) 'The role of immigrants in the CANDIDE I.O. model'. *Canadian Immigration and Population Study.*

DAVIS, N. N. W. and M. L. GUPTA (1968) Labour Force Characteristics of Post-War Immigrants and Native-Born Canadians, 1956—1967. *Special Labour Force Studies No. 6* (Ottawa: Dominion Bureau of Statistics).

DAVISON, R. V. (1966) *Black British: Immigrants in England* (London: Oxford University Press).

DEMERS, R. (1974) *Immigration and Job Vacancies* (Ottawa: Manpower and Immigration Research Projects Group).

DENTON, F. T., A. L. ROBB AND B. G. SPENCER (1980) *Unemployment and the Labour Force Behaviour of Young People: Evidence from*

Select Bibliography and References

Canada and Ontario (Toronto: University of Toronto Press).

DEUTSCH, KARL W. (1953) (1966) *Nationalism and Social Communication*, 2nd edn (Cambridge. Mass.: MIT Press).

deVRIES, J., and F. G. VALLEE (1980) *Language Use in Canada: 1971 Census Analytical Report* (Ottawa: Statistics Canada).

DOFNY, J., and A. AKIWOWO (eds.) (1980) *National and Ethnic Movements* (Beverly Hills: Sage Publications).

DOSMAN, E. J. (1972) *Indians: The Urban Dilemma* (Toronto: McClelland & Stewart).

D'OYLEY, VINCENT (1977) 'Another Note on the Education of Urban West Indian Black Canadians', *Interchange*.

DRIEDGER, LEO, (ed.) (1978) *The Canadian Ethnic Mosaic* (Toronto: McClelland & Stewart).

DURKHEIM, E. (1947) *The Division of Labor in Society* (Translated from the French by George Simpson) (Chicago, Ill.: The Free Press).

ECONOMIC COUNCIL OF CANADA (1978) *For a Common Future: A Study of Canada's Relations with Developing Countries* (Ottawa: Supply and Services).

EDWARDS, R. C., M. REICH & D. M. GORDON (1975) *Labour Market Segmentation* (Lexington: D. C. Heath).

EISENSTADT, S. N. (1955) *The Absorption of Immigrants* (London: Routledge & Kegan Paul).

ELLIOTT, JEAN L. (ed.) (1971) *Native Peoples: Minority Canadians, 1* (Toronto: Prentice Hall).

ELLIOTT, JEAN L. (ed.) (1983) *Two Nations, Many Cultures: Ethnic Groups in Canada* (Scarborough, Ontario: Prentice-Hall).

EMPLOYMENT AND IMMIGRATION CANADA (1980) *Annual Report 1979–80* (Ottawa: Employment and Immigration Canada).

EMPLOYMENT AND IMMIGRATION CANADA (1981) *Annual Report to Parliament on Immigration Levels, 1981* (Ottawa: Employment and Immigration Canada).

ENCEL, SOLOMON (1970) *Equality and Authority: A Study of Class, Status and Power* (Melbourne: Cheshire).

ENLOE, CYNTHIA H. (1973) *Ethnic Conflict and Political Development* (Boston: Little, Brown).

ENLOE, CYNTHIA H. (1986a) *Police, Military and Ethnicity: Foundations of State Power* (New Brunswick/London: Transaction Books).

ENLOE, CYNTHIA H. (1986b) *Ethnic Soldiers: State Security in Divided Societies* (Harmondsworth: Penguin Books).

ETZIONI, A. (1968) *Active Society: A Theory of Societal and Political Processes* (New York: The Free Press).

ETZIONI-HALEVY, EVA (1985) *The Knowledge Elite and the Failure of Prophecy* (London: George Allen & Unwin).

FANON, F. (1965) *The Wretched of the Earth* (Harmondsworth: Penguin).

FENNER, F. J. (1971) 'The Environment' in John Wilkes (ed.), Australian Institute of Political Science, *How many Australians? Immigration and Growth* (Sydney: Angus and Robertson).

FISHER, N. W. F. (1982) 'Immigration and Australian Labour Markets:

196 *Select Bibliography and References*

Issues and Evidence' in D. Douglas (ed.) *The Economics of Australian Immigration* (Sydney: Sydney University Extension Programme).

FOOT, PAUL (1969) *The Rise of Enoch Powell* (Harmondsworth: Penguin Books).

FORCESE, DENNIS P. (1975) *Canadian Class Structure* (Toronto: McGraw-Hill Ryerson).

FORD, G. W. (1977) 'Employment' in A. F. Davies, S. Encel and M. J. Berry, *Australian Society: A Sociological Introduction* (Melbourne: Longman Cheshire).

FROMM, ERICH (1941) *Escape from Freedom* (New York: Farrar & Rinehart).

FROMM, ERICH (1977) *The Anatomy of Human Destructiveness* (Harmondsworth: Penguin).

FURNIVALL, J. S. (1939) *Netheralnds India: A Study in a Plural Economy,* (Cambridge: Cambridge University Press).

FURNIVALL, J. S. (1956) *Colonial Policy and Practice* (New York: New York University Press).

GALBRAITH, J. K. (1971) *The New Industrial State* (Boston: Houghton Mifflin).

GELLNER, ERNEST (1983) *Nations and Nationalism* (Oxford: Basil Blackwell).

GIDDENS, ANTHONY (1976) *New Rules of Sociological Method* (London: Hutchison/New York: Basic Books).

GIDDENS, ANTHONY (1979) *Central Problems in Social Theory* (London: The Macmillan Press).

GIDDENS, ANTHONY (1984) *The Constitution of Society* (Cambridge: The Polity Press, with Basil Blackwell, Oxford)

GILROY, P. (ed.) (1982) Centre for Contemporary Cultural Studies, *The Empire Strikes Back: Race and Racism in '70's Britain* (London: Hutchinson).

GLAZER, NATHAN (1983) *Ethnic Dilemmas: 1964–1982* (Cambridge, Mass.: Harvard University Press).

GLAZER, N. and D. P. MOYNIHAN (1963) *Beyond the Melting Pot: Negroes, Puerto Ricans, Jews, Italians & Irish of New York City* (Cambridge, Mass.: MIT and Harvard University Press).

GLAZER, N., and D. P. MOYNIHAN (1975) *Ethnicity: Theory and Experience* (Cambridge, Mass.: Harvard University Press).

GOLDLUST, J. and A. H. RICHMOND (1974a) 'A Multivariate Model of Immigrant Adaptation', *International Migration Review,* 8:2, 193–224.

GOLDLUST, J. and A. H. RICHMOND (1974b) *Multivariate Analysis of Immigrant Adaptation. A Study of Male Householders in Metropolitan Toronto* (Toronto: York University Ethnic Research Programme).

GOLDLUST, J. and A. H. RICHMOND (1977) 'Factors Associated with Commitment to and Identification with Canada', in W. Isajiw (ed.) *Identifies: The Impact of Ethnicity on Canadian Society,* (Toronto: Peter Martin)

GOLDLUST, J. and A. H. RICHMOND (1978) 'Cognitive and Linguistic Acculturation of Immigrants in Toronto: A Multivariate Analysis', *Ethnic Studies,* 2, 1, 2–17.

Select Bibliography and References

GOLDSTEIN, J. E. and R. M. BIENVENUE (1980) *Ethnicity and Ethnic Relations in Canada* (Toronto: Butterworths).

GORDON, M. M. (1964) *Assimilation in American Life* (New York: Oxford University Press)

GORDON, M. M. (1978) *Human Nature, Class and Ethnicity* (New York: Oxford University Press)

GRANT, R. and S. WELLHOFER (eds.) (1978) *Ethno-nationalism, Multinational Corporations and the Modern State* (Colorado: University of Denver).

GREEN, A. G. (1976) *Immigration and the Post War Canadian Economy,* (Toronto: Macmillan).

GUINDON, HUBERT (1978) 'The modernization of Quebec and the Legitimacy of the Canadian State', in D. Glenday, N. Guindon and A. Turowetz (eds), *Modernization and the Canadian State* (Toronto: Macmillan)

GURR, T. R. (1970) *Why Men Rebel* (New Jersey: Princeton University Press).

HABERMAS, JURGEN (1976) *Legitimation Crisis* (London: Heinemann)

HAINES, D., D. RUTHERFORD, and P. THOMAS (1981) 'Family and Community Among Vietnamese Refugees', *International Migration, Review* XV. 1/2, 310–19.

HARRIS, J. and T. WALLACE (1983) *To Ride the Storm: The 1980 Bristol 'Riot' and the State* (London: Heineman).

HARTMAN, P. and C. HUSBAND (1974) *Racism and the Mass Media* (London: Davis-Poynter).

HAUSER, PHILIP (1970) 'Zero Population Growth', *Population Index*, vol. 36, 4. (Oct.–Dec.).

HAWKINS, FREDA (1972) *Canada and Immigration: Public Policy and Public Concern* (Montreal: McGill-Queens Press).

HAWKINS, FREDA (1974) *Immigration Policy and Management in Selected Countries* (Ottawa: Manpower and Immigration).

HAWKINS, FREDA (1982) 'Multiculturalism in Two Countries: The Canadian and Australian Experience' *Journal of Canadian Studies*, 17, 1 64–80.

HAWTHORN, H. B., and M. A. TREMBLAY (1966) *A Survey of the Contemporary Indians of Canada* (2 vols) (Ottawa: Queen's Printer)

HEAD, WILSON (1975) *The Black Presence in the Canadian Mosaic,* (Toronto: Ontario Human Rights Commission)

HEAD, WILSON (1980) *Adaptation of Immigrants in Metro Toronto: Perceptions of Ethnic and Racial Discrimination* (Toronto: York University).

HEATH, ANTHONY (1976) *Rational Choice and Social Exchange* (Cambridge: Cambridge University Press)

HECHTER, MICHAEL (1975) *Internal Colonialism: The Celtic Fringe in British National Development, 1536–1966* (London: Routledge & Kegan Paul).

HENRY, FRANCES (1973) *Forgotten Canadians: The Blacks of Nova Scotia* (Toronto: Longmans)

HENRY, FRANCES (1978) *The Dynamics of Racism in Toronto* (Toronto: York University).

198   *Select Bibliography and References*

HIGLEY, J., D. DEACON and D. SMART (1979) *Elites in Australia* (London: Routledge & Kegan Paul).

HIRO, DILIP (1973) *Black British, White British* (Harmondsworth, Penguin Books).

HOFFMANN-NOWOTNY, H–J. (1979) 'A Macrosociological Approach Toward a General Explanation of Migration and Related Phenomena', paper presented at the Conference Center, Bellagio, Italy.

HOFFMANN-NOWOTNY, H–J (1981) 'A Sociological Approach Toward a General Theory of Migration', in M. M. Kritz, *et al.* (eds), *Global Trends in Migration: Theory and Research on International Population Movements* (New York: Center for Migration Studies, 64–83.

HUGHES, D. and E. KALLEN (1974) *Anatomy of Racism: Canadian Dimensions* (Montreal: Harvest House).

HURD, W. BURTON (1965) *Ethnic Origin and Nativity of the Canadian People: 1941 Census Monograph* (Ottawa: Queen's Printer)

HUSBANDS, CHRISTOPHER T. (1983) *Racial Exclusion and the City: the Urban Support for the National Front* (London: George Allen & Unwin).

ISAAC, L., E. MUTRAN and S. STRYKER (1980) 'Political protest orientations among Black and White adults', *American Sociological Review* 45, 191–213.

ISAAC, L. and W. R. KELLY (1981) 'Racial insurgency, the State, and welfare expansion: Local and national level evidence from the post-war United States', *American Journal of Sociology* 86:6 1348–86.

ISAJIW, W. W. (1970) 'Definitions of Ethnicity', *Ethnicity*, 1, 1111–24.

ISAJIW, W. W. (1981) *Ethnic Identity Retention* (Toronto: Centre for Urban and Community Studies, University of Toronto, Research Paper, 125.

ISAJIW, W. W. and T. MAKABE (1982) *Socialization as a Factor in Ethnic Identity Retention* (Toronto: Centre for Urban and Community Studies, University of Toronto, Research Paper, 134).

JANSEN, C. J. (1981a) *The Italians of Vancouver: A Case Study of Internal Differentiation of an Ethnic Group* (Toronto: Institute for Behavioural Research, York University).

JANSEN, C. J. (1981b) *Education and Social Mobility of Immigrants: A Pilot Study focussing on Italians in Vancouver*, (Toronto: Institute for Behaviour Research, York University).

JEAN-BAPTISTE (1979) Jacqueline, *Haitians in Canada* (Ottawa: Supply and Services Canada).

JOHNSON, G. E. (1983) 'Chinese Canadians in the '70s: New Wine in New Bottles', in J. L. Elliott (ed.), *Two Nations, Many Cultures: Ethnic Groups in Canada* 2nd edition, (Toronto: Prentice Hall,) 393–411.

JUPP, JAMES (1984) *Ethnic Politics in Australia,* (Sydney: George Allen & Unwin).

KALBACH, W. E. (1981) *Ethnic Residential Segregation and its Significance for the Individual in an Urban Setting*, (Toronto: Centre for Urban and Community Studies, University of Toronto, Research Paper, 124).

KALBACH, W. E. and W. W. McVEY (1979) *The Demographic Bases of Canadian Society* (Toronto: McGraw-Hill Ryerson).

Select Bibliography and References 199

KALBACH, W. E., M. LANPHIER, D. RHYNE, and A. H. RICHMOND (1984) *Ethnogenerational Factors in Socioeconomic Achievement in Toronto: The Second Generation in the 1970's* (Toronto: Institute for Social Research, York University).

KALDOR, MARY (1978) *The Disintegrating West* (Harmondsworth: Penguin Books).

KALLEN, E. and M. KELNER (1983) *Ethnicity, Opportunity and Successful Entrepreneurship in Canada*, (Toronto: Institute for Behavioural Research, York University).

KALLEN, EVELYN (1982) *Ethnicity and Human Rights in Canada* (Toronto: Gage)

KELLY, W. R. and D. SNYDER (1980) 'Racial violence and socioeconomic changes among Blacks in the United States', *Social Forces*, 58: 739–60.

KERNER, OTTO (1968) *National Advisory Commission on Civil Disorders: Report* (Washington, DC: US Government Printing Office).

KERR, CLARK, J. T. DUNLOP, *et al.* (1960) *Industrialism and Industrial Man: The Problems of Labour and Management in Economic Growth*, (Cambridge: Harvard University Press).

KERR, CLARK (1983) *The Future of Industrial Societies: Convergence or Continuing Diversity?* (Cambridge: Harvard University Press).

KHLEIF, B. B. (1980) *Language, Ethnicity and Education in Wales* (The Hague: Mouton Publishers).

KRALT, JOHN (1976) *Language in Canada: 1971 Census Profile Study*, Bulletin 5.1–7 (Ottawa: Statistics Canada)

KUBAT, DANIEL, (ed.) (1979) *The Politics of Migration Policies*, (New York: Centre for Migration Studies).

KUBAT, DANIEL (ed.) (1984) *The Politics of Return: International Return Migration in Europe*, (Rome & New York: Center for Migration Studies).

KUBAT, D. and H–J. HOFFMANN-NOWOTNY (1982) 'International and internal Migration: towards a New paradigm', in T. Bottomore, S. Nowak and M. Sokolowska, (eds), *Sociology: State of the Art*, (London: Sage).

KUMAR, KRISHAN (1976) 'Industrialism and Postindustrialism: Reflections on a Putative Transition', *Sociological Review*, 24:3, 439–78.

KUMAR, KRISHAN (1978) *Prophecy and Progress: The Sociology of Industrial and Post-Industrial Society* (Harmondsworth: Penguin Books).

LAI, VIVIEN (1970) *The Assimilation of Chinese Groups in Toronto*, unpublished MA thesis, (Toronto: York University).

LAM, LAWRENCE (1982) 'Chinese-Canadian Families in Toronto', *International Journal of the Sociology of the Family*, 12:1, 11–32.

LAM, LAWRENCE (1983) *Vietnamese-Chinese Refugees in Montreal* unpublished Ph.D. dissertation (Toronto: York University).

LANPHIER, MICHAEL (1979) *A Study of Third World Immigrants* (Ottawa: Economic Council of Canada).

LANPHIER, MICHAEL (1981) 'Canada's Response to Refugees', *International Migration Review*, 17:1, 4–33.

Select Bibliography and References

LANPHIER, MICHAEL (1983) 'Refugee Resettlement Models in Action', *International Migration Review* 15:1–2 113–130.

LAPIDUS, GAIL W. (1984) 'Ethnonationalism and Political Stability: The Soviet Case', *'World Politics*, XXXVI: 4, 555–80.

LAPORTE, PIERRE. (1983) 'Language Planning and the Status of French in Quebec', in Jean Elliott (ed.), *Two Nations, Many Cultures,* (Toronto: Prentice-Hall).

LAWRENCE, ERROL (1982) 'Just Plain Common Sense: The Roots of Racism', in CCCS, *The Empire Strikes Back; Race and Racism in 70s Britain* (London: Hutchinson) pp.47–94.

LEE, TREVOR (1977) *Race and Residence: The Concentration and dispersal of Immigrants in London* (Oxford: Clarendon Press)

LENIN, V. I. (1970) *Questions of National Policy and Proletarian Internationalism* (Moscow: Progress Publishers)

LENIN, V. I. (1984) *On Imperialism and Imperialists* (Moscow: Progress Publishers).

LIEBERSON, STANLEY (1961) 'A Societal Theory of Race and Ethnic Relations', *American Sociological Review*, 26 902–910.

LIEBERSON, STANLEY (1963) *Ethnic Patterns in American Cities* (New York: Free Press).

LIEBERSON, STANLEY (1981) *Piece of the Pie: Blacks and White Immigrants since 1880* (Berkeley: University of California Press).

LIEBERSON, S. and A. R. SILVERMAN (1965) 'The precipitants and underlying conditions of race riots', *American Sociological Review* 30:6.

MANNHEIM, KARL (1936) *Ideology and Utopia* (London: Routledge & Kegan Paul).

MARR, W. L. (1976) *Labour Market and Other Implications of Immigration Policy for Ontario.* (Toronto: Ontario Economic Council).

MARTIN, J. I. (1978) *The Migrant Presence* (Studies in Society, 2) (Sydney: George Allen & Unwin).

MASTERS, R. D. (1983) 'The Biological Nature of the State', *World Politics*, XXXV: 2, 161–93.

MATA, FERNANDO (1983) 'The Latin American Immigration to Canada, 1946–1981', paper presented at the CALACS conference (Ottawa: Carleton University).

MATA, FERNANDO (1985) 'Latin American Immigration to Canada: Some Reflections on the Immigration Statistics', *Canadian Journal of Latin American and Caribbean Studies* X:20, 27–42.

McDIARMID, D. and D. PRATT (1971) *Teaching Prejudice: A content Analysis of Social Sciences Textbooks Authorized for Use in Ontario Schools* (Toronto: Ontario Institute for Studies in Education).

McLUHAN, MARHSALL (1964) *Understanding Media: The Extensions of Man* (New York: McGraw-Hill).

MILES, R. and A. PHIZACKLEA, (eds.) (1979) *Racism and Political Action in Britain* (London: Routledge & Kegan Paul).

MYRDAL, A. (1976) *The Game of Disarmament: How the United States and Russia Run the Arms Race* (New York: Pantheon Books).

MYRDAL, GUNNAR (1944) *An American Dilemma* (New York: Harper).

Select Bibliography and References

NAGATA, JUDITH A. (1974) 'What is a Malay?: Situation Selection of Ethnic Identity in a Plural Society', *American Ethnologist* 1: 2, 331–350.

NEUWIRTH, G. and L. CLARK (1981) 'Indochinese Refugees in Canada: Sponsorship and Adjustment', *International Migration Review* XV: 1–2, 131–140.

NORA, S., and A. MINC (1978) *The Computerization of Society* (Cambridge, Mass.: The MIT Press).

O'BRYAN, K. G., J. C. REITZ and O. M KUPLOWSKA (1976) *Non-Official Languages Study: A Study of Canadian Multiculturalism* (Ottawa: Supply & Services).

OCC, (ONTARIO CONSERVATION COUNCIL) (1972–73) *A Population Policy for Canada: The Proceedings of Two Seminars on the Need for a Population Policy: the Impact of People on the Environment* (Toronto: Ontario Conservation Council).

O'CALLAGHAN, MARION O. (1980) (ed.), *Sociological Theories: Race and Colonialism* (Paris: UNESCO).

OECD (1981) *Young Foreigners and the World of Work*, (Paris: OECD).

OPCS (1984) 'Labour Force Survey 1983: Country of Birth, Ethnic origin, Nationality and Year of Entry', *OPCS Monitor*, 18 Dec.

ORNSTEIN, M. D. (1981) 'The occupational mobility of men in Ontario', *Canadian Review of Anthropology*, 18:2, 183–215.

ORNSTEIN, M. D. (1982) *The Work Experience of Immigrants to Canada: 1969–1976* (Toronto: Institute for Behavioural Research, York University).

ORNSTEIN, M. D. and R. D. SHARMA (1983) *Adjustment and Economic Experience of Immigrants in Canada: 1976 Longitudinal Survey of Immigrants* Report to Employment and Immigration Canada (Toronto: Institute for Behavioural Research, York University).

PARAI, L. (1974) *The Economic Impact of Immigration* (Ottawa: Manpower and Immigration).

PARSONS, TALCOTT (1952) *The Social System* (London: Tavistock).

PATEL, D. (1980) *Dealing with Interracial Conflict: Policy Alternatives* (Montreal: The Institute for Research on Public Policy).

PEACH, CERI (1968) *West Indian Migration to Britain: A Social Geography*, (London: Oxford University Press)

PEARSON, D. G. (1981) *Race, Class and Political Activism: A Study of West Indians in Britain* (Farnborough: Gower)

PEPIN, JEAN-LUC and J. P. ROBARTS (1979) 'A Future Together: Observations and Recommendations', *Task Force on Canadian Unity* (Ottawa: Supply & Services Canada).

PETER, K. (1981) 'The Myth of Multiculturalism and Other Political Fables', in J. Dahlie and T. Fernando (eds), *Ethnicity, Power and Politics in Canada* (Toronto: Methuen) 56–67.

PETRAS, ELIZABETH (1981) 'The Global Labour Market in the Modern World Economy', in M. Kritz *et al.* (eds), *Global Trends in Migration*, (New York: Center for Migration Studies) 44–63.

PHILPOTT, STUART (1973) *West Indian Migration: The Monserrat Case*, (London: Athlone).

PHIZACLEA, A. and R. MILES (1981) *Labour and Racism* (London: Routledge & Kegan Paul, 1981).

202 *Select Bibliography and References*

PICHE, V., S. LAROSE and M. LABELLE (1983) *L'Immigration Caraibeenne au Canada et au Quebec: Aspects Statistiques* (Montreal: Centre de Recherches Caraibe, Universite de Montreal).

PITMAN, WALTER (1977) *Now is Not Too Late: Report submitted to the Council of Metropolitan Toronto by the Task Force on Human Relations* (Toronto: Metro Council).

PIVEN, F. F. and R. A. CLOWARD (1971) *Regulating the Poor: The Functions of Public Welfare* (New York: Vintage).

PORTER, JOHN (1965) *The Vertical Mosaic: An Analysis of Social Class and Power in Canada* (Toronto: University of Toronto Press).

PORTER, JOHN (1975) 'Ethnic pluralism in Canadian perspective', in N. Glazer and D. P. Moynihan (eds), *Ethnicity, Theory and Experience*, Cambridge, Mass.: Harvard University Press) 267–304.

PORTES, A. (1981) 'Modes of Structural Incorporation and Present Theories of Labor Immigration', in M. Kritz, *et al.* (eds) *Global Trends in Migration*, (New York: Center for Migration Studies) 279–297.

PRICE, CHARLES, (1974) *The Great White Walls are Built: Restrictive Immigration to North America and Australasia, 1836–1888.* (Canberra: Australian National University Press).

PRICE, CHARLES (1975) 'Australian Immigration: A Review of the Demographic Effects of Post-War Immigration on the Australian Population', *Research Report No. 2 of the National Population Inquiry* (Canberra: Australian Government Publishing Service).

PRICE, CHARLES (1979) *Australian Immigration, A Bibliography and Digest*, no. 4 (Canberra: Australian National University).

PRICE, CHARLES (1980) 'International Migration: Contribution to Growth and Distribution of the Australian Population', Paper presented at a conference on the Population of Australia (Canberra: September).

PRICE, CHARLES (1984) *Birthplaces of the Australian Population, 1861–1981,* Working Papers in Demography 13 (Canberra: Australia National University).

PRICE, CHARLES (1985) 'Refugees and Mass Migration: Australia', paper presented at the meetings of the International Sociological Association, Research Committee on Migration (Dubrovnik, June).

PRICE, CHARLES and J. M. MARTIn (1976) *Australian Immigration: A bibliography and Digest* (Canberra: Australian National University).

PRYCE, K. (1979) *Endless Pressure, A Study of West Indian Life-Styles* (Harmondsworth: Penguin Books).

RAMCHARAN, SUBHAS (1974) 'The Adaptation of West Indians in Canada', Doctoral thesis (Toronto: York University).

RAMCHARAN, SUBHAS (1976) 'Analysis of the Perception of Discrimination by West Indians in Toronto', *Rikha*, 3:3

RAMCHARAN, SUBHAS, (1982) *Racism: Nonwhites in Canada* (Toronto: Butterworths).

RAMPTON, A. (1981) *West Indian Children and Our Schools*, Interim report of Committee (London: HMSO).

RAO, L., A. H. RICHMOND and J. ZUBRZYCKI (1984) *Immigrants in Canada and Australia, vol. 1: Demographic aspects and Education* (Toronto: Institute for Social Research, York University).

Select Bibliography and References 203

REEVES, FRANK (1983) *British Racial Discourse: A Study of British Political Discourse about Race* (Cambridge University Press).

REITZ, J. G. (1980) *The Survival of Ethnic Groups* (Toronto: McGraw-Hill Ryerson Ltd).

REITZ, J. G. (1982) *Ethnic Group Control of Jobs:* Research Paper #133 (Toronto: Centre for Urban & Community Studies).

REITZ, J. G., L. CALZAVARA and D. DASKO (1981) *Ethnic Inequality and Segregation in Jobs,* Research Paper #123 (Toronto: Centre for Urban & Community Studies).

REX, JOHN (1970) *Race Relations in Sociological Theory* (London: Weidenfeld and Nicolson).

REX, JOHN (1973) *Race, Colonialism and the City* (London: Routledge & Kegan Paul).

REX, JOHN (1979) 'Sociology, theory, typology, value standpoints and research', in J. Rex, S. Tomlinson *et al.*, *Colonial Immigrants in a British City* (London: Routledge & Kegan Paul)

REX, JOHN (1981) *Social Conflicts: A Conceptual and Theoretical Analysis* (London: Longmans).

REX, JOHN and ROBERT MOORE (1967) *Race, Community and Conflict: A Study of Sparkbrook* (London: Oxford University Press).

REX, JOHN and SALLY TOMLINSON *et al.* (1979) *Colonial Immigrants in a British City: A Class Analysis* (London: Routledge & Kegan Paul).

RHYNE, DARLA (1983) *Visible Minority Business in Metropolitan Toronto* (Toronto: Ontario Human Rights Commission).

RHYNE, DARLA, W. KALBACH, *et al.* (1983) *Ethnogenerational Factors in Socioeconomic Achievement in Toronto: The Second Generation During the 1970s* (Toronto: Institute for Behavioural Research, York University).

RICHARDSON, ALAN (1967) 'Theory and Method for the Psychological Study of Assimilation', *International Migration Review*, 2:1, 1–30.

RICHARDSON, ALAN (1974) *British Immigrants and Australia, A Psycho-social Inquiry*, (Canberra: Australian National University Press).

RICHMOND, ANTHONY H. (1950) 'Economic insecurity and stereotypes as factors in Colour Prejudice', *Sociological Review*, 17, 147–70.

RICHMOND, ANTHONY H., (1960) 'Applied Sociology and Public Policy Concerning Racial Relations in Britain', *Race*, 1:2, 14–26.

RICHMOND, ANTHONY H. (1967) *Post War Immigrants in Canada*, (Toronto: University of Toronto Press).

RICHMOND, ANTHONY H. (1969) 'Sociology of migration in industrial and post-industrial societies', in J. A. Jackson (ed.), *Migration: Sociological Studies 2*, (London: Cambridge University Press).

RICHMOND, ANTHONY H. (1973) 'Race Relations and Behaviour in Reality', in P. Watson (ed.) *Psychology and Race* (Harmondsworth: Penguin Books).

RICHMOND, ANTHONY H. (1974a) 'Migration, Ethnicity and Race Relations', in G. Tapinos (ed.), *Demographic Research in Relation to International Migration* (Paris: CICRED).

RICHMOND, ANTHONY H. (1974b) *Aspects of the Absorption of Immigrants* (Ottawa: Manpower & Immigration).

204 *Select Bibliography and References*

RICHMOND, ANTHONY H., (1975) 'Canadian Immigration: Recent Developments and Future Prospects', *International Migration*, 13:4, 163–182.

RICHMOND, ANTHONY H. (1976) 'Urban conflict in Britain and Canada: A comparative perspective', in S. E. Clark and J. Obler (eds.), *Urban Ethnic Conflict: A Comparative Perspective* (Chapel Hill: University of North Carolina) 164–204.

RICHMOND, ANTHONY H. (1975–76) 'Black and Asian Immigrants in Britain and Canada: Some Comparisons', *New. Community*, 4: 4, 501–516.

RICHMOND, ANTHONY H. (1978) 'Migration, Ethnicity and Race Relations', *Ethnic and Racial Studies* 1:1, 1–17.

RICHMOND, ANTHONY H. (1981) 'Environmental Conservation: A New Racist Ideology?' in R. S. Bryce-Laporte (ed.), *Sourcebook on the New Immigration*, (New Jersey: Transaction Books).

RICHMOND, ANTHONY H. (1981a) 'Immigrant Adaptation in a Post Industrial Society', in M. M. Kritz, C. B. Keely, and S. M. Tomasi (eds.), *Global Trends in Migration: Theory and Research on International Population Movements* (New York: Center for Migration Studies, 298–319.

RICHMOND, ANTHONY H. (1981b) *Comparative Studies in The Economic Adaptation of Immigrants in Canada* (Toronto: Institute for Behavioural Research, York University).

RICHMOND, ANTHONY H. (1982a) 'Canadian Unemployment and the Threat to Multiculturalism', *Journal of Canadian Studies*, 17:1, 81–92.

RICHMOND, ANTHONY H. (1982b) (ed.), *After the Referenda: The Future of Ethnic Nationalism in Britain and Canada* (Toronto: Institute for Behavioural Research, York University).

RICHMOND, ANTHONY H. (1983) 'Immigration et Diversité Culturelle au Canada et en Australie' presented at colloquium, University of Paris, Val de Marne, Créteuil, France.

RICHMOND, ANTHONY H. (1984a) Special Issue: After the Referenda: The Future of Ethnic Nationalism, *Ethnic and Racial Studies*, 7:1.

RICHMOND, ANTHONY H. (1984b) 'Ethnic Nationalism and Postindustrialism' *Ethnic and Racial Studies*, 7:1, 4–18.

RICHMOND, A. H., and J. GOLDLUST (1977) *Family and Social Integration of Immigrants in Toronto* (Toronto: Institute for Behavioural Research, York University).

RICHMOND, A. H. and W. E. KALBACH (1980) *Factors in the Adjustment of Immigrants and their Descendants* (Ottawa: Ministry of Supply and Services).

RICHMOND, A. H. and G. L. RAO (1977) 'Recent Developments in Immigration to Canada and Australia: A Comparative Analysis', *International Journal of Comparative Sociology* 17, 183–205.

RICHMOND, A. H., and R. B. P. VERMA (1978) 'Income Inequality in Canada: Ethnic & Generational Aspects', *Canadian Studies in Population*, 5 25–36.

RICHMOND, A. H. and F. RICHMOND (eds.), *Immigrants in Canada and Australia*, vol. 1. *Demographic Aspects and Education* vol. 2. *Econo-*

Select Bibliography and References

mic Adaptation vol. 3. *Urban and Ecological Aspects* (Toronto: Institute for Social Research, York University).

RICHMOND, A. H. and J. ZUBRZYCKI (1984) *Immigrants in Canada and Australia: Economic adaptation,* (Toronto: Institute for Social Research, York University).

RICHMOND, A. H. and J. ZUBRZYCKI (1981) 'Occupational Status in Canada and Australia: A Comparative Study of the Native and the Foreign Born', in R. F. Thomasson (ed.), *Comparative Social Research: An Annual Publication,* vol. 4 (JAI Press) 91–110.

ROGERS, ROSEMARIE (1978) *On the Process of International Migrants', Integration into Host Societies: A Hypothesis and Comments* (Cambridge: Centre for International Studies, Massachusetts Institute of Technology).

ROGERS, ROSEMARIE (1981) 'Incentives to Return: Patterns of Policies and Migrants' Responses', in M. K. Kritz, C. B. Keely, and S. M. Tomasi, (eds.), *Global Trends in Migration: Theory and Research on International Population Movements* (New York: Center for Migration Studies) 338–364.

ROSE, RICHARD (1971) *Governing Without Consensus* (London: Faber & Faber).

ROSE, S., L. J. KAMIN, and R. C. LEWONTIN (1984) *Not In Our Genes: Biology, Ideology and Human Nature* (Harmondsworth: Penguin).

ROTHSCHILD, JOSEPH (1981) *Ethnopolitics: A Conceptual Framework* (New York: Columbia University Press).

ROYAL COMMISSION ON BI-LINGUALISM & BI-CULTURALISM (1970) *The Other Ethnic Groups* (Vol. 4) (Ottawa: Queen's Printer).

SAID, ABDUL & L. R. SIMMONS (1976) *Ethnicity in an International Context* (New Brunswick, New Jersey: Transaction Books).

SALTER, M. J., (1978) *Studies in the Immigration of the Highly Skilled* (Canberra: Australian National University Press).

SAMPSON, A. (1977) *The Arms Bazaar. The Companies, the Dealers, the Backers: From Vickers to Lockheed* (London: Hodder & Stoughton).

SAUNDERS, G. S. (1978) 'The Labour Market Adaptation of Third World Immigrants', in Economic Council of Canada, *For a Common Future. A Study of Canada's Relations with Developing Countries* (Ottawa: Supply and Services, Canada).

SCARMAN, Rt. Hon. Lord (1981) *The Brixton Disorders: Report of a Special Commission* (London: HMSO, Cmnd. 8427).

SCIENCE COUNCIL OF CANADA (1976) *Population, Technology and Resources,* Report no. 5 (Ottawa: Supply and Services, Canada).

SERAFINI, S., and M. ANDRIEU (1980) *The Information Revolution and its Implications for Canada* (Hull, Quebec: Supply and Services Canada).

SHARMA, R. D. (1980) *Trends in the Demographic and Socio-economic Characteristics of Metropolitan Toronto* (Toronto: Institute for Behavioural Research).

SHARMA, R. D. (1981a) 'Perceived Difficulties of Foreign-born Population and Services of Agencies' unpublished report (Toronto: Institute for Behavioural Research, York University).

206 *Select Bibliography and References*

SHARMA, R. D. (1981b) 'A Multivariate Analysis of Difficulties Reported by Long Term Third World and non-Anglophone Immigrants, in Toronto Three Years or More' unpublished report (Toronto: Institute for Behavioural Research, York University).

SMILEY, DONALD (1981) *The Canadian Charter of Rights and Freedoms* (Ontario Economic Council).

SMITH, ANTHONY D. (1971) *Theories of Nationalism* (London: Duckworth)

SMITH, ANTHONY D. (1973) *Concept of Social Change: a Critique of Functionalist Theory* (London: Routledge & Kegan Paul).

SMITH, ANTHONY D. (1976) *Social Change: Social Theory and Historical Process* (London: Longman).

SMITH, ANTHONY D. (1979) 'Towards a Theory of Ethnic Nationalism', *Ethnic and Racial Studies*, 2:1 21–37.

SMITH, ANTHONY D. (1981a) 'War and Ethnicity: the role of warfare in the formation . . .', *Ethnic and Racial Studies*, 4:4 375–97.

SMITH, ANTHONY D. (1981b) *The Ethnic Revival in the Modern World* (Cambridge: Cambridge University Press).

SMITH, ANTHONY D. (1983) *State and Nation in the Third World: The Western State and African Nationalism* (Sussex: Wheatsheaf (Harvester)).

SMITH, ANTHONY D. (1984) 'Ethnic Persistence and National Transformation', *British Journal of Sociology* XXXV:3 452–61.

SMITH, T. E. (1981) *Commonwealth Migration: Flows and Policies* (London: Macmillan).

SMOLICZ, J. J. (1979) *Culture and Education in a Plural Society* (Sydney: Curriculum Development Centre).

SPENCER, HERBERT (1967) *The Evolution of Society* (Chicago: University of Chicago Press).

STATISTICS CANADA (1979a) *International and Inter-provincial Migration in Canada* (Ottawa: Statistics Canada, Catalogue 91–208).

STATISTICS CANADA, (1979b) *Annual Elements of Population Growth, Canada 1955–56 to 1978–79* Catalogue 91–201 (Ottawa: Statistics Canada).

STATISTICS CANADA (1984) *Canada's Immigrants* Cat. 99–936 (Ottawa: Statistics Canada).

STONE, JOHN (ed.) (1979) Special Issue: Internal Colonialism, *Ethnic and Racial Studies*, 2:3.

SWANN, MICHAEL (LORD) (1985) *Education for All* (London: HMSO, Cmnd. 9453).

SZYMANSKI, A. (1978) *The Capitalist State and the Policy of Class* (Cambridge, Mass.: Winthrop).

TAFT, RONALD (1966) *From Stranger to Citizen* (London: Tavistock).

TAEUBER, K. E. and A. F. TAEUBER (1965) *Negroes in Cities* (New York: Aldine Press).

THOMAS W. I. and F. ZANIECKI (1918) *The Polish Peasant in Europe and America* (Chicago: University of Chicago Press) 2 vols.

TOFFLER, A. (1970) *Future Shock* (New York: Random House).

TOFFLER, A. (1981) *The Third Wave* (New York: Bantam Books).

Select Bibliography and References

TOMASI, S. M. (1981) 'Sociopolitical Participation of Migrants in the Receiving Countries', in M. M. Kritz, C. B. Kelly and S. M. Tomasi (eds.), *Global Trends in Migration: Theory and Research on International Population Movements* (New York: Center for Migration Studies) 320–337.

TOMLINSON, SALLY (1983) *Ethnic Minorities and British Schools* (London: Heinemann).

TOMLINSON, SALLY (1984) *Home and School in Multicultural Britain* (London: Batsford).

TONNIES, F. (1957) *Community and Society* trans. and ed. L. P. Loomis (East Lansing, Mich: Michigan State University Press).

TOURAINE, A. (1971) *The Post-Industrial Society* (New York: Random House.

TROPER, HAROLD (1972) *Only Farmers Need Apply: Official Canadian Government Encouragement of Immigration from the United States, 1896–1911*, (Toronto: Griffin House).

TURRITTIN, A. H. (1974) 'Social Mobility in Canada: A Comparison of three Provincial Studies and some Methodological Questions'. *Canadian Review Sociology and Anthropology*, Special Issue, 163–86.

VAN DEN BERGHE, PIERRE (1975) *Man in Society: A Biosocial View* (New York: Elsevier).

VAN DEN BERGHE, PIERRE (1981) *The Ethnic Phenomenon* (New York: Elsevier).

VAN DEN BERGHE, PIERRE (1983) 'Ethnic Melting Pots or Plural Societies?' *Australian & New Zealand Journal of Sociology* 21:2, 238–252.

VANNEMAN, R. D. and T. F. PETTIGREW (1972) 'Race and relative deprivation in the urban United States', *Race*, 4: April, 461–86.

VILLEMEZ, W. T. and C. H. WISWELL (1978) 'The impact of discrimination on the internal size distribution of Black income: 1954–74. *Social Forces*, 56, 1019–34.

WALLERSTEIN, I. (1974) *The Modern World System* (New York: Academic Press).

WARBURG, GABRIEL (1978) *Islam, Nationalism and Communism in a Traditional Society* (London: Cass).

WATSON, J. L. (ed.) (1977) *Between Two Cultures: Migrants and Minorities in Britain* (Oxford: Basil Blackwell)

WEAVER, SALLY M. (1983) 'The Status of Indian Women' in Jean Elliott (ed.), *Two Nations, Many Cultures* (Toronto: Prentice-Hall).

WESTELL, ANTHONY (1979) 'Frank talk needed on immigration', *Toronto Star*, (15 September).

WEBER, MAX (1946) *Max Weber: Essays in Sociology,* trans. and ed. H. H. Gerth and C. W. Mills (London: Oxford University Press).

WILSON, EDWARD O. (1975) *Sociobiology: The New Synthesis* (Cambridge: Harvard University Press).

WIRTH, LOUIS (1936) 'Types of Nationalism', *American Journal of Sociology*, XLI, 723–737.

WONG, LLOYD (1984) 'Canada's Guestworkers: Some Comparisons of Temporary Workers in Europe and North America', *International Migration Review*, 18: 185–89.

Select Bibliography and References

YOUNG, CHRISTABEL (1980) 'Characteristics of the Young Migrant Labour Force,' unpublished paper (Canberra: Department of Sociology, Australian National University).

ZIEGLER, B. M. (ed.) (1953) *Immigration: An American Dilemma* (Boston: D. C. Heath).

NAME INDEX

Abella, Rosalie S. 132
ACPEA (Australian Council on Population and Ethnic Affairs) 15, 16
Adorno, T. W. 157–8
Akiwowo, A. 168
Anderson, G. M., 60
Andrieu, M. 175, 185
Axworthy, Lloyd 114

Banks, J. A. 46
Banks, Margaret A. 126
Banton, Michael P. 25, 44–5, 97, 157
Barber, C. L. 79
Barth, F. 142
Basavarajappa, K. G. 87, 131
Bell, D. 1, 3, 173
Benyon, John 21
Berry, J. N. 116
Blainey, G. 17
Blau, Peter 157
Blauner, Robert 178
Boldt, M. 130
Bonacich, Edna 35
Borovoy, A. A. 117
Borrie, W. D. 15, 104
Bostock, William 18
Breton, Raymond 108, 136, 179
Brown, Colin 22
Brown, Craig 180
Bryce-Laporte, R. S. 79
Buchignani, Norman 91, 132
Bullivant, Brian M. 17, 53
Bulmer, Martin 31
Burgess, E. W. 31
Burnet, Jean 107, 129
Burnley, I. H. 36

Calzavara, L. 114
Cameron, David 173
Castles, S. 25, 34, 60

CCCS (Centre for Contemporary Cultural Studies) 40
Chan, Kwok 90
Chow, Maria 90
Christie, L. T. 60
Clark, L. 53
Clement, Wallace 14, 34, 108, 116
Clodman, J. 86, 109, 113, 121
Cloward, R. A. 120
Cohen, P. S. 168
Collins, D. 117
Con, Harry 90
Connor, Walker 143, 151
Cox, D. 16
Cox, O. C. 167
CRE (Commission for Racial Equality) 19, 40
Cummings, S. 121

Darroch, G. 116
Darwin, Charles 148
Dasko, D. 114
Davey, Alfred 23
Davies, G. W. 68
Davis, N. N. W. 71, 73
Davison, R. B. 23
Deacon, D. 17
Demers, R. 68
Denton, F. T. 67, 80
Deutsch, Karl W. 151, 171
DeVries, J. 63
Dofny, J. 168
Driedger, Leo 133
Durkheim, E. 31, 32, 169

Economic Council of Canada 113
Edwards, R. C. 35, 121
Eisenstadt, S. N. 33
Employment and Immigration Canada, 68

209

210 *Name Index*

Encel, Solomon 17
Enloe, Cynthia H. 161–3
Etzioni, A. 41
Etzioni-Halevy, Eva 3

Fanon, F. 158
Fenner, F. J. 103
Fisher, N. W. F. 67
Foot, Paul 101
Forcese, D. P. 115
Ford, G. W. 67
Frazier, Franklin 31
Fromm, Erich 157–8
Furnivall, J. S. 33–4

Galbraith, J. K. 173
Gellner, Ernest 142, 151–2
Giddens, Anthony 5, 39, 41–2
Glazer, Nathan 2, 156, 167
Goldlust, J. 36, 51, 54, 55, 88, 113
Gordon, M. M. 33
Grant, R. 147
Green, A. G. 69, 109
Guindon, Hubert 180
Gupta, M. L. 71, 73
Gurr, T. R. 119

Habermas, J. 5
Haines, D. 53
Hartmann, P. 23
Hauser, Philip 105
Hawkins, Freda 16, 58, 69
Head, Wilson 116
Heath, Anthony 157
Hechter, Michael 154, 178
Henry, Frances 12, 116
Higley, J. 17
Hiro, Dilip 120
Hoffmann-Nowotny, H.–J. 30, 31
Hughes, D. 117
Husband, Charles 23

IBR (Institute for Behavioural Research) 115
Indra, D. M. 132
Isaac, L. 119, 120
Isajiw, W. W. 63, 64, 142

Jean-Baptiste, Jacqueline 89
Johnson, G. E. 90
Jupp, James 17

Kalbach, W. E. 12, 36, 54, 60, 86, 88, 107, 111–2, 115, 131
Kaldor, Mary 174, 184
Kalin, R. 116
Kallen, Evelyn 57, 117, 133
Kamin, L. J. 150
Kelly, W. R. 120
Kelner, M. 57
Kerner, Otto 121
Kerr, Clark 1
Khleif, B. B. 180
Kosak, G. 34, 60
Kubat, Daniel 12, 30, 37, 52
Kumar, Krishan 3, 173
Kuplowska, O. M. 107

Lai, Vivien 90
Lam, Lawrence 90
Lanphier, C. Michael 82, 85
Lapidus, Gail W. 153
Laporte, Pierre 128
Lawrence, Errol 22
Lenin, V. I. 34, 152–3, 167
Lewontin, R. C. 150
Lieberson, Stanley 33, 121, 135
Long, J. R. 130
Lynch, J. 46

McCallum, J. C. P. 79
McDiarmid, D. 117
McLuhan, Marshall 2
McVey, W. W. 107
Makabe, T. 64
Malthus, Thomas R. 30, 148
Mannheim, Karl 101
Marr, W. L. 68
Martin, J. I. 16, 61
Marx, Karl 30–1, 34, 152–3, 167
Masters, R. D. 149
Mata, Fernando 85–6
Miles, R. 21, 65
Minc, A. 175
Moore, Robert 35
Moynihan, D. P. 2, 156, 167
Mutran, E. 119

Name Index

Myrdal, A. 172
Myrdal, Gunnar 135, 137

Nagata, Judith A. 142
Neuwirth, G. 53
Nora, S. 175

OECD (Organisation for
  Economic Co-operation and
  Development) 13
OCC (Ontario Conservation
  Council) 103
OPCS (Office of Population,
  Census and Surveys) 19
Ornstein, M. D. 86–7, 113, 116

Park, Robert 31–3
Parai, L. 68, 109
Parsons, Talcott 168
Patel, D. 117, 119, 120
Pepin, Jean-Luc 125
Peter, K. 108
Petras, Elizabeth 9
Pettigrew, T. F. 119
Phizacklea, A. 21, 65
Piche, V. 89
Pitman, Walter 117
Piven, F. F. 120
Porter, John 14, 115
Portes, A. 34
Powell, Enoch 101
Pratt, D. 117
Price, Charles 15, 18, 79, 98,
  101
Pryce, K. 65

Ramcharan, S. 88–9, 116
Rampton, A. 24
Rao, L. 15, 36, 102
Reitz, J. G. 59, 107, 108, 114,
  167, 185

Rex, John 5, 21, 35, 44, 60, 97,
  155
Rhyne, Darla 87
Richardson, Alan 33, 55
Richmond, Anthony H. 1, 2, 9,
  12, 15, 16, 21, 36, 42, 44,
  46, 54–6, 58, 60, 65, 86, 87,

88, 102, 110, 111–13, 114, 115
116, 120, 164, 183, 184, 185
Robarts, J. P. 125
Robb, A. L. 67, 80
Rogers, Rosemarie 55, 62
Rose, Richard 145
Rose, S. 150

Said, Abdul 151
Salter, M. J. 68
Sampson, A. 172
Saunders, G. S. 78
Scarman, Rt Hon. Lord 21, 61
  65
Science Council of Canada 104
Serafini, S. 175, 185
Sharma, R. D. 87, 88, 113
Silverman, A. R. 121
Simmons, L. R. 151
Smart, D. 17,
Smiley, Donald 125
Smith, Anthony 41, 59, 159–60,
  164, 171
Smolicz, J. J. 17, 54
Snyder, D. 120
Spencer, B. G. 67, 80
Spencer, Herbert 31, 148
Statistics Canada 11, 12, 79, 90
  110
Srivastava, R. 133
Stonequist, E. V. 31
Stryker, S. 119
Swann, Michael (Lord) 24
Szymanski, A. 121

Taft, Ronald 33
Taylor, D. M. 116
Thomas, W. I. 31
Toffler, A. 1, 3, 175
Tomasi, S. M. 52
Tomlinson, Sally 21, 35, 60,
  155
Tonnies, F. 170
Touraine, A. 1, 173
Troper, Harold 98, 133
Turrittin, A. H. 116

Valentine, V. F. 108
Vallee, F. G. 63

Name Index

212

Van Den Berghe, Pierre 148–50, 156
Vanneman, R. D. 119
Verma, R. B. P. 9, 87, 115, 131
Villemez, W. T. 121

Wallerstein, I. 173
Warburg, Gabriel 170
Watson, J. L. 65
Weaver, Sally M. 130
Wellhofer, S. 147
Westell, Anthony 117

Weber, Max 31, 32, 169
Wilson, Edward O. 148
Wirth, Louis 31
Wiswell, C. H. 121
Wong, Lloyd 82, 85

Young, Cristabel 67, 77, 80

Zaniecki, F. 31
Ziegler, B. M. 98
Zubrzycki, Jerzy 15, 16, 36, 86

Subject Index

acculturation   33, 35–6, 49–66 *passim*
achievement   *see* education
active mobilisation   46
adaptation   30, 33, 36, 47, 49–66 *passim*, 86–8, 183
affirmative action   66, 134
aggression   158
  see also violence
alienation   6, 8
Alberta   13,
America North,   31–32, 60, 138
  American immigrants   16, 185
  dilemma   135–6
  Latin   85–86
  way of life   50
  see also United States
anomie   6
Asia   11, 83
  Asian immigrants   13, 15–17, 21–3, 63, 81–92 *passim*, 90–1, 101, 131–3
assimilation   16, 31–2, 100, 127, 155, 167
Australia   10, 15–18, 25, 50, 67–80 *passim*, 96, 101, 103
authority   4, 7, 8, 39
  authoritarianism   6, 7, 9, 181
  authorities,   7
  defined   187
automation   1
  see also computers, technology

baby-boom   3
  see also population
Bangladesh   23, 90
bilingualism   12, 108, 126–8
biosocial theories   148–50
black(s)   21–3, 98, 101, 121, 133, 178
  see also Caribbean, West Indian
brain drain   91

Britain   13, 18–24, 25, 40, 96, 101, 145, 177
  see also United Kingdom
British   1–6
British Columbia   13
bureacracy   2

Canada   1, 10–14, 15, 18, 25, 50, 67–80 *passim*, 96, 103–5, 107–23 *passim*, 125–37 *passim*, 155, 177
capitalism   5, 164, 172, 176, 178
Caribbean   19, 21, 83, 88–9
  see also black, West Indian
change   7, 29–47 *passim*
charismatic   *see* authority
Charter of Human Rights   125–38 *passim*
Chicago School of Sociology   31–4
citizen(ship)   52
  defined   187
class,   6, 7, 8, 21, 23
  defined   187
client-state
  defined   187
  see also state, super-power
coercion   6–8, 39, 43–4, 47, 147, 158, 180
cognitive dissonance   7
Colombia   86
colonial(ism)   7, 9, 10, 33, 154–5
Commonwealth   18–19, 21–2, 102
communication(s)   1, 2, 9, 20, 50 60, 119, 151, 175–6, 178, 180–1, 185
communism   164, 176, 178
competition   31, 42–3, 11, 49
  defined   187
computers   20, 185
  see also technology

213

Subject Index

conflict 1–5, 6, 8–9, 12, 14, 17, 19, 31, 42–4, 49–65 *passim*, 95, 119, 135–8, 141, 159
  defined 187
consciousness 154, 176
consensus 41–4, 125
  defined 187
conservatism 6–7, 46, 120
Constitution Act 125
consumer behaviour 56–58
contradiction(s) 4–5, 9, 13, 19, 42–4, 47
  defined 187
cooperation 43
  defined 187
core 9, 58, 154, 173
  see also metropolis, periphery
CPR (Canadian Pacific Railway) 95,
crime 6
critical theory 5, 38–9
crisis *see* conflict
culture 49–65 *passim*, 143–4
  popular 56–58

defence 4
  see also war
de-industrialisation 4, 6
  see also post-industrial
    delegitimation *see*
    legitimation
demographic *see* population
deportation 9
deviance 6
dilemma 125–38 *passim*
discrimination 14, 21–2, 35, 47, 66, 108, 120, 122, 133, 137
    see also prejudice, racism
dissensus 6, 43–44,
  defined 187

economic
  adaptation 86–8
  insecurity 120, 184
  problems 108
  see also global economy
Ecuador 86
education 12, 15, 17, 23–4, 53–5, 131, 152, 156, 180
    see also qualifications

elite(s) 13–14, 34, 160, 164, 175, 179–80
emigration *see* migration, immigration
Empire 19
  see also Commonwealth
environmental conservation 95–105 *passim*
equality 4, 10, 14, 16, 115, 129, 132
  of opportunity 6, 23, 54, 96, 107
  see also class
ethnic
  conflict 1, 8, 42, 116–23, 136–8, 165
  definition of 142, 182, 188
  enclave 59, 183
  identity 50, 63
  media 16, 56
  nationalism 38, 58–9, 141–82 *passim* (defined 188)
  origin defined 188
  pluralism 155–56 (*see also* multiculturalism)
  soldiers 163,
  solidarity 6, 8, 160–61
  stratification 17, 115–16
ethnonational group,
  defined 188
Europe 15, 25
European Common Market 19–20
expellees *see* refugees

fascism, defined 188
foreign-born *see* immigration
francophone 10, 126–7
  see also French, Quebec
France 40, 50, 59
French 14
  see also francophone
functionalist 32, 36, 41, 45, 167
.
gemeinschaft 2, 170, 175–6, 181
  defined 188
generation 25, 61–65, 115
gesellschaft 2, 171–2, 175–6, 181
  defined 188

Subject Index

ghetto 183
global system 5, 9, 14, 25, 41, 46, 48, 165
  economy 9, 65, 167–68,
  village 2
government *see* state
Greece 12
  Greek immigrants 15, 16, 63
guestworkers 10, 49, 51

Haitian immigrants 89
Harmondsworth 21
hegemony 108, 129
  defined 188
hinterland 9, 58, 13, 154
  see also perpiphery
human rights 9, 14, 96, 125–38
  passim, 156
    see also justice

ideology 95–105 *passim*, 107,
  141–2, 146, 169, 175, 184
  defined 188
immigration 1, 10–12, 15–17,
  19–23, 49–65 *passim*, 67–80
  passim, 95–105 *passim*, 130–1
  defined 18
  illegal 10
  see also migration
imperialism 33–4, 42, 152–3, 178
Indian immigrants 19, 23, 90
Indians *see* native peoples
industrial(ism) 9–10, 167
  see also post-industrial
inequality *see* equality
information 1, 185
  see also communications
inflation 6–7, 172
injustice *see* justice, oppression,
  coercion
inner cities 4
integration *see* social integration
internal colonialism, 154–5, 178
  see also colonialism, core,
    periphery
internalisation 7
Inuit 11
  see also native peoples
Italy 11–12

Jamaica 84
  see also Caribbean, West Indian
Japanese 133
Jews 14, 15, 63, 145
jingoism 7
  defined 188
justice 14, 119, 133
  see also human rights

language 63–4, 126–8
  see also bilingualism,
    multiculturalism
law and order 6, 8, 22, 120
Lebanon 77, 85
legitimation 4, 5, 39–40, 151,
  163, 169, 180
  crisis 6, 8
  defined 188
  dual 160

McCarran Act 99
majority 6, 7, 8
marginal man 32
mass communications *see*
  communications, media
Marx(ism) 21, 34–5, 41, 152–5,
  167
media 18, 55–6, 60, 119, 133–4
Metis 11
  see also native peoples
metropolitan 12, 154, 173
  areas 37, 73–77
  see also core, periphery
Mexicans 10
migration 1, 2, 8–9, 29–47
  passim, 44–48, 81–92 *passim*
  defined 188
  see also immigration
militarism *see* war
military 6, 37, 41, 161, 175, 182
  see also war
minority 6, 7, 8, 14, 133, 135,
  141, 167
mobilisation 46, 151–2, 162
  defined 189
modernisation theories 59,
  150–2, 159, 161–2
Montreal 10, 127
multicultural(ism) 1, 10, 12, 16,
  66, 95–137 *passim*, 107–23

Subject Index

Multicultural(ism) *cont'd*
  passim, 125–38 *passim*, 183
    defined 189
multilingual *see* multicultural
multinational(ism) 5, 143, 153,
  171–81 *passim*
    corporations 5, 6, 34, 138,
      164, 168, 173
    state 144–5 (defined 189)
multivariate models 36–7, 118,
  159–64
Muslim immigrants 15

nation 142–4
  defined 189
  nation-state 5–6, 168, 171,
    179–80 (defined 189)
  see also state
National Front 23
nationalism 6, 7, 22, 38, 141–82
  passim
    defined 189
    see also ethnic nationalism
national sovereignty 1, 179, 182,
  186
    defined 189
native peoples 11, 107, 129–30,
  146, 184
NATO 19
network(s) 1, 2, 35, 51, 175, 180
  see also communications
New Zealand 16, 77

opposition 14, 42–4, 47, 137
  defined 189
oppression 8–9, 158
  see also coercion, conflict

Pakistani immigrants 19, 23, 84,
  90
paradigms 30, 147–8
  see also theories
periphery 9, 38, 58, 154, 173
  see also core, hinterland
pluralism 33, 36, 63, 92, 96,
  155–6
    see also multiculturalism
police 118
politics 17, 38, 47–8, 52, 108, 147

political autonomy
  (defined 189;
  controls 37, 47, 99;
  development 161–62;
  integration 168–70)
polity 5, 9
  see also global, state
polyethnic 10, 42, 50, 66, 143,
  146, 153
    nation defined 189
    see also multicultural
population 105–6, 109–11
Poland 185
Portugal 12
post-industrial(ism) 1–3, 8, 14,
  20, 23, 24–5, 35–7, 42, 164,
  167–81 *passim*, 173–6
    defined 189
poverty 3, 12
power 3, 14, 19, 38, 39–40, 43,
  46, 50, 108, 137, 169–70,
  173–4, 176–9
    defined 189
prejudice 12, 21–22, 47, 61, 96,
  108, 116, 122, 158
    see also racism
protests 6, 8
  see also conflict, riots

qualifications 15, 24, 86, 131
  see also education
Quebec 10, 126–8

race, defined 189
  relations cycle 32–3
racism 6, 7, 12, 19, 22, 25,
  93–137 *passim*, 97, 116–20,
  125–38 *passim*, 132–6, 184
    defined 190
radicalism 6
rational choice 25, 45–6, 157
receiving countries 49–65 *passim*
recession *see* unemployment
refugees 12, 15, 18, 49, 52–3,
  65, 81–2, 85, 122, 131, 183
regions 13, 79, 181
  see core, periphery
regionalism 8
  defined 190

Subject Index

reification 7
  see also systems
relative deprivation 119,
religion 64, 107, 145, 170–7
  passim
re-migration 2, 34, 62, 83
  see also migration
reserve army 21, 34, 45
revolution 3, 9, 42, 162
riots 3, 6, 8, 45
robotics 1, 20
  see also computers

satellite *see* communications
segregation 21, 119
  see also ethnic enclave
separatism 6, 8, 180
  see also ethnic nationalism,
    regionalism, Quebec,
    Welsh social
  action 44–6
  change 7, 20, 40–2
  Darwinism 148, 150
  disorders 6, 7, 45
  integration 49, 51, 59–65, 88,
    92, 123, 168–70
  mobility 23, 59, 96, 116
  networks 35, 51, 60, 62
  science 141–65 *passim*
  structure 40–2
sociology 29–47 *passim*
sovereignty 9, 182
  association 147, 190
  defined 190
Soviet Union 138, 153
state 7, 145, 167, 170–4
  defined 190
  see also sovereignty
status, defined 190
stratification 17
  see also class
stress 7
strikes 6
  see also protests
structuration 41–2
  defined 190
superpowers 3, 6, 14, 37–8, 48,
  174, 185
    defined 190

supranational *see* suprastate
suprastate 6, 165, 167, 173, 175
  178, 181–2
  see also state
Switzerland 25
system(s) 1, 5, 7, 40–2, 159–64
  passim
symbolic values 42, 136

technology 1–5, 20, 174–6
technological redundancy *see*
  unemployment
    see also computers, post-
    industrialism
temporary workers 2, 13, 61,
  81–2, 110–11
  see also guestworkers
terrorism 3, 6, 8, 14, 48, 165,
  176
theories 5, 38
  of migration 27–47 *passim*
  of ethnic nationalism 141–65
    passim
Third World 1, 10–11, 15, 40,
  78–80, 81–91 *passim*, 96, 114,
  122, 160–1, 168, 176
Toronto 10, 74–5, 88, 183
transilient 2, 45
  defined 190
transportation 1, 151
  see also communications
Turkey 17

under-achievement *see* education
unemployment 3, 4, 13, 18, 20,
  49, 67–80 *passim*, 96, 107–23
  passim, 131, 172, 183–84
United Kingdom 10, 19, 50, 59,
  102, 145
    see also Britain
United States 10, 13, 14, 33, 35,
  96, 50, 102, 121, 128, 155,
  177
    see also America
utopia 146
  defined 190
  see also ideology

Subject Index

verbindungsnetzschaft 2, 174–5,
  181, 185
  defined 190
Vietnamese 18, 52, 84–5, 90
violence 6–7, 116–20, 152, 157,
  184
  see also conflict
visible minorities 14, 65–6, 87,
  132–5
  defined 190
  see also minorities, racism

war 3, 14, 18, 47–8, 67, 81, 99,
  160–1, 171, 174, 177, 182
  civil 8, 118, 162, 176
welfare state 4, 5, 34
Welsh nationalism 146, 154
West Indian 23–24, 89
  see also black, Caribbean
work ethic 5
world *see* global

zero population growth (ZPG)
  105
  see also population